FEMINISM
AGAINST CISNESS

EMMA HEANEY
EDITOR

FEMINISM

ASTERISK Gender, Trans-, and All That Comes After
A series edited by Susan Stryker, Eliza Steinbock, and Jian Neo Chen

AGAINST CISNESS

Duke University Press   Durham and London 2024

© 2024 DUKE UNIVERSITY PRESS. All rights reserved
Project Editor: Liz Smith | Designed by Aimee C. Harrison
Typeset in Garamond Premier Pro by Westchester Publishing Services

Library of Congress Cataloging-in-Publication Data
Names: Heaney, Emma, editor.
Title: Feminism against cisness / edited by Emma Heaney.
Other titles: Asterisk (Duke University Press)
Description: Durham : Duke University Press, 2024. | Series: Asterisk |
Includes bibliographical references and index.
Identifiers: LCCN 2023033120 (print)
LCCN 2023033121 (ebook)
ISBN 9781478030454 (paperback)
ISBN 9781478026228 (hardcover)
ISBN 9781478059431 (ebook)
Subjects: LCSH: Transgender people. | Cisgender people. | Gender
nonconformity—Political aspects. | Gender identity—Political aspects. |
Feminism. | Feminist theory. | Queer theory. | BISAC: SOCIAL
SCIENCE / LGBTQ Studies / Transgender Studies | SOCIAL SCIENCE /
Feminism & Feminist Theory
Classification: LCC HQ77.9 .F46 2024 (print) | LCC HQ77.9 (ebook) |
DDC 306.76/8—dc23/eng/20231108
LC recordavailableathttps:// lccn.loc.gov/2023033120
LC ebook recordavailableathttps:// lccn.loc.gov/2023033121

Cover art: Creighton Baxter, *Meeting Morgan at the Horizon*, 2021.
Acrylic, ink, and watercolor on paper, 11 × 7.25 in. Courtesy of the artist.

For Susan Stryker

CONTENTS

ix   Acknowledgments

1   Introduction. Sexual Difference without Cisness
        EMMA HEANEY

I. TRANS POLITICS

37   1 On Trans Use of the Many Sojourner Truths
         CAMERON AWKWARD-RICH

56   2 1970s Trans Feminism as Decolonial Praxis
         MARGAUX L. KRISTJANSSON AND EMMA HEANEY

II. TRANS HISTORY

83   3 Trans Feminine Histories, Piece by Piece, or,
         Vernacular Print and the Histories of Gender
         GRETA LAFLEUR

108 4 Denaturing Cisness, or, Toward Trans History as Method
         BEANS VELOCCI

III. TRANS THEORY

135　5　Two Senses of Gender Abolition:
　　　Gender as Accumulation Strategy
　　　KAY GABRIEL

158　6　Faceless: Nonconfessions of a Gender
　　　MARQUIS BEY

IV. ANTI-TRANS POLITICS

175　7　Assuaging the Anxious Matriarch:
　　　Social Conservatives, Radical Feminists, and
　　　Dark Money against Trans Rights
　　　JOANNA WUEST

197　8　Caring for Trans Kids, Transnationally, or,
　　　Against "Gender-Critical" Moms
　　　JULES GILL-PETERSON

217　9　Generic Deductiveness:
　　　Reasoning as Mood in the Stoner Neo-Noir
　　　GRACE LAVERY

241　　Afterword. Toward a Feminism for the Living
　　　DURBA MITRA

251　　Contributors
257　　Index

ACKNOWLEDGMENTS

First, the contributors thank Elizabeth Ault and Benjamin Kossack for all the work, patience, kindness, and skill that they brought to this project. Thanks to Eliza Steinbock, Jian Neo Chen, and everyone else whose work contributes to the ASTERISK series at Duke. The two reviewers were such steady anonymous friends to this project. Thank you for the time you took to engage so thoughtfully and for holding us to your high standards.

This book wouldn't exist without the fierce mind and brilliant heart of Susan Stryker. This is true as a narrow practical matter, but on a broader scale, her work has made space for trans feminist thought in (and adjacent to) the academy. This book is dedicated to her, for making a place where none was before and inviting so many to come and be there together.

EMMA HEANEY

INTRODUCTION

Sexual Difference without Cisness

> Who, we might ask, is truly on the outside
> of heteronormative power—maybe most of us?
> —CATHY COHEN, "PUNKS, BULLDAGGERS,
> AND WELFARE QUEENS"

> Sex is one of the few social interactions I choose
> that reminds me of my unending penetrability.
> —BILLY-RAY BELCOURT,
> *A HISTORY OF MY BRIEF BODY*

*C*isness is feminism's counterrevolution. Historically, it is the concept that recasts sex as a biological fact following political challenges to the sanctity of sex as an ordained social order. Because cisness ontologizes sex as a binary of bodily forms, it orients the definition of feminism away from a revolution in the hierarchy of values that would overturn, for instance, the priority of accumulation over reproduction and domination over care toward female emancipation as an individual affair. This feminism offers women the opportunity to advance in the current patriarchal hierarchy of values. Cisness casts as feminist victories the existence of female CEOs who lord over feminized workers and the sacralized image of the mother doing double duty that obscures the mass reality of dwindling social support for the work of mothering. To adapt Monique Wittig's classic and clarifying formulation: cisness obfuscates the reality *women* with the fiction *woman*.[1]

Part of the power of cisness as ideology is its presentation as self-evident empiricism, but the protocols of its enforcement are not straightforward. Rather than a pure binary of men and women, cisness produces myriad racialized and classed categories of people whose communal indifference to the bourgeois mores of sex is deemed aberrant. The mutually reinforcing structures of coloniality, white supremacy, patriarchy, caste, and class reproduce the distinction between the powerful who do sex correctly and the masses who do sex incorrectly and therefore must be managed or punished. The claim to sexed propriety made by colonizers, settlers, enslaving societies, and bourgeois elites has been a significant component of power for the past five hundred years. To say cisness is feminism's counterrevolution is to say that cisness is the ableist apprehension of bodies into good and bad, the colonial destruction of kinship structures, the white supremacist obliteration of personhood in the service of capital extraction, and a component of bourgeois antipathy for the poor, working, and racialized people of the world.

The chapters that compose *Feminism against Cisness* foreground this racial, class, and colonial history at the heart and center of the enforcement of cisness. This scholarship addresses patriarchy without reifying the categories—woman and man—that do its brutalizing work. This feminist critique militates against misogyny by recognizing that the category of cis woman is not patriarchy's only target. From the mid-nineteenth century to the early twentieth century, first organs, then hormones, and finally chromosomes became the medical bottom line of assigned sex. But before, during, and after this period of medicalization, these structures and substances have never determined who is subjected to feminizing violence, as any femme sixth grader who has walked the gauntlet of a middle school hallway can tell you. Solidarities that stem from feminizing violence are not natural, eternal, or total, but sites of political alliance with both the potential to transform social relations and the inevitable internal contradiction that such solidarities always contain. Each chapter in this collection makes a case for feminism's practiced or potential divestment from the naturalizing logic of cisness. The chapters are thus able to map the relations among patriarchy, white supremacy, settler colonialism, and capitalism that jointly establish gender as a principal way in which our lives are regulated and limited. These chapters encourage feminists to turn away from dialogue with transphobes and turn toward one another to pose questions raised by trans life, history, and liberatory formations whose answers are necessary to understanding the operation of sex and gender *tout court*.

This volume considers feminism's most trenchant claims to be that assigned sex does not determine the qualities or value of any human being and that bourgeois domination and racializing regimes have relied on the illusion that it does. The constant renewal of cis social ordering is therefore necessary to the counterrevolutionary containment of the revolutionary potential of feminist self-assertion to shake the foundations of not just gender, but white supremacist heteropatriarchy. The enforcement of cisness creates racialized, classed, and colonial fissures in the gendered solidarities that bourgeois patriarchy wrought. Therefore, exposing the ideological operation of cisness is one way to dethrone the white bourgeois formations that have too often been inaccurately characterized as defining feminism. We locate our lines of engagement among those whose thought promulgates gender liberation for all, a project that is defined not by a march forward out of a benighted past, but often by the reinvigoration of modes of collective life that the individualist, colonial, bourgeois logic of individual rights have stigmatized and driven underground.

This introduction proposes that each chapter in this volume addresses the simultaneity of cisness as a bifurcating and hierarchizing ideology that is fundamental to racial, colonial, and class formation. In each case, the thought legacies and political desires of feminism form their author's inquiry. Scholarly and popular framings of generational conflict, of the supposed opposition between deference and innovation, have long obscured the actual genealogy of feminist thought and action. You'll find no waves here. To say these contributions are new is to say that they welcome stores of knowledge, experience, and thought that have long been part of practices that produce sex and gender freedom, but that have often been viewed as additive, marginal, or even antagonistic to something called feminism. What follows offers a theory of sexual difference without cisness to systematize the theoretical contribution of this volume's chapters.

This collection's inquiry begins in 1970 with the words of two best friends spoken across a kitchen table in New York City.[2] These friends, nineteen-year-old Sylvia Rivera and twenty-six-year-old Marsha P. Johnson, gathered to be interviewed by the journalist Liza Cowen for a segment Cowen was research-ing on the topic of cross-dressing for the noncommercial New York City radio station WBAI.[3] The conversation swiftly moves away from a dialogic exchange with their interviewer as the two subjects begin speaking to each other about their lives and commitments.[4] Against the hiss of the radiator, Johnson says that she would prefer to partner with a gay man, "because I don't care for heterosexual men as a husband. . . . They're too . . . too masculine for me." Rivera interjects: "They're just too oppressive; be more realistic about it." To this, Johnson doesn't really respond, turning to talk about growing up and becoming a woman:

> JOHNSON: I could always talk like a woman. I could always act like a woman. I could always do things that women would do because I was raised by my mother. Like, I could wash . . . iron . . . cook . . . sew . . .
>
> RIVERA: [cutting in] That's very oppressive toward women.
>
> JOHNSON: Well, that's what they're good for doing. . . .
>
> RIVERA: [cutting in] Ewwww, stop!
>
> JOHNSON: That's what they always do. That's what my mother did. Well, some women don't do that, but my mother was poor; she had to do it all herself.

Rivera responds with a succinct and forceful feminist analysis of domestic work and male oppression:

> I, as a person, don't believe that a transvestite or a woman should do all the washing, do all the cooking, and do everything that's forced on by the bourgeois society and the establishment that women *have* to do this. I don't believe in that; that's all a lot of baloney. If you have a lover, or you have a friend that you really care for, you split everything down fifty-fifty. If you don't feel like doing it, you just don't do it. Let *him* do it because this is what we're all trying to get across. Men are oppressive. They just oppress you in all different ways.

We are sadly denied Marsha P. Johnson's response to Rivera's comments, if there was one, but what the archive provides us here is plenty. In this ex-change, Johnson is tasked by the topic and format of the interview to provide an account of her sense of her own sex. She describes the hormones she takes and the resulting "handful" of "bosom" growth; she discusses her plans to pursue genital surgery, a "sex change" in her terms.[5] But her comments cited above reveal that even before she arrived in New York City at seventeen and started pursuing these medical services, womanhood meant an identification with the strong Black woman who raised her and, in particular, with that woman's labors. Her sex identity emerged from this affinity. Womanhood was the inclination to and fact of receiving an education in those labors through her bond with her mother: an identity born of skill transmission. Not every child who gravitates toward a parent's gendered skills will find the grounding for a sex identity in that affinity, of course, but such identification is one material way in which the abstraction called sex materializes in the consciousness of individuals, both for those whom we call cis and those whom we call trans.

Rivera and Johnson's exchange is, in a sense, an orthodox instance of consciousness-raising, the paradigmatic political practice of 1970s American radical feminism, modeled after the Chinese communist revolutionary feminist practice of "speaking bitterness."[6] Through open autobiographical storytelling, Johnson reflects on the household tasks that ground her identity as a woman. Rivera purports to correct her, saying that this definition is oppressive to her and the rest of "us," raising Johnson's consciousness to the reality that she and other women are "good for" more than just domestic labors. But, before Rivera's interjection, Johnson was already producing feminist analysis from a 1970s feminist vantage and, specifically, from a Black feminist vantage. All over the world, women were observing that womanhood itself is the social expression of reproductive labor.[7] Black feminists and other working-class women were noticing the social structures through which this labor was distributed, not evenly across all categories of women, but especially tasked to racialized and low-wage women—poor women, like Johnson's mother—thus producing not an internally homogenous "womanhood" but a striated category of sex produced through racialized and classed internal contradictions. This analysis led to, for instance, the politicizing of welfare provision and the conditions and operations of public housing during the period that followed.[8]

The materialist feminist dialectic is alive in this exchange between Rivera and Johnson: shared feminized labors are the necessary work of life-giving in Johnson's mother's home. In Rivera's experience and analysis, the feminization of these labors is the dreadful and dehumanizing burden on which white supremacist bourgeois patriarchy is premised. Both seemingly opposed perspectives are true as simple statements; the analytical truth is their synthesis: to destroy patriarchy would be to free these, the only necessary labors, from their gendered and racialized character, to communize them, to free the world's efforts from the production of surplus value and bourgeois identities and refocus these efforts on the tasks that sustain and reproduce life. This would mean the general recognition of the value of Johnson's mother's labors as the only real form of value.[9] The embrasure of the dialectic tension between valorizing and refusing domestic labor recognizes the production and progression of contradictions, rather than the adjudication of who is right, as the political mode that matches how history moves.[10]

But if sex is only a question of labors and the social categories that the uneven valuation of labors produce, then how to engage the knowledge that Johnson makes when she describes her body and the processes that she is helping her body to undergo? Is it true, as Judith Butler writes, that bodily structures, adipose deposits, and organs, to the extent that we can cognate them, are "indissociable from discursive demarcations"?[11] Is there nothing in bodily dwelling that is not capturable by the ideological constraints of the word? Are the tools of materialist feminism adequate to the task of addressing these questions? And aren't we, in the year 2024, sick of asking these questions and getting only unsatisfactory, vague conciliations that have different feminist theories in their own orbits, agreeing to disagree? These are well-worn questions in the history of feminist inquiry since the 1990s, but there is yet to be a satisfactory theoretical formulation to answer them. This introduction, informed by the analyses of the chapters gathered in this collection, proposes an analytic of sexual difference without cisness to finally reconcile the evident linguistic substance of all social identities with the embodied experiences that fall out of thought when sex is viewed as only the lived instantiation of words.

If the historical materialism of Rivera and Johnson's exchange provides the first half of this articulation, then an interview conducted by the historian Eric Marcus nineteen years later, in 1989, in Sylvia Rivera's Terrytown apartment, provides the second: entry into an essential materialist, feminist analysis of the body. Rivera tells her story of leaving her grandmother's house in the Bronx when she was eleven after finding her grandmother in tears because the neighborhood gossips were calling Sylvia a *pato*.[12] The child found her way to Times Square, where she began to engage in the survival sex work that would be her source of income for many years to follow. Marcus queries her on whether she actually engaged in sex work at such a young age. Rivera responds: "You can sell anything out on the streets. You can sell men, young boys, and young women. There's always a customer out there and they are the ones that are sick. I remember just going home and just scrubbing myself in the tub with hot water saying: 'oh these people touched me.' I mean the sleaze. Even if they weren't old. They could have been young."[13] The need that the child Sylvia Rivera felt to scrub her skin after sexual encounters with— how should we refer to them? sex work clients? assaulters? the most local instance of a social system that left an eleven-year-old kid with no resource but access to her body to exchange in order to attain the necessities of barest life?—provides a deep investigation of the material reality of sex. That is, if we understand sex, as I propose we do, as the embodied experience produced by the comingling of two kinds of social relations. On the one hand there are affinities that pull you toward identification with people situated on one or the other side of the sex binary; this is how Marsha P. Johnson and many others come to sex.

On the other hand, there are social relations that subject you to one or the other term in a symbolic binary of penetrator and penetrated; this distinction sexes or sexualizes a body in ways that track you as female/feminine or male/masculine. To feel dirtied by sexual use, to need to trade access to one's body for certain resources, to routinely feel oneself positioned as the object through which someone else can reproduce their own identity as sexually dominant over you: these bodily sensations define sexual difference for those positioned as feminized, penetrable terms in that binary. This social positioning has very little to do with the act of sex, although sex, sexualization, and sexual attraction are intensified points of articulation for this ideological positioning because the penetrability of the body serves as the organizing ontological premise for sex. Men, both cis and trans, can be penetrated and can even invite penetration. But to be a man is to be able to escape association with penetrability as an organizing structure of your extra-sexual social life, as a public quality, let's say. A person might even endure the most symbolically laden form of penetration, rape, but not wear a social identity that is haunted by rape, a disjointed gender experience that creates its own devastating emotional legacies. Conversely, a person might never have been raped but wear a social identity that associates her with this form of penetration as she walks home in the evening to a chorus of catcalls or as she navigates daily gendered relations at work and in her private life.

Rivera's scrubbing is, then, a practice of sexual difference, arising from the emotional and physical states that attend feminization. Her experience demonstrates that these conditions do not solely adhere to the bodies, life experiences, and communal histories of those assigned female at birth. Rivera's status as a minor, her race, and her trans femininity all subject her to the conditions that make her feel the need to scrub. The interview places this practice in the context of her broader vulnerability to arrest, assault, maltreatment in sexual relationships, and rape; this vulnerability is produced by the transversal relation between the different terms of her identity.[14] Her race and transness foreclose her from the kinds of protections that a white supremacist society purports to provide women and children, implicitly defined as white and cis.[15] This and similar materially grounded experiences provide the context for understanding the social practices that cis society views as the actual markers of Rivera's gender: that she is drawn to the feminine name of Sylvia; to feminine kinship terms like "mother" and "half-sister in struggle"; to the pronouns she/her/hers; and to feminine clothing, hairstyles, and makeup.[16]

The social order in which she exists sees and reflects her identity to such a uniform extent that when she is misgendered, she reads this as a willful shaming. Her account of one such experience, inflicted by gay male leftists, vivifies misgendering itself as a feminizing form of subjection:

> I was at the demonstration when the gay people charged the United States with genocide. . . . [T]his person . . . starts off *Mr*. Ray Rivera . . . *Mr*. Rivera likes to be called by his transvestite friends as Sylvia. This is very oppressive. Everyone calls me Sylvia. . . . I've had this name for nine years, straight or gay. Even on my job, the girls, the women, that I used to work with called me Sylvia. . . . It's not just transvestites that called me Sylvia or consider me or treat me as she. . . . People respect you. This is respect.[17]

In recounting this and other experiences, Rivera and Johnson occupy the infrastructure of the interviews, removing their lives from articulation in the "issue" of cross-dressing, in the first instance, or as some periphery or subset of LGBT life in the second. Their lives were not phenomena to be examined from the outside or issues to be debated: their lives were social processes in motion with relentlessly material bases: race, class, gender, and trans experience. Their comments reflect that feminization as a social process both adheres in and exceeds the category *woman*. The various operations of power that constrain those positioned as womanlike attain their power to diminish from the association it implies with *woman*, but it also attains a new kind of power to diminish because *womanlike* implies an inadequacy, that one is *not even*, properly, a woman.

We are left in need of a theory composed of two modalities of materialism: historical materialism and the materialism that emerges when historical categories order the way our bodies feel in the world. This theory reflects the reality of sex as not natural, not even necessarily uniform or consistent over time, but, yes, an ontological experience premised on the symbolic ordering of penetration to the extent that sex is felt, sensed, and experienced on the level of the substance of the body. This is over and against the false ontology that approaches, for instance, the vagina as the singular site of sexuating penetration and assembles a cast of organs, hormones, and chromosomes as the criteria of true womanhood. We need a theory of sexual difference without cisness. The following section provides a systematic accounting of this theory.

THE MATERIALIST DISARTICULATION OF SEXUAL DIFFERENCE FROM CISNESS

An ontological nature of bodies is that they are penetrable; sexual difference is the partitioning of bodies into penetrator and penetrated, an ideological ordering premised on the denial of universal penetrability. This binary of ideological categories does not adhere consistently to any type of body as we've seen, or even necessarily consistently to any individual body. Your sex can change regularly, to the extent that the same person can occupy the position of masculinist personhood during one period, in one relation, or even in one moment and then the position of feminized nonperson, excluded from being in another period, relation, or moment. This can occur just as a well body can become sick, either for a time or for evermore, and as a young body will certainly become old. A body that is racialized in one way in a given social context will be racialized differently or unmarked by racialization in another. A butch can experience masculinist priority amid community in the dyke bar and be feminized by harassers on the subway home. A woman CEO can rhetorically dominate a boardroom and be subject to brutal or subtle misogynist undermining by her husband at home. A white woman can flex her personhood by degrading a woman of color in a misogynist way, be she coworker or employee, even as she herself might be subject to tonally similar degradation in other contexts. A man of color might be punished or even killed for representing the very kinds of masculine qualities that protect and privilege his white male peer.[18] A boss of any gender might seek to shame and punish a subordinate in order to bolster the boss's masculinist authority. A transphobic woman can call attention to the genitals of a trans person and experience for the first time the thrill of engaging, on the masculinist side, in this long-standing misogynist tactic of calling embarrassing, feminizing attention to their target's genitals or other sexed structures.[19]

One's sex is the sum total of these machinations with the hierarchy of masculinity over femininity, and the maintenance of masculine priority for those in positions of class and racial power, as the stable social field in which these oscillations operate. Of course, many of us are more intractably and uniformly bound to one or the other position; a woman is much more likely to be tasked with the labors and associations that feminize a person than is a man. These machinations are rarely consciously manipulated. Rarely are the expectations and burdens produced by sexual difference articulated; rather, they permeate social life, creating feelings, impulses, and instantiating dynamics. Then there are those who inhabit categories of experience that are the most uniformly and intractably bound to the violent degradation that adheres to femininity in a misogynist society. Examples include sex workers, poor and working-class women, single mothers, women on welfare, and women in service-sector jobs.

Accounting for the reality of these operations and the lives that they ensnare requires the clear theoretical articulation of the relation of two concepts: sexual difference and cisness. Sexual difference is the social organization of the supposedly biologically derived terms of the sex binary into a hierarchy of persons and qualities: masculine/male (active, cerebral, spiritual, agential) over feminine/female (passive, emotional, material, dependent).[20] Cisness is the biologizing ideology that these social roles of sexual difference adhere to assigned sex based on the appearance of genitals at or (via prenatal imaging technologies) before birth. In other words, cisness is the idea that those identified as girls at birth are naturally inducted into the social expectation that sexual difference sets for the feminine and likewise for boys with the masculine. So, as is clear from these definitions, both sexual difference and cisness are ideological constructs, but of different types.

Sexual difference is an ideological construct that emerges from a material structure. The terms of this difference have been established by their differential relation to money. The category feminine/female is the social expression of the valuelessness of reproductive labor: cooking, cleaning, care for children and elders, gestation and lactation, and emotional care. All these activities are associated with wageless work and are devalued both when unwaged and when they are waged as feminized service-sector jobs. As I argue in *The New Woman*, trans femininity, in addition to being constructed around this historical structure of reproductive labor, emerged from association with a particular form of waged reproductive labor: sex work, the particular class and racial character of which has been accounted for in an extensive body of fine scholarship.[21] The persistent criminalization of this form of work sets it apart from other feminized work, and by extension sets apart the forms of social life it produces from the category of cis womanhood.[22]

This valuelessness then adheres in a more ideated form. The feminine, devalued materially, is ontologized as sexual penetrability. The availability of feminized people for degraded and degrading sexual penetration establishes a mutually reinforcing equation among penetrability, submission, and degradation. To say sexual difference is material is different than saying sexual difference is natural or eternal: far from it. It is, in fact, to say the opposite: that as material conditions change, so too would the ideological status of persons and qualities whose value is established by the rubric of sexual difference. Currently, however, it is a dominant structure that determines the real experience of our lives.

Cisness, in contrast, has no material basis of its own, only the one it attains via its imbrication in sexual difference. This may sound counterintuitive, because the ideology's relation to the physical structure of our bodies produces the impression of a real basis in chromosome, flesh, follicle, hormone, muscle, and organ. But consider the following concrete, material example: a vagina is a structure composed of skin, mucous membrane, muscle, and other tissues. Its functions are real, are important, and require attention. Further, the possessor's relation to this structure is so laden with ideology that she might feel, even on the highly affecting level of sensation and bodily self-awareness, that this structure actually grounds her sex identity. In the negative, she may experience her vagina, for example, as the source of her body's vulnerability to rape.

But we know that vaginas, in themselves, are no more vulnerable to or inviting of sexual assault than other bodily structures that can be penetrated. We know this because people without vaginas are also vulnerable to rape and disproportionately so, according to certain group-forming attributes. Trans women, racialized people, gay men whose gender expression communicates (or is interpreted as) effeminacy, incarcerated people, enslaved people, workers in a subordinate labor position, children, disabled people, people who are economically precarious and/or experiencing homelessness, sex workers, gender-nonconforming and trans masculine people whose trans status is known or has been revealed: all of these populations are disproportionately vulnerable to rape and are not categorically defined by having vaginas.[23] What is the quality that explains this disproportionate vulnerability across these vastly disparate social categories among people with all forms of genitals and combinations of secondary sexual characteristics? The answer to this question is the rapist's perception of their victim as actually, properly, or potentially socially positioned as powerless. This social positioning is then reinforced in its relation to the feminine through the use of the tactic of sexual assault with its historically produced relation to the feminine. That is to say, the production of disproportionate vulnerability to assault is the rapist's enforcement and reproduction of the ideology of sexual difference. This social positioning has defined the category *woman* historically, but its effects have never been limited to those assigned female at birth, to those who identify as women, or even to those socially recognized as women.

Any adequate account of that social process must recognize that the qualities that position an individual in this structural relation to their rapist might have nothing to do with what we commonly think of as biological sex or even gender, as the history of racialized gender violence in the United States makes plain. An enslaved person's vulnerability, for instance, is produced by an ideology of anti-Blackness and the white supremacist legal, cultural, and political structures that allowed and administrated slavery. The claim here is precisely *not* that enslaved people experienced routinized sexual assault because slavery positioned enslaved people *as women*. Such a claim would preserve a distinction between "woman" and "the enslaved," naturalizing womanhood as whiteness and obscuring the point altogether. Rather, the claim is that sexual difference itself, the ability to withhold power based on a perceived or enforced relation to the feminine, can operate as a racializing tactic. Likewise in the case of Black women's experiences under the conditions of chattel slavery and in its afterlives, the foreclosure from feminization, the enforcement of conditions and punishments that among whites were reserved for men, was also a constitutive sexuating operation of racialization.[24] Far from being a new observation, one has only to read the primary literature of the experience of enslavement in the American chattel system or the theoretical articulations of scholars that stem from that history in order to understand this reality.

As one consequential example of the operation of sexual difference without cisness drawn from this historical context, consider Harriet Jacobs's narrative of her enslavement and self-emancipation, *Incidents in the Life of a Slave Girl* (1861). Jacobs's story provides a detailed analysis of the role of routinized sexual assault in the lives and logics of slavery; she is compelled by the structural imperative of the genre, despite deep reticence and disinclination to do so, to use her own experience as a representative example. She describes the terror that attends enslaved girls' twelfth birthdays when they can expect these abuses to become a daily fact of their lives, and she details the strategic choices that enslaved girls and women made to lessen the devastation of this constant menace.

Jacobs includes descriptions of the woman who is married to her enslaver posing as her husband and whispering sexual things in Jacobs's ear as she sleeps in order to investigate her husband's infidelity, as she views his behavior. In this dynamic, a white cis woman sexually abuses Jacobs, demonstrating the operation of sexual violence as a racializing violence.[25] That is also to say that the white woman inflicts feminization as a tactic of racialization, her masculinist position in sexual difference here produced by her whiteness, thus illuminating the way sexual difference operates independently of cisness. The bourgeois white woman who uses sexual assault as a racializing attack and the Black woman who is consigned to manual labor or punishment on a chain gang— indeed, the labor and punishment histories of women who are not white and bourgeois—demonstrate that "womanhood" is a racialized and classed category, as Talitha L. LeFlouria has demonstrated via historical argumentation.[26]

Jacobs also discusses an enslaved male friend named Luke whose male enslaver compels him to engage in "freaks . . . of a nature too filthy to be repeated" for the enslaver's sexual satisfaction.[27] Sexual precarity has different iterations for Jacobs and Luke based on their social positioning as a woman and a man and as a result of Jacobs's capacity for pregnancy. An analytic of sexual difference without cisness allows us to understand the solidarity between Jacobs and this male friend that is produced by the common state of sexual precarity that their enslavement inflicts on both of them.[28] That common precarity produces the solidarity bond that explains Luke sharing his experience with Jacobs and her resulting deep empathetic identification with her friend, whose bodily experience she well understands.[29] Theirs is a bond that cuts across cisness, demonstrating the "transversal relation," in C. Riley Snorton's terms, between Blackness and sex.[30]

To take another example: likewise in the case of children, it is not analytically precise to say that children are *like* women in their common vulnerability to sexual assault.[31] Rather, an ideology of sexual difference that imbues the feminine with—in fact *defines* the feminine as—powerlessness reproduces itself through the sexual abuse and assault of children who are in a materially powerless relation to adults. The vulnerability of children is both categorical and internally differential, depending on additional social factors.

The way these factors cut across cisness is clarified by juxtaposing accounts from two recent memoirs. First, Kiese Laymon's *Heavy* (2019) addresses his experience of sexual abuse by a babysitter when he was eight years old. His abuser, a woman in her twenties, forces her breasts into his mouth, a form of forced penetrative sexual contact.[32] Laymon explains that his emotional response to this abuse is formed by his identity as a fat boy. The experience produces many muddled feelings, including insecurity about his body's softness and worry about what his adult abuser will think about how he smells. This experience occurred because of his material positioning as a child. His feelings about this abuse are embodied, but rather than a social relation to femininity, he feels uncertainty around his fatness and desirability. He doesn't have adequate language or conceptual structure for the experience, except to feel a vague connection between his abuse and the normalized way in which his male peers treat the girls in their social world. When these boys go off into a bedroom to serially sexually assault a peer girl, a practice they call "running the train," Laymon "stood there wondering why the shallow grunts and mini-squeaks coming from the boys in Daryl's room made [him] want to be dead. [He] didn't know, but [he] assumed some kind of sex was happening."[33] The adult Laymon contemplates the fact that his child self couldn't access connection to these girls whom the boys socially coerce into sexual service because these girls experience him as one of those boys. The memoir conveys both embodied commonality between those who experience sexual assault and the way that cisness obscures that similarity and therefore precludes the expression of solidarity across the border that the ideology imposes.

Janet Mock's *Redefining Realness* (2011) documents her experiences of sexual abuse and her adult project of finding language to analyze her experience, which also began when she was eight years old. For several years she was abused by the teenaged son of her mother's boyfriend, who lived in the house with her. Mock analyzes that a child like her, a trans feminine child, is much more likely to be targeted for this kind of abuse than a child such as Laymon who is not considered (and doesn't experience himself as) feminine. Her adult reckoning, like Laymon's, includes negotiating the way that abuse felt like an affirmation of her desirability and girlhood, activating the sense of herself as a girl that had exclusively been acknowledged previously through punishment and censure by adults.

Looking at the important similarities and differences between these experiences—both the common penetrability of these children's bodies and the differential exposure to the risks that this universal fact of bodies poses to each in a misogynist society—clarifies the way that sexual difference structures the experience. For Laymon, his status as a minor makes his body vulnerable; his identity as a boy and eventually a man forms how those experiences affect him in the long run. For Mock, her femininity, trans status, and status as a minor make her body vulnerable. The fact that the first two identities persist beyond childhood explains the recurrence of these abuses in later life. Also, the view of Mock's body as sexualized, subject to scrutiny, and violable continues to shape her life in a much more pronounced and public way than is the case for Laymon, as their stories go on to tell.

The transversal relation produced here by childhood, drawing together the experiences, produced by sexual difference, of a cis boy/man and a trans girl/woman, provokes the theoretical articulation of sexual difference without cisness. Most obviously, the noncausal relation between assigned sex and lived sex means that Mock is positioned as a girl in these dynamics; sexual difference operates independently of assigned sex, a reality that exposes the ideological status of cisness. This fact of trans life, however, helps us understand the opaque point that sexual difference can also operate within other vectors of social power: race, class, age, and disability, not only trans status. Contrasting these accounts of experience exposes abuse and rape as social and historical, not biological, harms. This seems like a truism too obvious to bother stating, but we haven't fully accounted for this truth in a theoretical denaturalization of cisness as I aim to do here.

Sexual difference serves not only as a structure of bodily dispossession and social violence but also as a structure of pleasure and identification. Here too, while sexual difference orders social relations, cisness is not its basis. In the positive, women who have uteruses and ovaries are encouraged to view these organs as the source of experiences of maternity. Anyone who mothers a child whom they did not gestate knows the ideological nature of that claim. But mothering, the provision of care associated through history with gestators, is still marked as feminine by this historical accretion, regardless of who undertakes that role. Therefore, as communist feminist Sophie Lewis argues, "mothering" is a form, a labor, a verb over and against the identity noun *mother*; the verb "[designates] people who do mothering without necessarily being mothers."[34] Mothers, in contrast,

> have, after all, historically both brought down oppressive regimes and built them. On the one hand, maternal feminists, maternalist activists and femonationalists (so-called mothers of the nation) have served for centuries as prime movers of world-systemic evils such as white supremacy, spearheading imperial and settler-colonial projects of "racial uplift" and eugenics. On the other, as we've seen, dispossessed mamas, mamis, othermothers and

queer motherers have consistently posed a formidable threat to capitalism and the state. The dialectic in question is . . . more properly articulated not as a contradiction in the soul of every mother, but as a structural matter of colonially imposed scarcity; of planetary whiteness and its abolition; of the war between social reproduction "from below" and class society's reproduction from above; of motherhood's very invention and design, finally, as an institution to render indigenous and formerly enslaved people "kinless."[35]

This is the anti-essentialism that has too often been misconstrued as essentialism. To say that fatherhood is a relation of property and that mothering is a practice of care is to say that these sexed roles are fully circumscribed in the changeable conditions of history. It is also to say that these "maternalist activities" do not spring from any particular configuration of somatic traits or bodily processes, both enjoining all who would do the work of mothering and also creating a standard for what qualifies as mothering beyond the act of gestating or bearing the legal designation of mother.

Such a theory also clarifies previous theorizations of embodiment that have often been dismissed as essentialist. Luce Irigaray theorizes *woman* as the reality of difference against the masculinist consolidation of the subject as singular, possessed of bodily integrity, and agential. This distinction is produced by the projection of woman as absence, both in an existential sense, as nonbeing, and as a sex in a physical sense, marked by the absence and passivity that this masculinist logic projects onto the structure and manifold activities of vaginas. In fact, Irigaray theorizes, the feminine is the multiple, the internally different; vagina as metaphor speaks to this diffuse, proliferating difference, the paradigmatic form of which, for Irigaray, is sexual difference.[36]

Sexual difference without cisness allows us to name the historical reality that this internally different Irigarayan vaginality, a feeling of diffusion both in sexual sensation and in identitarian sensation (to feel different even from oneself, in Irigarayan terms), has never been restricted to those assigned female at birth. To illuminate this reality we can consult a long archive of trans women's writing that describes the experience of penetrability as a positive sexual and sexed quality of their bodies. These accounts are available from the sexological archive of the latter nineteenth century to recent work. Consider just two: the early twentieth-century account of the life of a Brooklyn street fairy named Loop-the-loop and the recent autobiographical writings of the historian Jules Gill-Peterson.

The first narrative was published by a US Army doctor in the *American Journal of Urology and Sexology* in 1917. The narrative is composed of the doctor's reflections on physical examinations and interviews with Subject 23, a fairy named Loop-the-loop who was born in rural Pennsylvania in 1883 and lived in New York as a sex worker at the time of the doctor's examinations. The doctor describes Loop-the-loop's genitals and concludes that they were perfectly "normal" and "virile." He is therefore confused and angry when Loop-the-loop "invited ... attention to the fine development of his breasts, whereas there was not the slightest evidence of gynecomasty."[37] The doctor goes on to report that Loop-the-loop "was laboring under the honest conviction that his anus was indeed an aborted vagina—a most extraordinary delusion."[38] Loop-the-loop confirms this bodily self-understanding by reporting that she "avoids the danger of a brutal coitus" that might result in "tearing [her] very small vagina." The doctor interprets these comments as evidence that she has "lost ... every sense of shame; believing himself designed by nature to play the very part he is playing in life, it was truly remarkable to hear this nervous, loquacious, foul-mouthed and foul-minded 'fairy' of the most degraded slums of a multi-millioned city chatter about his experiences, just as though he were talking about the rearing of fancy pigeons, or anything of a similar nature."[39] So precisely here we see the expert dismissing the subject's understanding of her body as delusion. Despite harassment by police and the scorn that marks the doctor's report, Loop-the-loop felt that her "instinct [was] not congenital" and that she "sees no immorality in it; there is no desire for alteration in his nature, and so fierce is the sexual impulse in his case that he claims to be practically insatiable."[40] The reality of the lives of street fairies cannot enter into the doctor's understanding. This doctor believes that Loop-the-loop's life is criminal and wants Loop-the-loop to believe that her life and body are an affliction. Her contentment with her body, her relationships, and her life break the very operation of the medical encounter where the patient is supposed to seek the expertise and aid of the doctor.

The second account is from Gill-Peterson's "Estro Junkie," in which she outlines the bodily and identitarian practices of her hormonal regime. She writes,

> How can I explain what is happening to me, when I puncture the small round progesterone ball with a different needle, before lubricating it and stuffing it inside my ass? What can I do about my desire for it to make my boobs go from Cs to Ds? ... What kind of feminist am I today: a feminist hooked on progesterone, or a transgender body hooked on feminism? I have

no other alternative but to revise my classics, to subject those theories to the shock that was provoked in me by the practice of taking progesterone. To accept the fact that the change happening in me is the metamorphosis of an era.

Except, it's not. There is no real change in my feminism, merely its tactical defense from the bad faith fascists who send me death threats in its name. There is no revision of my classics by the mundane fact of putting a hormone oil capsule inside my ass each day. . . . There is no shock, there is no era inaugurated. . . .

My breasts may be swelling and my libido running hot, but that was also true before I started progesterone. Yes, I can fuck my boyfriend hard, and nearly indefinitely, with my girl dick. Castrated as I am, we can even share the intimate pleasure of me cumming inside him without any of the usual anxieties. But no era is born of this congress. . . . I am far more concerned that the flat fact of my taking hormones to maintain this body is reason enough to be treated as disposable, expendable, and contemptible by those who have nothing better to do than visit hate upon the marginal to secure their station.[41]

In this passage, Gill-Peterson does many things. First, simply, she narrates her body on her own terms with no doctor to receive, censor, or translate. She is not beholden to the medical model's logic of change nor must she dodge a doctor's attempted erasure of trans women's embodiment from the historical record. She remarks the active elements of female embodiment: swelling, desiring. Gill-Peterson's body acts on the world, on her boyfriend, and on her own consciousness. Her description of her body destroys the mutual exclusion of penetrability and ability to penetrate, revealing the universal ability of bodies to do both, by one moment "stuffing" a capsule into her ass and the next stuffing herself into her boyfriend's body. Her description of sexual relationality detaches the acts of penetration from the bodily ordering that cisness rests on, from the binaries active/passive, subject/object, presence/absence, showing us that penetration is an offering and beckoning penetration is an act. Finally, castration here is an enlivening, affirming, possibility-producing experience that does not inaugurate a new era, life, or person but is one event in the becoming of the body that writes these words.

Perhaps most importantly, however, penned by a historian who is working on a manuscript that tells the story of the many ways that trans women have outfitted their bodies for themselves in the twentieth century, Gill-Peterson's personal account disrupts the conceptual apparatus that has held trans women in a perpetual state of novelty, always brand new, always too new to be allowed to exist.[42] This history, throughout the entire span of trans women regarded and depicted as categorically distinct from cis women, has presented trans women, as Gill-Peterson goes on to say, as "mere allegory, reduced at the same time to the too literal, she is what has no space in which to mean, and so she knows . . . what materialism really demands."[43] In Gill-Peterson's ability to know that she is doing this, the text does inaugurate a new era, not of a personal history but of a collective one. This is not to say that a trans woman is doing something for the first time here; to claim that would be to collaborate in producing the collective amnesia stretching from Loop-the-loop to Janet Mock and encompassing the texts of thousands of their sisters and siblings, and this writing knows that bodily experience is relentlessly historical. Rather, again, Gill-Peterson is positioned here, in history, both to narrate her body as it speaks to her *and* to envision the audience who can read her. This audience is not categorically cis and she needn't translate for the benefit of a supposed cis readership. All the trans women's writing to which Gill-Peterson has been audience has readied the way for this historical emergence. It is that same audience that we constitute, anticipate, and hope to expand and bolster with this volume.

FEMINISM AGAINST CISNESS

Every chapter in this collection helps to clarify the knot of the two materialisms that have structured this introduction: first, society is ordered around a hierarchy of value stemming from monetization of work with the corollary devaluation of reproductive labor. Second, sexual difference is a social hierarchy organized by the reproduction of the link between penetrability and subordination; its animating premise, proffering a homology between cisness and bourgeois whiteness, is one of its most potent weapons. Each chapter, departing from a place of knowing these things, pushes forward political, historical, and theoretical thought that reflects the real terrain of sex, gender, and sexuality, unobscured by the ideology of cisness.

In chapters that focus on the politics of trans identities, Cameron Awkward-Rich, Margaux L. Kristjannson, and I redraw the lines of communication away from cis people and among trans people and trans historical genealogies. Awkward-Rich's "On Trans Use of the Many Sojourner Truths" investigates the image of Sojourner Truth addressing the audience of the 1851 Women's Rights Convention, an event that has had a long and varied life. Her famous question—"Ain't I a woman?"—has for decades circulated in a variety of feminist contexts as a contestation of narrow, misogynist, and white supremacist conceptions of *woman*. It's not surprising, then, that this image of Truth has been likewise put to use in twenty-first-century contestations of trans-exclusionary feminisms (and plain trans misogyny under the guise of feminist concern). Foregrounding the example of Joy Ladin's 2016 TEDx talk, titled, of course, "Ain't I a Woman?," Awkward-Rich's chapter thinks critically about this relatively new trans life of Sojourner Truth. In particular, it queries the rhetorical moves and effects of Truth's invocation in white trans contexts, arguing that these invocations rely on a structure of analogy with and displacement of race. In turn, this structure of argument works to obscure the extent to which cis sex/gender—that is, sex/gender as a stable, binary configuration—was and is a racial project. Further, the chapter takes seriously the likelihood that Truth never actually posed her membership as "woman" as a question. Using the long-standing debate about whether Truth ever asked her famous question as a context, it suggests that (white) trans feminist investment in nonetheless invoking Truth as the question "Ain't I a woman?" can teach us something about the racist logics of liberal trans feminism. But, rather than turning away from the most popular image of Sojourner Truth as a resource for Black trans feminism, the chapter concludes with a turn toward two Black trans feminist potentials embedded within it.

In "1970s Trans Feminism as Decolonial Praxis," Kristjannson and I proceed from writings by trans feminine people active in 1970s Trans Liberation political projects in New York City, Philadelphia, and Miami. We write in the ongoing life of an anti-Black and settler colonial order, where trans feminine life and resistance continue under the conditions set by the murderous logics of sexual violence, murder, disappearance, and the carcerality of everyday life. In this scene of ongoing dispossession, settler states offer trans inclusion as the promise of the next frontier of civil rights struggle. Agents of this state position legislation, such as the trans bathroom bills, as the representative form of anti-trans violence and recommend legal challenges. As important as these legal efforts are in protecting trans access to public space, delimiting trans struggle to the promise of inclusion in state protection is revealed to be also an effort to conscript trans people into the reproduction of the settler nation that has always been structured by enslavement, genocide, and bureaucratic and carceral enforcement of cisness.

In historical chapters, Greta LaFleur and Beans Velocci take the concepts that emerge from these political formations and bring them to bear on archives. LaFleur's "Trans Feminine Histories, Piece by Piece, or, Vernacular Print and the Histories of Gender" reads eighteenth- and nineteenth-century settler newspaper reports that refer to, gesture toward, or describe the experiences of self-castration. The strategies that appear in these reports are variegated, creative, and, to the one, partial, depicting approaches to trans womanhood that include everything from modifications to modes of dress to what might amount, in our own time, to hormone adjustment. None of the reports are longer than a few hundred words, at best, and many of them are rendered in the judgmental and/or disciplinary language of strict settler gender systems and gendered racial expectations. The chapter has two aims: first, it showcases these reports as narratives important to the ongoing project of writing thicker and more robust trans feminist histories of eighteenth-century North American cultures; second, the chapter takes these reports as a point of departure for sketching out a trans feminist historiographic method for the study of early periods that combines care, creativity, and historical research methods sensitive to a complex knot of eighteenth-century realities (colonialism, multiple and competing understandings of gender diversity, racialization and enslavement, gendered discipline, etc.). Central to the chapter is the assumption that erasing or undermining the claims of trans women to womanhood has been a prerogative of traditional methods for writing history, including (or especially) women's and queer history, but that some scholarship in women's and queer history nonetheless offers us some tools to undo assumptions of cisness, cis sexist epistemological principles that inform historical research.

Velocci's "Denaturing Cisness, or, Toward Trans History as Method" counters arguments that transness is a newfangled invention and therefore an illegitimate way of being. Historians of transness and nonacademic trans people alike have sought to locate trans individuals in the past to prove that they have always existed in some way or another. But while this approach promises contemporary validation of identities, it has several unintended consequences. First, because trans history developed out of a history of sexuality paradigm that focuses on genealogies of contemporary categories and demands tight historicization of identities, it continuously runs up against the problem of defining "who counts" as a subject of trans history. This insistence on a coherent and recognizable trans subject presupposes an ontological gender stability that runs contrary to transness itself. Second, a minoritizing search for trans people in the past unintentionally reproduces a cis/trans binary—in that model, throughout history, most people's gender identity or social role has naturally mapped onto their sexed body, in contrast to trans people who are distinct for their lack of fit. This renders invisible the way that that *all* sex and gender—including what is regarded as cisgender, or non-trans—has constantly failed to fit into normative taxonomies. Cisness itself had to be actively constructed as arguments about racialized and classed sexual difference, scientific study of sex that revealed constant bodily anomalies, and quotidian violations of gender norms constantly threatened to undermine the idea of a coherent, stable, and binary sex system. It is, in fact, cisness that cannot ever be adequately defended. Third, the very attempt to legitimize contemporary transness through an insistence on a trans historical transness takes for granted that the best way to defend something in the present is to show that it has always existed. This chapter, then, in addition to arguing that cis normativity is itself a historical construct, also pushes back against the impulse to historicize transness at all, offering an alternative trans historical temporality that values change and fluidity over stability.

In theoretical chapters, Kay Gabriel and Marquis Bey provide conceptual tools for understanding the present state of trans life and how it might move through revolutionary futures. Gabriel's "Two Senses of Gender Abolition: Gender as Accumulation Strategy" asks what contribution does the struggle for trans liberation have to this communist horizon? To pose this question raises immediately the vexed relationship between class struggle and so-called identity politics. This chapter aims to understand the totalizing, rather than particularizing, force of political movement from one or another standpoint of social identity. The Hungarian philosopher Georg Lukács introduced *standpoint* as a category in order to think the differential perspectives onto capitalist totality that class positions enable. In a Lukácsian attempt to account for the capitalist production of sexual identity, Kevin Floyd in *The Reification of Desire* has argued that this production of identity—a reification in the sense of the freezing and solidification of a stable position out of a historical process—enables a particular, historically situated, and critical knowledge of capitalist totality: "To think sexuality in reification's terms is to begin to see the way in which reification refers to a social dynamic that opens critical vantages on the totality of capital as much as it closes them down."[44] The author pursues an analogous argument from a specifically transsexual perspective. This chapter says *transsexual*, versus *trans* or *transgender*, advisedly. Gabriel's aim is to foreground the sphere of embodiment that transsexuality bears on—where "embodiment" signals the social dimension of signification that any particular body partakes in.

Bey's "Faceless: Nonconfessions of a Gender" unfolds in a first-person perspective. Their chapter yearns for a gendered subjectivity of facelessness. They know that their body, read as cis too often, read as Black nearly always, and rarely understood as what that impossible nexus entails, is made to confess certain things. Indeed, Foucault says elsewhere that sociality is structured by the demand to confess oneself as a way to coerce truth from deviant criminality. To refuse the gender binary is a criminal act, and trans antagonism—a violence that manifests along a spectrum from head-shaking disapproval to death—is at base a vociferous coercion to confess. The aim in this chapter is to pose this question: What happens when one's body belies what they wish it to be? For those of us who are read as cis, have not undergone the alterations potent with gendered signification, and are not trans(gender) in a sense that registers with how such an identity is made tentatively legible, what claim do we have to a gendered subjectivity that is in fact a nonconfession, a confessional refusal, a desire for facelessness? And how might (their) Blackness muddy the already muddy waters of gender alignment, that uneven epidermis indexical of an anoriginal lawlessness lacerative of the "cis" of cisgender, intimate with the "trans" of transgender? In this they have only a byzantine desire for a way of moving in the world and among others on grounds unstable, being and becoming a nobody, a faceless being not without gender per se—oh, how known it is that one has a gender, one everyone assumes and insists on and demands of them, ontologically—but with a subjectivity that vibrates away from perinatal circumscription. In a desire for facelessness and confessional refusal, they are intrigued by the contours of the engendered world when living unto a way of being that is not coerced to confess its gendered self or confined to the normative registers of the body-made-legible.

If Gabriel and Bey provide a glimpse at utopian horizons where the knot of compulsory cisness, capital, and anti-Blackness is undone, Joanna Wuest and Jules Gill-Peterson document impediments to such futures. Wuest's "Assuaging the Anxious Matriarch: Social Conservatives, Radical Feminists, and Dark Money against Trans Rights" addressed the recent and strange convergence of Christian legal organizations, conservative foundations and nonprofits, Trump administration officials, and trans-exclusionary radical feminists (TERFs). These social conservatives and radical feminists have joined forces in legislative and judicial conflicts over the rights of physicians and therapists to treat gender-nonconforming and transgender youth as well as over inclusionary bathroom access policies. Though it resembles past partnerings of feminists and conservatives who allied against pornography and for the victims of violent crime, the coalition's mobilization of feminist, antiracist, and even intersectional arguments against the very notion of trans experience and identity heralds the advent of a new social conservative feminist political logic. The Family Policy Alliance, for instance, has unveiled its own version of #MeToo feminism with its "Ask Me First" campaign, which champions the voices of cis women and (presumably cis) children and uses them in ballot referenda and legislative campaigns against trans rights. Additionally, the Alliance Defending Freedom (ADF), the country's largest, most well-funded right-wing Christian litigation group, has funded TERF groups like the Women's Liberation Front and has worked with them across a range of legal battles and public education events. In doing so, the ADF has centered a POC cis-female plaintiff to make an appeal to the rights of racialized (cis) women against trans women (styled in part as the ever-creeping specter of the opportunistic cis-male predator). Thus, at its core, this coalition is prepared to levy the principles of feminism, womanhood, intersectional antiracism, and diversity and pluralism more broadly against the expansion or erosion of sex and gender as social categories. This chapter tracks the emergence of this series of partnerships and campaigns and interrogates the rhetorical and ideological transformations that have attended them.

Gill-Peterson's "Caring for Trans Kids, Transnationally, or, Against 'Gender-Critical' Moms" names and indicts the transnational network of anti-trans political alliances in the United States and United Kingdom that targets children explicitly for harassment, bullying, and legislative and administrative violence. Trans children find themselves in the crosshairs of a series of anti-trans political fronts: state legislative efforts in the United States to make trans-affirmative healthcare a *crime*, and to ban trans children's participation in education and organized sports; the saturation of UK corporate media outlets with moral panic stories about trans children, leading to the imperiling of reforms to the country's Gender Recognition Act; the circulation of pseudoscientific theories like "Rapid Onset Gender Dysphoria"; and the invocation of trans children as moral degeneracy incarnate by right-wing movements with white supremacist and authoritarian goals. This diffuse field of anti-trans movements has in common the stimulus that children are far more culturally and legally vulnerable to political violence than adults.

To produce a political analysis of this varied field of actors, this chapter focuses on the most respectable of such crusaders: so-called gender-critical moms, who have organized around the aggrieved identity category of "mom" or "mommy." Using a sentimental political mode in the United States and

United Kingdom from which white women, as mothers, have long bene-fited, these well-funded, organized groups claim to be sincerely alarmed at the supposed growing ranks among their children who are coming out as trans. Although their "critical" understanding of "gender ideology" is based in a series of easily falsifiable claims, this chapter aims not to prove them wrong or catch them in a lie, which would do little to challenge their current clout and respectable veneer. Instead, as a contribution to the political analysis of white supremacy embedded in cis normativity and trans-exclusionary feminism, this chapter places gender-critical moms in the larger context of resurgent reactionary, authoritarian, and ethnonationalist political movements in both countries. What does it mean, the chapter ultimately asks, that white women are the respectable face of a politic invested in the fantasized outcome of exposing trans children to social and literal death?

Grace Lavery's "Generic Deductiveness: Reasoning as Mood in the Stoner Neo-Noir" models what trans feminist analysis can do with the trans-misogynist conditions established by the political actors that Wuest and Gill-Peterson describe. To capture and theorize the particular condition of trans women under the present circumstances of unprecedented historical surveil-lance, this chapter examines the epistemic ambivalence and erotic deflation of what it calls the "stoner neo-noir" subgenre of Hollywood cinema. The genre's principles were, Lavery suggests, sketched in the classic 1970s noir revival movies (Polanski's *Chinatown* and, especially, Altman's *The Long Goodbye*) but became a staple of studio output in the 1990s (with the Coen Brothers' *The Big Lebowski*) and into the present (with Paul Thomas Anderson's adap-tation of *Inherent Vice* and the recent *Under the Silver Lake*). These movies share more than a stoned protagonist (a detective, or "dick") and a Southern Californian location: crucially, they depart from traditional noir by emplot-ting mysteries that, while they may have conventional solutions, provoke un-ruly and metaphysical speculations into the nature of suspicion, depicting and perhaps even promoting a lethargic air of deductiveness that exceeds (indeed, only partly overlaps with) the mysteries delineated by plot, applying itself rather to the ambient, affectively muted condition of social reality as mediated by the phenomenological experience of the dick. "Generic deduc-tiveness" aligns the double-deductiveness of the stoned dick, solving both a particular mystery and the mystery of reality itself, with the curious condition of the trans woman positioned as theorist of a general condition while simulta-neously charged with resolving a plot whose particulars are all-too-intimately known. Although she stops short of claiming a causal relationship, Lavery also examines narrative echoes and reverberations between the stoned dick as protagonist of neo-noir and the contemporary (that is, the 1970s to the present) emergence of a feminist critique of Freud's abandonment of the seduction theory—a fateful decision to elevate fantasy above plot in the causal scheme psychoanalysis attributed to the development of the sexual subject.

WHO IS ON THE OUTSIDE OF CISNESS?

The epigraphs that begin this introduction demonstrate a lineage of this thought. Cohen's seminal essay "Punks, Bulldaggers, and Welfare Queens" lays out, by simply looking around at the real conditions of history in her present, that heterosexuality is a minoritarian structure of power and not actually a lived social norm for most people. The essay springs from Cohen's resistance to the way that white queer radicals in the early 1990s were drawing a simple and antagonistic political line between queers and straights (or breeders as the misogynist parlance often had it). Looking around her life and the people in the neighborhoods where she felt safe and seen, Cohen noticed that there was not such an easy line. Black women, Black families, and other people of color were held outside the protections of heteropatriarchy, taxonomized by gender and sexuality through terms like *welfare queen* as categorically as any subgroup of queer people. Rather than dissipating the force of political resistance to heteropatriarchy, for Cohen, this fact expands its force, indicating the material basis for a web of solidarity that reached the vast majority of people.[45]

To adapt Cohen's essential formulation, we might ask who is on the outside of cisness? The literal answer: every single one of us, because even those who are called cis only own that title through the maintenance of nervous denial about the way bodies work.[46] Despite this universal non-cisness of bodies, however, groups of people are radically differentially socially positioned in relation to this fact. People who are racialized or poor, people with disabilities, and, most overtly, people who are called trans or gender nonconforming: these are the people made to bear all the weight of the universal non-cisness of bodies because they are made to represent that fact. That is why, for so many decades of the twentieth century, culture, in the United States and other colonizing/colonized contexts, created a substantial archive of media that presented trans women as a joke, a sign of panic, or, simply, dead.[47] This genocidal cultural imaginary and the particular representational forms that constitute it (which include presenting trans women as seductive forces up until the revelation of genitals, the emphasis on the comical nature of trans women's very existence, and the centrality of images of trans women who are abused or murdered) index the stakes of being thus laden with the role of representing something about bodies that cis people do not want to admit.

But, then, who is outside of sexual difference? The answer is none of us. Cis or trans; men, women, nonbinary people: all of our sex and gender experience is devilishly bound by its symbolic field. Billy-Ray Belcourt is talking about the act of sex when he says that "sex is one of the few social interactions I choose that reminds me of my unending penetrability" in his book of essays *A History of My Brief Body*.[48] But, this introduction argues, the experience of sexed embodiment is also (and relatedly) a reminder of our "unending penetrability." We are simply differentially positioned regarding this universal penetrability of bodies, which is the material reality of sex. All of us live in bodies that are interpreted in the terms set by this ideological formation, more or less able to deny or deflect our body's penetrability. Those who are called women are tasked with representing this universal reality, but that signifier *woman* is only shorthand for the object of feminization, a category that can be mobilized in many ways, as this introduction has demonstrated. Each of us has other identities that are not as a subsidiary, modifying, secondary, or additive but constitutive of and transversal to sex, this field of meaning in which our bodies circulate. Belcourt, like Irigaray, models embrasure of the unending penetrability of bodies as the only true resistance to a historical formation that renders the penetrable person expendable or nonexistent. Belcourt's beautiful sentence begins with sex and ends with penetrability; "I choose" is the hinge at the center. To be able to choose how we all manage our penetrability is the ur-goal of feminist political struggle, in a sense, and this is a question of material conditions and practices. Queer and trans life, historically, has known this reality of bodies intimately and elaborately, even as those cultural formations are also striated with masculinist refusal, necessitating the assertion of the feminine embrasure of penetrability here too. Herein lies one significant distillation of the mutually constitutive nature of feminist and queer/trans struggle.

This introduction has attempted to outline a theory that allows us to push past the impasse, set up by the misrecognitions of queer theory as it emerged in the early 1990s. It is cisness, not the historical category *woman*, that limited feminist revolutionary horizons. When woman is a conceptual or political problem, it is a racial and class problem. Whiteness and cisness, co-emergent and inextricable historical formations, are the impediment to gender liberation. The strands of queer liberation that orbited academic queer theory in the early 1990s couldn't see this, and so woman became the bad object and femininity the field of expression that came to represent gender expression *tout court*. In much the way that Cohen observes that this moment posed heterosexuals as the problem, while sidestepping the way that *the heterosexual* only really serves as an alibi for the claim to the natural sexual propriety of whiteness, these same operations rushed to femininity and woman as the problem. They sidestepped the way that these formations serve as alibis for whiteness and accumulation and even in this sense only to the same extent as are masculinity and maleness. Cisness is the true crux, foundation, and ideological substrata of all this gendered ordering.

The phrase "feminism against cisness" ought to be a redundancy and *Feminism against Cisness* seeks to make that imperative plain going forward. Feminism should be definitionally against cisness. For people to assert femininity for its own aesthetic and social possibilities not for the small compensation of gender-normative, which is to say racial and class, benefit is to militate against cisness. For women to march together, to gather unmediated by men, to, in their being together, reject the hierarchy imposed by sexual difference is to attack cisness. For trans people to march together, to work out the antagonisms internal to trans community, unmediated by cisness, to, in their being together, reject the hierarchy imposed by cisness, and in transgender publicness and mutual recognition reveal cisness as only an ideology that manages us for whiteness and capital accumulation, is to end cisness. For all to assert the queerness and femininity of reproductive labors, because, not in spite, of their position against the state of the world as it is, organized by capital accumulation and the extractive violence that allows such accumulation: this is simply a substantial component of any program that can claim the mantle of feminism.

NOTES

1 "'Woman' is there to confuse us, to hide the reality 'women.'" Monique Wittig, "One Is Not Born a Woman," in *The Straight Mind*, 16.
2 Gill-Peterson, "It's Not Enough to Celebrate Transgender Women of Color during Pride."
3 For the audio and a transcription of the interview, see Rivera, "Bonus Episode—From the Vault: Sylvia Rivera and Marsha P. Johnson, 1970."
4 This impression is strengthened by the fact that the interviewer's questions have mostly been edited out of the surviving copy of the interview, which was discovered on a reel-to-reel tape in a box in the basement of the Lesbian Herstory

Archive in Brooklyn in 2019. There is also a third person in the interview, who's identified as Victor.

5 See Greta LaFleur's contribution to this collection for a provocation regarding the many methods of body modification that the historical archive holds.

6 Mitchell, *Woman's Estate*, 62.

7 Fortunati, *Arcane of Reproduction*.

8 See Williams, *Politics of Public Housing*; and Kornbluh, *Battle for Welfare Rights*.

9 For an elaboration of this communist analysis of reproductive labor, see Gleeson and O'Rourke, "Introduction." See also O'Brien, "To Abolish the Family."

10 See Kay Gabriel's contribution to this collection for a thorough and new articulation of the relation between transsexual embodiment and the instrumentalization of gender for capital accumulation.

11 Butler, *Bodies That Matter*, 235.

12 *Pato* is Spanish-language slang for faggot, as Rivera explains.

13 Rivera, "Sylvia Rivera—Part 2."

14 Snorton, *Black on Both Sides*.

15 See Jules Gill-Peterson's contribution to this collection for a fulsome historical and theoretical account of this racial mobilization of the idea of women and children.

16 Rivera, "Transvestites."

17 Rivera, "Bonus Episode—From the Vault: Sylvia Rivera and Marsha P. Johnson, 1970."

18 See Greta LaFleur's work in progress *A Queer History of Sexual Violence*, which addresses the early American use of castration as a punishment for a variety of racialized and classed criminalized behaviors and conditions.

19 See Joanna Wuest's contribution to this collection for an account of the political alliances that compose the transnational circuit of transphobic political action that seeks to popularize gestures such as this one.

20 I work with a long-established feminist analysis of sexual difference. See, for example, Simone de Beauvoir's analysis of the biologizing of social difference in service of the creation and maintenance of woman as a secondary, othered term to the unmarked male universal in *The Second Sex*. See also Luce Irigaray's theory of sexual difference articulated in *This Sex Which Is Not One*. In this text, Irigaray argues that the history of Western philosophical thought from Plato to Freud has been built around a supposedly universal subject who is in fact gendered male. This subject is produced through contrast with woman in this philosophical system; her unreason and intractable material embodiment provide the Other through which universal Man is aggrandized. The political philosopher Carole Pateman uses the phrase "the law of male sex-right" to describe men's social and political priority and that "sexual mastery is the primary means through which men affirm their manhood," with rape as the "primal scene" through which this power is confirmed. Pateman, *Sexual Contract*, 3.

21 For a small sampling of the scholarship on the relation of sex work to race and class, see Blair, *I've Got to Make My Livin'*; Chin, *Cosmopolitan Sex Workers*;

Levine, *Prostitution, Race and Politics*; Walkowitz, *Prostitution and Victorian Society*; and Wong, *Transpacific Attachments*.

22 Heaney, *The New Woman*, 20.

23 The scholarship documenting the disproportionate vulnerability to sexual assault and abuse among these demographic groups is extensive; what follows is a small sampling. For quantitative analysis of sexual assault and abuse in children, see Gewirtz-Meydan and Finkelhor, "Sexual Abuse and Assault in a Large Sample of Children and Adolescents." For analysis of incidence of sexual assault among disabled populations, see Andrews and Veronen, "Sexual Assault and People with Disabilities." For an analysis of sexual assault of incarcerated women, see Harts-field, Sharp, and Conner, "Cumulative Sexual Victimization and Mental Health Outcomes among Incarcerated Women." For a statistical analysis of incidence of sexual assault among populations of queer and trans people, see Langenderfer-Magruder et al., "Sexual Victimization and Subsequent Police Reporting by Gender Identity."

24 See Cameron Awkward-Rich's essay in this collection for an analysis of how Sojourner Truth, both her actual situation as a self-emancipated, formerly enslaved orator and her presentation by subsequent generations of commentators, reflects negotiation of this transversal relation between Blackness and gendered treatment.

25 For a careful and clarifying historical analysis of white women as managers of plantation labor and finances, an analysis that provides the necessary historical materialist context and corollary for this white woman's behavior, see Glymph, *Out of the House of Bondage*. For an account of Black women's exclusion for the rhetoric of protection and maternity that formed the experience of many bourgeois white women, see Morgan, *Laboring Women*.

26 For a careful and clarifying account of convict labor as a racialized form of punishment used against Black women, see LeFlouria, *Chained in Silence*. Thank you to Scottie Streitfeld for drawing my attention to this book during our discussion hosted by the Queer Theory Reading Group at UC-Irvine.

27 Jacobs, *Incidents in the Life of a Slave Girl*, 214.

28 The other side of Spillers's argument regarding the ungendering of flesh; this history produces solidarities of the feminized. Spillers, "Mama's Baby, Papa's Maybe."

29 See Marquis Bey's contribution to this collection for a theoretical parsing of the "facelessness" that adheres in the non-cis operation of Blackness.

30 Snorton, *Black on Both Sides*.

31 As, for example, Shulamith Firestone does in chapter 4, "Down with Children," in *The Dialectic of Sex*.

32 Laymon, *Heavy*, 23.

33 Laymon, *Heavy*, 16–17.

34 Lewis, "Mothering against the World." See also O'Brien, "To Abolish the Family."

35 Lewis, "Mothering against the World."

36 See Irigaray, *This Sex Which Is Not One*.

37 Shufeldt, "Biography of a Passive Pederast," 453.

38 Shufeldt, "Biography of a Passive Pederast," 454.

39 Shufeldt, "Biography of a Passive Pederast," 455.

40 Shufeldt, "Biography of a Passive Pederast," 455.

41 Gill-Peterson, "Estro Junkie."

42 Jules Gill-Peterson, "Gender Underground: A History of Trans DIY" (manuscript in progress). For an account of this consistent, recurrent claim to the "newness" of trans life, see Heaney, "Preface," in *The New Woman*, xv–xvii.

43 Gill-Peterson, "Estro Junkie."

44 Floyd, *Reification of Desire*, 20.

45 Cohen's work exemplifies and portends the articulation of queer of color critique as well as a wealth of political and cultural organizing from the late 1990s to the present that, in centering BIPOC LGBT people, inherently avoids the kind of whitewashed political and intellectual imaginary that Cohen critiques. Recent political formations including the Undocuqueer movement, which centers the needs of LGBT migrants against an advocacy discourse that often privileges the bonds of nuclear families; anti-pinkwashing groups that fight back against the use of the presence of the forms of LGBT life and civil rights discourses that are legible to Americans and Western Europeans as a cover for the continuation of racist and Islamophobic policies, colonial expansions, and imperialist wars that diminish the life chances of people of all sexual and gender identities in targeted territories; and Queer Muslim political and cultural projects that allow for the articulation of LGBT perspectives and priorities without slipping into the Islamophobia that mainstream LGBT spaces have been too willing to tolerate or even foster. See Margaux Kristjannson's and my contribution to this collection for a partial historical genealogy of this kind of political work.

46 See Beans Velocci's contribution to this collection for a thorough historical analysis of the eugenicist history of how cisness attained this primacy.

47 For an overview of this cultural landscape through film and television, see the film *Disclosure: Trans Lives on Screen*, dir. Sam Feder (Netflix, 2020).

48 Belcourt, *History of My Brief Body*, 72.

BIBLIOGRAPHY

Andrews, Arlene Bowers, and Lois J. Veronen. "Sexual Assault and People with Disabilities." *Journal of Social Work and Human Sexuality* 8, no. 2 (1993): 137–59.

Belcourt, Billy-Ray. *A History of My Brief Body*. Columbus, OH: Two Dollar Radio, 2020.

Blair, Cynthia M. *I've Got to Make My Livin': Black Women's Sex Work in Turn-of-the-Century Chicago*. Chicago: University of Chicago Press, 2018.

Butler, Judith. *Bodies That Matter: On the Discursive Limits of Sex*. New York: Routledge, 1993.

Chin, Christine B. N. *Cosmopolitan Sex Workers: Women and Migration in a Global City*. Oxford: Oxford University Press, 2013.

Cohen, Cathy J. "Punks, Bulldaggers, and Welfare Queens: The Radical Potential of Queer Politics?" *GLQ* 3, no. 4 (1997): 437–65.

Firestone, Shulamith. *The Dialectic of Sex: The Case for Feminist Revolution*. New York: Farrar, Straus and Giroux, 2003.

Floyd, Kevin. *The Reification of Desire: Toward a Queer Marxism*. Minneapolis: University of Minnesota Press, 2009.

Fortunati, Leopoldina. *The Arcane of Reproduction: Housework, Prostitution, Labor and Capital*. Translated by Hilary Creek. Brooklyn, NY: Autonomedia, 1995.

Gewirtz-Meydan, Ateret, and David Finkelhor. "Sexual Abuse and Assault in a Large Sample of Children and Adolescents." Crimes against Children Research Center, Family Research Laboratory, University of New Hampshire, 2020.

Gill-Peterson, Jules. "Estro Junkie." *Sad Brown Girl*, March 3, 2021. https:// sadbrowngirl.substack.com/p/estro-junkie.

Gill-Peterson, Jules. "It's Not Enough to Celebrate Transgender Women of Color during Pride. It's Time to Learn Their History." *The Lily*, June 24, 2021. https:// www.thelily.com/its-not-enough-to-celebrate-transgender-women-of-color -during-pride-its-time-to-learn-their-history/.

Gleeson, Jules Joanne, and Elle O'Rourke. "Introduction." In *Transgender Marxism*, edited by Jules Joanne Gleeson and Elle O'Rourke, 1–32. London: Pluto Press, 2021.

Glymph, Thavolia. *Out of the House of Bondage: The Transformation of the Plantation Household*. Cambridge: Cambridge University Press, 2008.

Hartsfield, Jennifer, Susan F. Sharp, and Sonya Conner. "Cumulative Sexual Victimization and Mental Health Outcomes among Incarcerated Women." *Dignity: A Journal on Sexual Exploitation and Violence* 2, no. 1 (2017). https://doi.org/10 .23860/dignity.2017.02.01.11.

Heaney, Emma. *The New Woman: Literary Modernism, Queer Theory, and the Trans Feminine Allegory*. Evanston, IL: Northwestern University Press, 2017.

Irigaray, Luce. *This Sex Which Is Not One*. Translated by Carolyn Burke. Ithaca, NY: Cornell University Press, 1985.

Jacobs, Harriet. *Incidents in the Life of a Slave Girl*. New York: Penguin, 2000.

Kornbluh, Felicia Ann. *The Battle for Welfare Rights: Politics and Poverty in Modern America*. Philadelphia: University of Pennsylvania Press, 2007.

Langenderfer-Magruder, Lisa, N. Eugene Walls, Shanna K. Kattari, Darren L. Whitfield, and Daniel Ramos. "Sexual Victimization and Subsequent Police Reporting by Gender Identity among Lesbian, Gay, Bisexual, Transgender, and Queer Adults." *Violence and Victims* 31, no. 2 (2016): 320–31.

Laymon, Kiese. *Heavy: An American Memoir*. New York: Scribner, 2018.

LeFlouria, Talitha L. *Chained in Silence: Black Women and Convict Labor in the New South*. Chapel Hill: University of North Carolina Press, 2015.

Levine, Philippa. *Prostitution, Race and Politics: Policing Venereal Disease in the British Empire*. New York: Taylor and Francis, 2013.

Lewis, Sophie. "Mothering against the World: Momrades against Motherhood." *Salvage Journal*, September 18, 2020. https://salvage.zone/articles/mothering-against-the-world-momrades-against-motherhood/.

Mitchell, Juliet. *Woman's Estate*. London: Verso, 2015.

Mock, Janet. *Redefining Realness: My Path to Womanhood, Identity, Love and So Much More*. New York: Atria Books, 2014.

Morgan, Jennifer L. *Laboring Women: Reproduction and Gender in New World Slavery*. Philadelphia: University of Pennsylvania Press, 2011.

O'Brien, M. E. "To Abolish the Family: The Working-Class Family and Gender Liberation in Capitalist Development." *Endnotes* 5 (2019): 360–417.

Pateman, Carole. *The Sexual Contract*. Stanford, CA: Stanford University Press, 1988.

Rivera, Sylvia. "Bonus Episode—From the Vault: Sylvia Rivera and Marsha P. Johnson, 1970." Transcript of interview with Liza Cowan. *Making Gay History*, December 27, 2019. https://makinggayhistory.com/podcast/bonus-episode-from-the-vault-sylvia-rivera-marsha-p-johnson-1970/.

Rivera, Sylvia. "Sylvia Rivera—Part 2." Transcript of interview with Eric Marcus. *Making Gay History*, October 22, 2017. https://makinggayhistory.com/podcast/sylvia-rivera-part-2/.

Rivera, Sylvia. "Transvestites: Your Half Sisters and Half Brothers of the Revolution." *Come Out*, Winter 1972.

Shufeldt, R. W. "Biography of a Passive Pederast." *American Journal of Urology and Sexology* 13 (1917): 451–60.

Snorton, C. Riley. *Black on Both Sides: A Racial History of Trans Identity*. Minneapolis: University of Minnesota Press, 2017.

Spillers, Hortense J. "Mama's Baby, Papa's Maybe: An American Grammar Book." *Diacritics* 17, no. 2 (1987): 65–81.

Walkowitz, Judith R. *Prostitution and Victorian Society: Women, Class, and the State*. Cambridge: Cambridge University Press, 1982.

Williams, Rhonda. *The Politics of Public Housing: Black Women's Struggles against Urban Inequality*. Oxford: Oxford University Press, 2004.

Wittig, Monique. *The Straight Mind: And Other Essays*. Boston: Beacon Press, 1992.

Wong, Lily. *Transpacific Attachments: Sex Work, Media Networks, and Affective Histories of Chineseness*. New York: Columbia University Press, 2018.

PART I
TRANS POLITICS

CAMERON AWKWARD-RICH

ON TRANS USE OF THE   I

MANY SOJOURNER TRUTHS

> What is used most can be mostly missing.
> —SARA AHMED, *WHAT'S THE USE*

In May 1851, a tall Black woman stood onstage at a women's rights convention in Akron, Ohio. In the most familiar historical memory of this scene, the woman, Sojourner Truth, bared her arm and its "tremendous muscular power" to a crowd of hostile white men and women.[1] Her arm, in turn, bore the trace of her history of enslavement and labor, a history that cast her outside of true womanhood. Thus, when, from this position, Truth asked the crowd "Ain't I a woman?" we can understand her to have been "authorizing her experiences under slavery as proof of [the] underlying illogicality" of a notion of universal womanhood that depended on race- and class-based elisions for its coherence.[2]

Over a century and a half later, a tallish white woman stands onstage and rhetorically bares her body and its history to a crowd of mostly, we can assume, non-trans women and men.[3] In this instance, the woman is poet and scholar Joy Ladin and the stage is the setting of her January 2016 TEDx talk. Ladin's talk was conceived and delivered against the backdrop of a flurry of high-visibility mainstream publications that pitted cis and trans womanhood against one another under the guise of feminist concern. Elinor Burkett's June 2015 *New York Times* op-ed "What Makes a Woman?," for example, responded to the public transition of Caitlyn Jenner by putting familiar trans-antagonistic feminist logics on display.[4] In the tradition of Janice Raymond—though perhaps unknowingly or ambivalently so—Burkett used the occasion of Jenner's coming out to lament that "the transgender movement" is "undermining women's identities, and silencing, erasing or renaming [their] experiences" by forcefully reinstalling a patriarchal image of "woman"; that, in short, trans women must actively erode liberal feminist conceptions of "woman" in order to be counted as such. Confronting this and other, even more hostile, negations of her womanhood by means of her body's bared history, Ladin takes up Truth's question "Ain't I a woman?" as both her title and refrain.[5]

How ought we think about the relationship between these two scenes, these two women onstage, situated on either side of historical and social divisions? There are, undoubtedly, many ways to pursue this question. One might, for example, take Truth's trans resonance as evidence of "a structure of black feminism as always already encompassing trans radical feeling."[6] Likewise, one might focus on the "transitivities of blackness and transness" as what enables trans takeup of Truth's question in the first place.[7] Such a reading would allow for an understanding of Black and trans abjection as not analogous, but related outcomes of the ideological role of binary sex/gender in securing and reifying white racial dominance. Following this line of thought, one might attend to the hostile forces confronting both Truth and Ladin, emphasizing the interconnection of white supremacist and trans-antagonistic thought.

While each of these insights informs what follows, ultimately this chapter positions its twinned opening scenes as illustrative of the fraught nexus between Black feminism and a kind of trans (and anti-trans) feminist conversation that requires, for its coherence, "the stability of cis."[8] Or, to put it another way, Ladin's use of Truth exemplifies one way in which transgender discourses often "instrumentalize Black feminism and disavow it simultaneously."[9] I would like to be clear from the outset that the simultaneous use and elision of (figures of) Black feminism is by no means a phenomenon peculiar to trans discourse, nor is Ladin's talk a particularly egregious, but merely a convenient, example. Ladin's talk, that is, offers an occasion to think with an old debate about the historical veracity of the popular version of Truth's Akron speech—indeed, several accounts contend that she never uttered the famous phrase—in order to query the relatively new trans life of the symbol of Sojourner Truth. To do so, it positions the symbol of Sojourner Truth and its circulation alongside the "fact of trans life" in order to, in part, illuminate how, as Emma Heaney puts it in the introduction to this volume, "sexual difference can also operate within other vectors of social power." Much of this chapter, therefore, retraces old ground in a trans attempt to arrive differently where Black feminist critique has already been.

"AIN'T I A WOMAN?"

The 2010s are often narrated as a remarkable decade for trans visibility in the United States, insofar as they ushered *the idea of* trans people into mainstream media and political life. In fact, public conversation about trans people and practices has occurred iteratively for well over a century, often in the form of sensationalized news reports, talk-show specials, and other forms of mass entertainment. While this sensationalized quality persists, the 2010s have also been marked by a strengthening discourse of trans normativity, which has enabled the folding of some, but by no means all or even most, trans people into the national imaginary as deserving subjects of rights. For this reason—along with a changed media environment, the mainstream incorporation of (a certain, very limited kind of) feminist/LGBT politics, and so on—debates that once took place most fiercely within feminist/queer subcultural worlds have come to preoccupy different spaces: the *Atlantic,* the *New York Times,* high schools, youth sports leagues, state congresses, the Supreme Court. In these spaces, trans worlds of sense, dense with histories of being under threat, are perpetually encountered as new and as, themselves, sources of threat.

Fundamentally at issue for both Ladin and Burkett is this encounter between dominant and trans worlds of sense. What might it mean, they are both asking, for dominant worlds of sense to encounter, accommodate (Ladin hopes), and perhaps be displaced (Burkett fears) by trans ones? If trans women (and men) are recognized, within *the* world and not only some trans, queer, and feminist worlds, as "paradigmatic women" (and men), what is the implication?[10] Further, how—using what language, what theory—might and ought such an encounter occur? In the structure of Burkett's article, Caitlyn Jenner functions as a harbinger of an antifeminist theory/language of "woman," one that narrows the category to innate differences in brain structure, nail polish, and "hoary stereotypes."[11] It's easy enough to see through the way Burkett uses the image of Jenner to actively construct two opposing notions of "woman" that necessarily contradict one another—one trans, one feminist; one narrow and grounded in stereotype; one expansive and grounded in experience—in order to rationalize cis sexism *as* feminism. But what is more vital and difficult, I think, is the intramural conversation that must unfold if we also attend to how Ladin likewise uses the image of Sojourner Truth to both set up and resolve a contradiction. Recruited "as a Trans* modifier of feminism," Sojourner Truth's famous question "indexes the contradiction of (white) feminist exclusion of black women, at the same time as it forges a space for the expansion of the category 'woman.'"[12] For this reason, Truth appears as both an antecedent and a horizon for contemporary trans/feminist negotiations of "woman"; she provides, at once, a past for present "fighting for representation within the term 'woman'" *and* a guarantee of the outcome of that struggle.[13]

In order to provide this function, Truth must operate within Ladin's talk as she long has within the (white) feminist imagination, as "a figure in remove" who is simultaneously instrumentalized and disavowed.[14] To illustrate: Ladin's talk opens with an invocation of Sojourner Truth onstage at the 1851 convention, asking her famous question. In this opening instance, "Ain't I a woman?" is attributed solidly to Truth, and Ladin narrates the question as a challenge to Truth's white audience to "expand their definition of 'woman' to include someone they had been taught to believe was physically, mentally, even spiritually different from themselves."[15] But, by the end of the talk, *Ladin* is the one asking her audience "Ain't *I* a woman?" That is, the talk both opens and closes with Truth's question, but, by the end, Truth is no longer, exactly, a historical figure to think with and alongside about the contingency of "woman." Rather, she becomes a position that can be occupied in order to close the debate.

Ladin is far from unique in her rhetorical instrumentalization of Truth. As Nell Irvin Painter has argued, this use of Truth as both a starting point to be displaced and an argument-stopping last word has been remarkably consistent from Truth's day to our own. From Harriet Beecher Stowe's circulation of Truth interrupting Frederick Douglass's 1852 speech in which he moved toward affirming the place of violence in abolition work, to her recruitment into poststructuralist feminist debates about—to put it reductively—"woman" as the foundation for feminism, to 2010s appeals to her Akron speech as the ground for discussions about trans women and girls' inclusion in "woman" in the context of administrative law and feminist discourse, "the colossal Sojourner Truth . . . with a few choice words, gives direction to muddled proceedings."[16] But, insofar as Truth is a position to be occupied that allows the speaker to extract and use the symbolic power of Black womanhood, what emerges from the quagmire is necessarily a reduction of what is at stake in "the proceedings."

There is, for example, an essay by Pat Griffin titled "Ain't I a Woman?" published in the 2012 collection *Transfeminist Perspectives*. Griffin's essay opens by quickly putting "Sojourner Truth's powerful demand that white feminist abolitionists in the nineteenth century expand their awareness to include the needs of black women" to work in the service of an exploration of issues surrounding the inclusion of trans and intersex women in sex-segregated sports in the twenty-first century.[17] One might be inclined to regard this application as mere rhetorical flourish or, even, an admirable attempt to narrate present trans feminist struggles as simply a "new" chapter in what Clare Hemmings would call "a Western feminist progress narrative."[18] But what Hemmings teaches us about such progress narratives is that they rely on particular temporal and affective structures for their coherence, ones "that situate black feminist critiques as essential to the transformation of Western [feminism], but ultimately as transcended," insofar as Black feminist critique is narrated as a definitionally unchanging "*catalyst* to a more general focus on difference."[19] Or, in Griffin's version of the progress narrative, first, white feminists were spurred by a confrontation with Truth to include Black women as subjects of feminism; now, they are likewise confronted with the demand to "expand their awareness to include the needs" of trans and intersex women. Implicit in this story is the relegation and fixing of Black feminist critique—and the situation that gave rise to it—to the past. Feminism, in this story, *used to be* insufficiently attentive to race but now it knows better, thanks to the intellectual labor of Black women that it no longer needs, except perhaps as a warning issuing from feminism's past about the need to continue incorporating difference in order to secure feminism's future.

As Hemmings notes, this kind of feminist storytelling produces a racist false conciliation, which works against an image of Western feminist theory as "a space of conflict or irresolution."[20] Indeed, a denial of the irresolution of the situation that prompted Black feminist critique structures Griffin's essay, insofar as race and racialization become more and more occluded as she moves from Sojourner Truth to trans/intersex athletes. At first, Griffin notes that early twentieth-century controversies about women's sports stemmed from anxieties about protecting impressable white womanhood from sport's "'masculinizing' effects on their appearance, behavior, and sexual interests that would prevent them from living as 'normal' women whose proper roles were wives and mothers."[21] That is, gendered regulation of female athletes was driven by *racial* anxieties about sport's imagined capacity to interfere with the reproduction of the white family unit by undoing the "unique achievement" of sexual and gendered dimorphism.[22] But, as Griffin's analysis turns to late twentieth- and twenty-first-century cases of trans and intersex athletes, race falls out of her analysis entirely, as if the operation of sexual difference through and as race ceased in the second half of the century. Or, perhaps more likely, as if the biological determinism that structures the intersex/trans debate under review has *replaced* rather than (also) *given new cover for* biologically determinist notions of race.

And, yet, there is an extensive bibliography that argues that race is "a ghost variable" haunting contemporary regimes of "sex"/"gender" testing in athletics.[23] As such, this work forcefully undermines the temporality implicit in Griffin's essay: far from having been replaced by the trans/intersex question, old narratives, myths, and anxieties about race and nation structure the terms by which this question is asked, and, therefore, they act as the constitutive outside to ongoing debates about which bodies belong in women's sport. For example, in an essay exploring the racial logics of the 2011 International Association of Athletics Federations (IAAF) rule governing participation of female athletes with "excessive . . . androgenic hormones (Testosterone)," Katrina Karkazis and Rebecca M. Jordan-Young note that the women who became objects of IAAF's sexed governance seemed to be "exclusively from the Global South, and all indications are that they are black and brown women."[24] Through a careful tracing of official IAAF discourse surrounding the policy, Karkazis and Jordan-Young demonstrate the ways and means by which a policy that "should be race neutral" was animated by racialist/nationalist assumptions about gendered aesthetics, medical modernity, the nature of advantage, and incidence of intersex among different populations.[25] There is a reason, that is, that the Black South African runner Caster Semenya features prominently as a case in Griffin's essay about trans/intersex athletes even though—and by Griffin's own admission—her intersex status was at the time based on "unconfirmed speculations."[26]

While it is outside the scope of this essay to give this argument its full due, I mean only to remind that the overrepresentation of nonwhite athletes among those subject to "sex verification" is both an outcome and a reinforcement of one of the core assumptions of Anglo-European nineteenth-century racial science and twentieth-century race thinking: that dimorphic sex/gender is an (evolutionary, social, medical) achievement, and that a "lack of social and biological differentiation between men and women marked blacks as black while also indexing their fundamental difference from and inferiority to whites."[27] As a result, the vanishing of race from trans feminist (and anti-trans) approaches to "the woman question"—in sports and elsewhere—contributes to an understanding of sexual dimorphism as a stable given (to the idea of 'sex' as cis) even though the transness of sex (its fundamental instability) must be presumed in order for "sex" to have become (and remain) a primary technology of racialization in the first place. That is, the vanishing of race helps to secure the cisness of sex so that trans/intersex can appear to only *just now* arrive to contest it.

As another representative, therefore, of a way of arguing that is sometimes called trans feminist, Ladin's move to simultaneously displace and occupy Truth raises questions about, among other things, the relationship between antiracist and trans feminist approaches to sex/gender. Specifically, it raises questions about the extent to which existing trans uses of Truth are *premised on* a displacement of race, of the ways and means by which we can understand cis sex/gender as a racial construct. In Ladin's talk, at the very least, the displacement of race is necessary for Truth to perform her function as a promise that "woman," by way of its contestation, will be expandable. After all, as Ladin tells it, "when Sojourner Truth asked 'ain't I a woman?', no one, then or in the past one hundred fifty years, answered 'no.'"[28]

As Painter and others have also pointed out, the use of Truth in various twentieth- and twenty-first-century political/intellectual projects has relied on a particular kind of not-knowing, ensuring that Truth "floats outside history, a symbol without a life."[29] Indeed, her life often contradicts the uses to which the symbol of her is put. In particular, there are two threads from Truth's biography whose obstruction enables the movement of invocation, displacement, occupation that structures these trans uses. First, the sense that Truth was ever able to securely occupy the category "woman"—that "no one . . . answered 'no'" to her famous question—requires an understanding of "woman" as a category that can (and, more to the point, *should*) be unlinked from its role within racial patriarchy. Such an assertation also requires the elision of one of the other confrontations for which Truth is known: in 1858, she bared her breasts to an audience in Indiana because several proslavery advocates in attendance made the charge that she was a man in disguise.[30] Far from being unquestioned, Truth's womanhood was and—if the contemporary treatment of powerful Black women is any indication—*would be* disputed, on every ground.

The second elision that has enabled trans uses of Truth is a widespread un-willingness to reckon with what it might mean that Truth herself likely never posed her membership to "woman" as a question in the first place. While it is impossible to know the precise wording of her Akron speech, it likely did not include the refrain "Ain't I a woman?" Though this question undoubtedly "became her signifier, her mark and the way that she enter[ed] history," a series of biographies published in the 1990s persuasively argued that Truth's famous question was not her question at all.[31] Rather, it was attributed to her over a decade after the fact by white abolitionist feminist Frances Dana Gage, who presided over the Akron meeting.

There are several existing accounts of Truth's Akron speech, two of which have often been juxtaposed in searches for the "authentic" representation.[32] The first was published in the Ohio *Anti-slavery Bugle* in June 1851 by Marius Robinson, who was serving as secretary for the Akron convention. The sec-ond, commonly known account authored by Gage was not published until twelve years after the fact, in 1863, and was reprinted in both Truth's *Narrative* (1875) and by Elizabeth Cady Stanton, Susan B. Anthony, and Matilda Joslyn Gage in *History of Woman Suffrage* (1881). While the two accounts share many features, they diverge in their description of Truth's linguistic style, narrative details, the inclusion of sentimental appeals to enslaved women's thwarted motherhood, and so on. Notably, only in Gage's account does Truth literally bare her arm and pose her womanhood as a rhetorical question; in Robinson's she insists, "I am a woman's rights. I have as much muscle as any man, and can do as much work as any man. I have plowed and reaped and husked and chopped and mowed, and can any man do more than that?"[33] In both formulations, we can understand Truth to have been "pointing out how gender emerges as much from such contingent social formations as plantation capitalism as from the biological body."[34] However, only in Gage's speech can Truth be interpreted as appealing to white women for inclusion within their concept of "woman." That is, while Truth's trans use has largely been limited to making appeals *to other feminists* to expand their definition of "woman," this was not necessarily, according to most of the available accounts, her concern.

In short, as Susan Stryker notes in her own trans use of Truth, "no defin-itive text of Truth's 1851 speech is extant"; the versions of Sojourner Truth that arrive to us in the present are necessarily mediated by others who have likewise put her to use, initiating the career of her lifeless symbol.[35] For that reason, what she may or may not have actually said is somewhat beside the point. Instead, the point is to ask what of value white feminists have extracted, from the 1860s onward, from this particular image of Sojourner Truth. Put another way: this version of Truth was proffered by a white feminist and has been persistently *useful* to white feminists in the project of both contesting and reestablishing "woman" as a coherent category necessary for feminist politics. Given this, trans feminist invocations of Truth as a defense against trans-exclusionary and trans-misogynistic logics merely continue this project. Which begs the question: What does this long-standing feminist attachment to the symbol of an ungendered Black body petitioning for representation as "woman" preclude?

While I will conclude by offering some suggestions toward an answer, I would first like to confess that this essay is, above all, a complaint. And, as a complaint, it is a response to a dynamic that recurs—a dynamic of which this very complaint is a part. We've all already been here before. So, to reiterate: Ladin's use of Truth is not a novel rhetorical move. It's one, in fact, that she borrows directly from Stryker who herself has noted that Truth's famous question is "perhaps apocryphal."[36] I cannot help, therefore, but be wary of the way in which complaint actually does not intervene in but rather lubricates the dynamics at play here, insofar as "complaints can . . . be stopped by the appearance of being heard."[37] In this case, Stryker's "perhaps apocryphal" both registers and dismisses the structure of my complaint, in advance of my having made it. For that reason, now that my complaint has been made, I will spend the brief remainder of this essay speculating about what it might open up if I abandon the mood of complaint and pursue instead some Black trans feminist potentials embedded in Truth's enunciations.

REINVENTING SOJOURNER TRUTH

While Nell Irvin Painter and Carleton Mabee's approaches were not identical, both these Truth biographers argued that all of the available evidence, when read "in good historian's fashion," suggests that the well-known version of Truth's Akron speech was a retrospective fabrication, that the original did not include the "Ain't I a woman?" refrain.[38] Painter, in particular, was concerned with the process by which Truth entered history stripped of all but a few cutting lines, a few confrontations, and how it was that a person became (and remains) a usable and useful "symbol without a life."[39] The attempt to restore accuracy to Truth's story, that is, was motivated by a historian's concern for the evidence, yes, but also by a Black feminist concern for the real person at the center of that story. It was an attempt to restore to Truth what—as a slave and then as a symbol—she has rarely, if ever, been granted: her "complex personhood," her *life*.[40]

Given my respect for these biographers' motives, I must admit that my complaint about the use of the perhaps apocryphal version of Sojourner Truth does not stem from any particular investment in adjudicating the real story with recourse to shared and shareable evidence. Indeed, I insist that taking the analytic capacities of *trans* seriously requires giving equal valuation to what might be considered unreal, merely felt, or not to—in the ruling episteme—exist.[41] My misgivings, therefore, about the (white) trans use of Truth is not due to evidence overlooked or the wishfulness that animates her circulation; instead, it is a wariness about how the force of the wish for one Truth crowds out other potentialities. Analogous to the way that a trans feminism reduced to endlessly petitioning for inclusion in "woman" through rebuttal of trans-exclusionary discourse inevitably reproduces white supremacist racial grammars—and diminishes the force of other iterations of trans feminism that harness the "anoriginal lawlessness" of *trans*—Sojourner Truth being made to ask, endlessly, "Ain't I a woman?" reduces her to a particular, familiar function.[42]

That is, as Black and women of color feminists have long argued, nonwhite (and, paradigmatically, Black) people are "symbolically and even theoretically excluded from sexual difference," and this exclusion is the necessary backdrop against which sexual difference animated by bourgeois whiteness comes into "relief."[43] Or, to put it more sharply, Black unsexing is a resource from which sex/gender is made. In the case of Sojourner Truth, her endless invocation as the question "Ain't I a woman?" should be understood as performative, insofar as it continually *creates* Black exclusion from sex/gender *through the appearance of contesting that exclusion*. It is, I suspect, for this reason that decades of argument have mostly not affected how Truth is used: the continual renewal of the resource of Black abjection from sex/gender has allowed generations of white women—from Truth's former owner, to Gage, to Ladin—to secure their claims to it.[44]

Of course, the differing contexts of each of these women is deeply meaningful: each of them arrives to the conflict over "woman" at different historical moments, with different personal and political stakes. But, in Deborah McDowell's words, "the repeated invocation of 'Sojourner Truth' functions not to document a moment in a developing discourse but to freeze that moment in time. Such a chronopolitics operates not so much as history but as an interruption of history, at least as black women might figure into it."[45] What never changes, after all, is Truth's role in the proceedings. Further, in trans contexts, this move actually reinforces the relegation of both Blackness *and* transness to sometime other than the present. Blackness gets stuck outside of time as a catalyst—that which provokes a reaction but does not, itself, undergo change—while transness is "futurity itself," arriving *just now* without a history of its own.[46]

At this juncture, it would be hubristic, to say the least, for me to claim to know a way out, to propose a mode of resolution. Instead, let me close by submitting into the long record on Truth and her "multiplicity of uses" two more stories, two bits of unresolved "critical fabulation" that might at least provide glimpses of other paths—[47]

Visibility

My first closing story isn't a story in which Sojourner Truth appears at all. It is, however, also a story about a brandished, muscular arm; a declaration of sex; and a coerced disrobing. In this story, which took place in San Francisco, California, in 1890—seven years after Truth's death—a Russian immigrant who answered to the name Mamie Ruble was arrested for wearing "male attire," in violation of the city's 1863 cross-dressing ordinance. When brought before the judge, Ruble protested the logic of their arrest by "refus[ing] to identify with available gender categories," insisting that they were "neither a man nor a woman" and had, in fact, "no sex at all."[48] To prove that the terms of neither sex nor the law applied to them, Ruble submitted their hand and arm into evidence. More precisely, they invited the judge to look at and feel their musculature, declaring, according to one report, "Why, just feel my arms, Judge. Are those the arms of a woman?" In response, the judge "blushed . . . in doubt of the judiciousness of feeling such a rugged-appearing arm." Ultimately, the police surgeon "conduct[ed] an investigation" and "reported that Mamie Ruble was a woman."[49] Ruble was declared insane and committed indefinitely to the Stockton Asylum where they died of tuberculosis only eight years later.[50]

Admittedly, Ruble's scene in court had little to do with Gage's rendition of Truth's speech at Akron other than, perhaps, the fact that many of the avowed women arrested under cross-dressing laws at that time were, like Gage, feminists invested in expanding what "woman" could mean. And, admittedly, the figures at the center of these stories are not obviously related; like Ladin and Truth, Truth and Ruble sit on either side of key historical, geographical, and social divisions. Still, insofar as it is a device that brings otherwise disparate figures into correspondence, these scenes certainly rhyme. And, once one registers the rhyme (the arm bared, the declaration, the coerced stripping that occurs just outside the scene), the question is how might our interpretation of Truth's speech change once we perceive these scenes as being linked?

One answer is that this pairing places the image of Sojourner Truth in proximity to trans masculinity—and transness generally—not only to trans womanhood. While others have preferred Robinson's version of Truth's speech for its likely nearer fidelity to what happened, I prefer it because of the ambivalence that Truth herself articulates vis-à-vis "joining the ranks of gendered femaleness."[51] (And, to be clear, I prefer this *not* because I think it is necessarily more true or more politically or theoretically efficacious; rather, it's because it begins to help me clarify something still murky about my own Black, trans masculine life.) Reading this way, one might notice that "woman" in Robinson's version of Truth is sometimes a *we*, sometimes a *they*. Indeed, rather than petitioning for the expansion of "woman" to include her despite her difference from white, middle-class norms, Truth proudly frames her musculature, her capacity for work, and her appetite as equivalent to "any man."[52] Both versions of the speech sharply contest terms of what we would now call cisness, but this version in particular disallows us from understanding Truth's exclusion from "true" gender as *only* injury to be contested. Indeed, and despite my earlier complaints, forms of Black political and cultural analysis motivated by what Treva Ellison calls "the promise of black gender," ones that refuse to understand ungendering as anything but an incapacitating injury and not also a resource for a motley solidarity-in-difference, have the effect of making transness (out to be) unlivable.[53] Simply, placing Ruble's scene next to Truth's reminds us that people have long struggled precisely for the right to *exit* the terms of "the colonial/modern gender system," have long lived, been made to live—with all that living entails—askance to its terms.[54]

From this perspective, interpretations that rely on the adjudication of sex/gender (was Truth "really" a woman and by what definition, was Ruble "really" neither?) merely reify cisness and reinforce cis-normative ways of reading. Taking for granted that—insofar as the assemblage of physical attributes, modes of living, self-narration, and cultural codes that govern sex/gender attribution in neither case seamlessly or stably congealed as F or M—neither Truth nor Ruble "were" "cis," what is notable about these rhyming scenes is how sharply they diverge in consequence. Ruble, it seems, lived relatively unnoticed until the eye of the law subjected them to the feminizing violence of "sex verification" and then committed them to an asylum for the rest of their life, whereas Truth spent years by necessity "living overexposed"—or, as she put it, "selling the shadow"—and was subsequently committed to history as a "symbol without a life."[55] One proposal, then: the correspondence and divergence of these scenes illustrate that racialized regimes of visibility differentially shape the experience of the "inhabitation of the un-gender-specific" in ways that are predictable and durable.[56]

Post-2014, the claim that visibility is a trap, especially for trans women of color, is unremarkable. But, perhaps, this kind of trans use of Truth both provides a prehistory for and modifies this claim, by underscoring that the "trap of the visual" is not merely or always *intensified* for racialized and feminized trans people.[57] Rather, there is a qualitative difference, a different kind of trap. Visibility, for Ruble, led to capture by the medicolegal system and an attempt to fix white sex/gender (in all senses of this phrase) by removing reminders of its ideological nature from view so as to prevent it from affecting the sex/gender stability of onlookers. All of this is condensed in the judge's "blush" when faced with "such a rugged-appearing arm." Truth's rugged arm, on the other hand, was not deemed improper or dangerous to regard; importantly, only in Gage's rewriting of the Akron speech was her arm explicitly uncovered. Subsequently, Gage's image of Truth has lived on as a figure whose muscular arm—reproduced by feminist posters, newspapers, and so forth—is continually used for the project of expanding womanhood. In this reading, what interrupts the rhyme of Truth/Ruble is not that one should be properly interpreted as cis and the other as trans, one a woman and the other nonbinary or no known thing. Rather, what interrupts the rhyme is the difference in the availability of white and Black gender nonconformity for (visual) use in the project of (re)constituting sex/gender.

And Yet

Thus far, I have stuck closely to white trans uses of Truth, but Black trans feminists have certainly and similarly put Gage's version of the Akron speech to work. In my final story, then, a tall Black woman stands onstage in Albany, New York. Less than a year prior, the woman's portrait appeared on the cover of a national publication, and her figure—statuesque, dignified, arms bared—came to visually represent the horizon of "America's next civil rights frontier." Onstage at Albany, she enumerates the forces that erode the livability of her people's lives—among them shame, murderous violence, unemployment, incarceration, harassment, and denial of identity and first-person authority—before flipping her hair and asking the question, which is not a question: "Yet, ain't I a woman?"[58]

This scene is taken from a recording of a lecture by Laverne Cox—titled, of course, "Ain't I a Woman?"—delivered to students at the University at Albany in 2015. What strikes me most about this moving image of Cox is how eerily it repeats, not merely rhymes with, the image of Sojourner Truth. For example, Sojourner, as Isabella, spent the first three decades of her life as a slave and then a free woman in a county roughly eighty miles south of the location of Cox's speech. The date of Truth's original speech coincides, as Cox reveals with relish, with Cox's birthday. Also, and most importantly, images of both women—alike in stature and grace—circulate in the national imaginary as portents of the expansion of "woman" and "human" to include, finally, their people as citizens deserving of rights. That is, while Cox employs Truth's pithy question to insist on her own womanhood despite occupying a "social context that would often deny it," what differentiates Cox's use of Truth from the other trans feminist uses I have reviewed is its tense, the time and duration it describes.[59] For Griffin and Ladin, Truth indexes the possibility—perhaps the inevitability—of change, whereas Cox's person, performance, and care to situate Truth in an ongoing Black feminist now emphasize continuity, the time of "the changing same."

In short, both Cox and Truth endure not only context-specific denials of interiority, authority, and gendered being but also the consequences of the racialized hypervisibility that, in small part, differentiated Ruble and Truth. And yet, of course, neither Truth nor Cox is reducible to the circulation of her image, even as both women made and make their living through that very circulation. In their analysis of the June 2014 *Time* cover that figured Cox as the fulcrum of "the transgender tipping point," Jian Neo Chen reads the dialectic between these two tenses, between image and living, between capture and what escapes: "We can view the magazine's insistence on capturing the full image of Laverne Cox from head to toe, in contrast to *Time's* usual close-up cover portraits, as exploiting the overwritten hyper-visibility of Black trans embodiment to mark American civil progress—and to renew a claim on the racially gendered Black body for the continued expansionism of the settler colonial nation-state. Cox's studied crossed stance, however, seems to offer a visual impasse in response to *Time's* demands."[60]

Following Chen, we might understand the impasse introduced by Cox's posture as analogous to the impasse introduced by her use of Truth. Both scenes, that is, forestall the folding in of Black trans embodiment into the narrative time of progress—American progress, Western feminist progress—by foregrounding all that has exceeded it. And what happens in the impasse? The very thing that Truth, Cox, and all manner of racialized, trans/feminized people are denied at every turn. Life. The "scramble for modes of living on."[61] Nearly everything, nothing much.

NOTES

1 Gage, "Reminiscences," 116.
2 McDowell, *"Changing Same,"* 161.
3 While it's possible to use *cis* and *non-trans* more or less interchangeably—and while *cis* has come to replace *non-trans* as the preferred terminology—I'm experimenting here with defaulting to *non-trans* when I am describing people who have not lived (and will not live) trans lives. In contrast, I use *cis* when I am describing *the idea* that sex/gender is, for some, a stable ground. Perhaps it will be a failed experiment, but I am for the meanwhile using this distinction to signal that, while there are myriad ways to live a non-trans life, myriad lived experiences of unstable sex/gender that are nonetheless not socially or personally apprehended as "trans," the appearance of stability that *cis* claims to index is an effect of the racial logics this chapter describes.
4 Burkett, "What Makes a Woman?" For a contextualization of Burkett's essay in the longer history of cis sexist feminism, see Heaney, "Women-Identified Women."
5 Ladin, "Ain't I a Woman?"
6 Gossett, "Blackness and the Trouble of Trans Visibility," 186.
7 Snorton, *Black on Both Sides*, 8.
8 Enke, "Education of Little Cis," 69.
9 Ellison et al., "We Got Issues," 166.
10 Bettcher, "Trapped in the Wrong Theory," 389.
11 Burkett, "What Makes a Woman?"
12 Green, "Troubling the Waters," 67.
13 Stryker, "(De)Subjugated Knowledges," 7.
14 McDowell, *"Changing Same,"* 162.
15 Ladin, "Ain't I a Woman?"
16 On Truth's interruption of Douglass, see Painter, *Sojourner Truth*, 160–61; and Stowe, "Sojourner Truth, the Libyan Sybil." For poststructuralist feminist uses of Truth, see Riley, "Does Sex Have a History?"; and Haraway, "Ecce Homo." For an essay that uses Truth as entryway into thinking about trans women's encounters with the administrative apparatus of the prison, see Andasheva, "Aren't I a Woman?"; and Painter, *Sojourner Truth*, 284.
17 Griffin, "'Ain't I a Woman?,'" 98.
18 Hemmings, *Why Stories Matter*, 35.
19 Hemmings, *Why Stories Matter*, 45, 44 (emphasis in original).

20 Hemmings, *Why Stories Matter*, 46.

21 Griffin, "'Ain't I a Woman?,'" 102.

22 Schuller, *Biopolitics of Feeling*, 59.

23 Karkazis and Jordan-Young, "Powers of Testosterone," 9.

24 The rule was stated in International Association of Athletics Federations, "IAAF Regulations," 111. See Karkazis and Jordan-Young, "Powers of Testosterone," 5.

25 Karkazis and Jordan-Young, "Powers of Testosterone," 5.

26 Griffin, "'Ain't I a Woman?,'" 104.

27 Magubane, "Spectacles and Scholarship," 770. On this point as it relates to trans of color critique studies, see also Gill-Peterson, *Histories of the Transgender Child*; and Snorton, *Black on Both Sides*.

28 Ladin, "Ain't I a Woman?"

29 Painter, *Sojourner Truth*, 261–62.

30 Painter, *Sojourner Truth*, 138–41.

31 Harris, "Finding Sojourner's Truth," 316.

32 See Mabee, *Sojourner Truth*; and Painter, *Sojourner Truth*. See also Washington, *Sojourner Truth's America*, for an updated, thoroughly sourced account of Truth's Akron speech.

33 "Women's Rights Convention: Sojourner Truth."

34 Ellison and Green, "Tranifest," 223.

35 Stryker, "(De)Subjugated Knowledges," 16.

36 Stryker, "What Does It Mean to Be a Woman?"

37 Ahmed, *What's the Use*, 160.

38 Painter, *Sojourner Truth*, 281.

39 Painter, *Sojourner Truth*, 261.

40 Gordon, *Ghostly Matters*, 4.

41 Hayward, "Don't Exist."

42 Bey, "Trans*-ness of Blackness," 278.

43 O'Grady, "Olympia's Maid," 14.

44 See Harris, "Finding Sojourner's Truth," 336–43; and Zackodnik, "'I Don't Know How You Will Feel When I Get Through.'"

45 McDowell, *"Changing Same,"* 163.

46 Halberstam, *In a Queer Time and Place*, 18.

47 Painter, *Sojourner Truth*, 262; Hartman, "Venus in Two Acts," 11.

48 Sears, *Arresting Dress*, 74–75.

49 "She Denied Her Sex."

50 Sears, *Arresting Dress*, 75.

51 Spillers, "Mama's Baby, Papa's Maybe," 229.

52 "Women's Rights Convention: Sojourner Truth."

53 Ellison, "Black Femme Praxis," 10.

54 Lugones, "Heterosexualism," 187. See also Lugones, "Toward a Decolonial Feminism," for a use of Truth I'm interested in: "Thus, the colonial answer to Sojourner Truth is clearly, 'no'" (745).

55 Gill-Peterson, "Feeling Like a Bad Trans Object"; Painter, *Sojourner Truth*, 198, 262.
56 Snorton, *Black on Both Sides*, 58.
57 Tourmaline, Stanley, and Burton, "Known Unknowns," xv.
58 Cox, "Ain't I a Woman?"
59 Cox, "Ain't I a Woman?"
60 Chen, *Trans Exploits*, 3.
61 Berlant, *Cruel Optimism*, 8.

BIBLIOGRAPHY

Ahmed, Sara. *What's the Use: On the Uses of Use*. Durham, NC: Duke University Press, 2019.
Andasheva, Faroat. "Aren't I a Woman? Deconstructing Sex Discrimination and Freeing Transgender Women from Solitary Confinement." *FIU Law Review* 12, no. 1 (Fall 2016): 117–50.
Berlant, Lauren. *Cruel Optimism*. Durham, NC: Duke University Press, 2011.
Bettcher, Talia. "Trapped in the Wrong Theory: Rethinking Trans Oppression and Resistance." *Signs: Journal of Women in Culture and Society* 39, no. 2 (Winter 2014): 383–406.
Bey, Marquis. "The Trans*-ness of Blackness, the Blackness of Trans*-ness." *TSQ* 4, no. 2 (May 2017): 275–95.
Burkett, Elinor. "What Makes a Woman?" *New York Times*, June 6, 2015. https://www.nytimes.com/2015/06/07/opinion/sunday/what-makes-a-woman.html.
Chen, Jian Neo. *Trans Exploits: Trans of Color Cultures and Technologies in Movement*. Durham, NC: Duke University Press, 2019.
Cox, Laverne. "Ain't I a Woman?" February 3, 2015. Video-recorded lecture. https://livestream.com/hvccstreaming/lavernecox/videos/75930275.
Ellison, Treva. "Black Femme Praxis and the Promise of Black Gender." *Black Scholar* 49, no. 1 (2019): 6–16.
Ellison, Treva, and Kai Green. "Tranifest." *TSQ* 1, no. 1–2 (2014): 222–25.
Ellison, Treva, Kai M. Green, Matt Richardson, and C. Riley Snorton. "We Got Issues: Toward a Black Trans*/Studies." *TSQ* 4, no. 2 (May 2017): 162–69.
Enke, Finn. "The Education of Little Cis: Cisgender and the Discipline of Opposing Bodies." In *Transfeminist Perspectives in and beyond Transgender and Gender Studies*, edited by Finn Enke, 60–77. Philadelphia: Temple University Press, 2012.
Gage, Frances D. "Reminiscences." In *History of Woman Suffrage Vol. 1*, edited by Elizabeth Cady Stanton, Susan B. Anthony, and Matilda Joslyn Gage, 115–17. New York: Fowler and Wells, 1881.
Gill-Peterson, Jules. "Feeling Like a Bad Trans Object." *Post45*, December 9, 2019. http://post45.org/2019/12/feeling-like-a-bad-trans-object/.
Gill-Peterson, Jules. *Histories of the Transgender Child*. Minneapolis: University of Minnesota Press, 2018.

Gordon, Avery. *Ghostly Matters: Haunting and the Sociological Imaginary.* Minneapolis: University of Minnesota Press, 2008.

Gossett, Che. "Blackness and the Trouble of Trans Visibility." In *Trap Door: Trans Cultural Production and the Politics of Visibility*, edited by Tourmaline, Eric A. Stanley, and Johanna Burton, 183–90. Cambridge, MA: MIT Press, 2017.

Green, Kai. "Troubling the Waters: Mobilizing a Trans* Analytic." In *No Tea No Shade: New Writing in Black Queer Studies*, edited by Patrick E. Johnson, 65–82. Durham, NC: Duke University Press, 2016.

Griffin, Pat. "'Ain't I a Woman?': Transgender and Intersex Student Athletes in Women's Collegiate Sports." In *Transfeminist Perspectives in and beyond Transgender and Gender Studies,* edited by Finn Enke, 98–111. Philadelphia: Temple University Press, 2012.

Halberstam, Jack. *In a Queer Time and Place: Transgender Bodies, Subcultural Lives.* New York: New York University Press, 2005.

Haraway, Donna. "Ecce Homo, Ain't (Ar'n't) I a Woman, and Inappropriated Others: The Human in a Post-humanist Landscape." In *Feminists Theorize the Political,* edited by Judith Butler and Joan W. Scott, 86–100. New York: Routledge, 1992.

Harris, Cheryl I. "Finding Sojourner's Truth: Race, Gender, and the Institution of Property." *Cardozo Law Review* 18, no. 2 (November 1996): 309–410.

Hartman, Saidiya. "Venus in Two Acts." *Small Axe* 12, no. 2 (June 2008): 1–14.

Hayward, Eva S. "Don't Exist." *TSQ* 4, no. 2 (May 2017): 191–94.

Heaney, Emma. "Women-Identified Women: Trans Women in 1970s Lesbian Feminist Organizing." *TSQ* 3, no. 1–2 (May 2016): 137–45.

Hemmings, Clare. *Why Stories Matter: The Political Grammar of Feminist Theory.* Durham, NC: Duke University Press, 2011.

International Association of Athletics Federations (IAAF). "IAAF Regulations Governing Eligibility of Females with Hyperandrogenism to Compete in Women's Competitions." April 12, 2011. https://www.sportsintegrityinitiative.com /wp-content/uploads/2016/02/IAAF-Regulations-Governing-Eligibility-of -Females-with-Hyperandrogenism-to Compete-in-Women's-Competition-In-force-as-from-1st-May-2011-6.pdf.

Karkazis, Katrina, and Rebecca M. Jordan-Young. "The Powers of Testosterone: Obscuring Race and Regional Bias in the Regulation of Women Athletes." *Feminist Formations* 30, no. 2 (Summer 2018): 1–39.

Keegan, Cáel M. *Lana and Lilly Wachowski: Sensing Transgender.* Urbana: University of Illinois Press, 2018.

Ladin, Joy. "Ain't I a Woman?" TEDx talk, January 7, 2016. Video. https://www .youtube.com/watch?v=goK2YvvQyEw.

Lugones, María. "Heterosexualism and the Colonial/Modern Gender System." *Hypatia* 22, no. 1 (Winter 2007): 186–209.

Lugones, María. "Toward a Decolonial Feminism." *Hypatia* 25, no. 4 (Fall 2010): 742–59.

Mabee, Carleton. *Sojourner Truth: Slave, Prophet, Legend.* New York: New York University Press, 1993.

Magubane, Zine. "Spectacles and Scholarship: Caster Semenya, Intersex Studies, and the Problem of Race in Feminist Theory." *Signs: Journal of Women in Culture and Society* 39, no. 3 (2014): 762–85.

McDowell, Deborah E. *"The Changing Same": Black Women's Literature, Criticism, and Theory*. Bloomington: Indiana University Press, 1995.

O'Grady, Lorraine. "Olympia's Maid: Reclaiming Black Female Subjectivity." *Afterimage* (Summer 1992): 14–15.

Painter, Nell Irvin. *Sojourner Truth: A Life, a Symbol*. New York: W. W. Norton, 1996.

Riley, Denise. "Does Sex Have a History? 'Woman' and Feminism." *New Formations* 1 (Spring 1987): 35–45.

Schuller, Kyla. *The Biopolitics of Feeling: Race, Sex, and Science in the Nineteenth Century*. Durham, NC: Duke University Press, 2017.

"She Denied Her Sex." *San Francisco Chronicle*, October 3, 1890.

Sears, Clare. *Arresting Dress: Cross-Dressing, Law, and Fascination in Nineteenth-Century San Francisco*. Durham, NC: Duke University Press, 2014.

Snorton, C. Riley. *Black on Both Sides: A Racial History of Trans Identity*. Minneapolis: University of Minnesota Press, 2017.

Spillers, Hortense. "Mama's Baby, Papa's Maybe: An American Grammar Book." In *Black, White, and in Color: Essays on American Literature and Culture*, 203–29. Chicago: University of Chicago Press, 2003.

Stowe, Harriet Beecher. "Sojourner Truth, the Libyan Sybil." *Atlantic*, April 1863.

Stryker, Susan. "(De)Subjugated Knowledges: An Introduction to Transgender Studies." In *The Transgender Studies Reader*, edited by Susan Stryker and Stephen Whittle, 1–17. New York: Routledge, 2006.

Stryker, Susan. "What Does It Mean to Be a Woman? It's Complicated." *Time*, March 5, 2020. https://time.com/5795626/what-womanhood-means/.

Tourmaline, Eric A. Stanley, and Johanna Burton. "Known Unknowns: An Introduction to *Trap Door*." In *Trap Door: Trans Cultural Production and the Politics of Visibility*, edited by Tourmaline, Eric A. Stanley, and Johanna Burton, xv–xxvi. Cambridge, MA: MIT Press, 2017.

Washington, Margaret. *Sojourner Truth's America*. Urbana: University of Illinois Press, 2009.

"Women's Rights Convention: Sojourner Truth." *Anti-slavery Bugle*, June 7, 1851.

Zackodnik, Teresa C. "'I Don't Know How You Will Feel When I Get Through': Racial Difference, Woman's Rights, and Sojourner Truth." *Feminist Studies* 30, no. 1 (Spring 2004): 49–73.

MARGAUX L. KRISTJANSSON

AND EMMA HEANEY

1970S TRANS FEMINISM 2

AS DECOLONIAL PRAXIS

The 2010s saw the codification of a set of priorities for mainstream trans politics in the United States. These priorities emerged when large queer and trans legal nonprofits took on cases brought by plaintiffs who were experiencing oppression in schools and workplaces as they tried to live their lives as trans people. The focus of the most prominent of these suits sought to guarantee access to bathrooms for children in public schools and to protect trans people from job discrimination and firing for trans status.[1] The prominence of these efforts led then vice president Joe Biden to identify trans rights as "the civil rights issue of our time" in a speech in 2012 and *Time* magazine to declare 2014 the "tipping point" for trans rights.[2] More recently, a backlash against this high-profile attention to trans rights has shifted legal strategy to defense as, all across the country and indeed the world, attempts to legislatively prohibit trans healthcare, exclude trans people from sports, and (in the United Kingdom) overturn gender self-ID policies have taken up the resources of legal organizations defending trans rights.[3] This proliferation of anti-trans legislative efforts dovetails with writings by a mostly UK-based cohort of academics with easy access to major publishing venues who claim that trans women pose a threat to cis women in prisons and domestic abuse shelters and so ought to be barred from those spaces. At the beginning of a new decade then, trans politics seems to have two sides: a progressive camp that works to expand state rights and protections via impact litigation, and a reactionary camp that works through legislatures, courts, and public opinion to deny trans people access to services and spaces.

But if you shift your view away from *Time* and the *Huffington Post*, another picture of contemporary trans struggle comes into view. This struggle aims to address the immediate needs of trans people for housing, medical care, protection from police violence, and support during incarceration. The practices that have developed to meet these aims are crowdfunding money for medical services and living expenses, crowdfunding bail funds and commissary funds for incarcerated queer and trans people, organizing rent strikes and tenants' rights groups, and organizing and participating in street protests regarding the deportations and police murders of Black people.[4] These practices sometimes produce events that attract significant media attention—the massive Brooklyn Black Trans Lives Matter demonstration in June 2020 was the most iconic manifestation of this—but the majority of this work takes place quietly, in small demonstrations and proliferating social media posts with links to places to share funds.[5]

These practices have been theorized from a trans perspective in the recent books *Trans Care* by Hil Malantino and *Mutual Aid* by Dean Spade. These books suggest we look for what we might call politics, not in the town hall forums, the ballot box, or in articles in newspapers of record, but in the activities that we are probably already engaged in every day to feed, clothe, and nurture each other, to manage addiction and illness, and to attain housing and necessary medical care. These skills that we often cultivate in our personal circles and with friends and family, the books suggest, are the same skills that, when scaled up, keep neighborhoods and communities alive and thriving. Where do we find the history of this kind of activity and analysis? How have previous generations understood the relation between these activities and queer and trans life? What kinds of collective life and care are effaced when trans archives are examined for contemporarily legible articulations of trans politics? Crucially, how can the practice of these activities of worldmaking and life-making work undo, rather than just maintain, the working of the settler colony—a political order founded by white settlers on Indigenous lands through conquest and genocide—and the economic and political system founded on the extraction of wealth from the labor of enslaved people on which it relies?

This chapter seeks answers to these questions by contextualizing these recent political activities with precedent writings by trans feminine people active in 1970s Trans Liberation political projects in New York City, Philadelphia, and Miami. We write this in the ongoing life of an anti-Black and settler colonial order, where trans feminine life and resistance continue under the conditions set by the murderous logics of sexual violence, murder, disappearance, and the carcerality of everyday life. In this scene of ongoing dispossession, the US settler state offers inclusion as the horizon that Biden imagines. Agents of this state position legislation such as the trans bathroom bills as the representative form of anti-trans violence and promise trans people protection by the state and its laws. As important as these legal efforts are in protecting trans access to public space, delimiting trans struggle to the promise of inclusion in state protection is revealed to be also an effort to conscript trans people into the reproduction of the settler nation that has always been structured by enslavement, genocide, and bureaucratic and carceral enforcement of cisness.

This chapter analyzes three trans feminist groups—Street Transvestite Action Revolutionaries (star), Radical Queens, and Transsexual Action Organization (tao)—in conversation with (and as part of) Black resistance and Native resistance, to identify three intertwined legacies of refusing such conscriptive gestures. First, we argue that, in these projects, trans feminine and gender-nonconforming people capacitated each other's flesh by sharing hormones, food, shelter, medical access, and autonomous spaces in an order that continually attempts to murder them or hasten their deaths. These practices kept and keep trans femininities and non-cis bodies alive. Second, we argue that trans women of color and street-based sex workers have worked to claim what Hortense Spillers calls the "monstrosity" of their racialized positioning outside normative gender. This claim is expressed when trans feminine people call each other "half-sisters," "queens," "girls," and "non-men," making these avowals and the solidarities they produce a position on the insurgent ground, disrupting not just the cis ordering of society but also the settler colonial and anti-Black order, which is the origin and regulatory life of that ordering. Third, in tracing 1970s trans movement solidarity with Puerto Rican, Black, and Indigenous anticolonial nationalisms, we reveal how trans feminisms have fundamentally interrupted the bodily formations and politics of the United States as a white settler colony.[6]

The ideology of cisness rests on two primary assumptions: (1) that human-ity is divided and reproduces through heterosexual pairings of biologically dimorphic bodies ("males" and "females," XX and XY); and (2) that these differences are everywhere socially relevant and hierarchically fileable into categories equivalent to "men" and "women." The historical process that generalizes cisness is the colonial dehumanization of collectivities and social forms that are not organized through cisness—evidenced in early European images and accounts depicting Indigenous and African women as mon-strously gendered.[7] Cisness was imposed and elaborated in the Americas through conquest and transatlantic slavery—as recent scholarship in Indig-enous and Black studies has illustrated. European colonizers came to Turtle Island and the Caribbean with cis hierarchies deeply embedded in their social organization and thought. By the time of the 1544 Valladolid debates, which marked the first instance of Europeans debating the morality of colonizers' treatment of Indigenous people, Spanish colonial apologist Juan Ginez de Sepulveda could posit that Taino people were "natural slaves" to Christians by way of analogy—as women are to men, as children are to adults. María Lugones argues that "the modern/colonial gender system—the biological dimorphism, the patriarchal and heterosexual organizations of relations" produced "race and gender" and sex as powerful fictions.[8] Lugones exposes how sex/gender and racial difference emerge together through colonial law, violence, and surgical mutilation of intersex bodies. From this premise, we argue that cisness was cultivated as a property of white bodies through slav-ery and genocide. The presence of cis bodies on stolen land depends on the elaboration of the gendered order of colonial rule. As such, settler cisness is one iteration of what Jodi Byrd calls a "transit of empire." Settler cisness func-tions with and through settlers treating "Indianness" as a transferable quality that can be evoked to legitimize European's claims to acquire Native "lands, territories, and resources." In turn, these transits produced colonial order by effacing bodily difference on stolen land.[9]

Understanding trans feminist struggle, then, requires situating it within the white supremacist orders that have sought to make non-cis bodies im-possible and trans lives unlivable on this continent. Spillers writes that the sociopolitical order of the New World, "with its human sequence written in blood, represents for its African and indigenous people a scene of actual mutilation, dismemberment and exile."[10] The United States came into being through genocide and the theft of Indigenous lands and because of the profits from chattel slavery that enriched the wealthy colonists who fought Britain for independence. At present, the United States continues to be a white supremacist polity predicated on anti-Black and anti-Indigenous violence. The trans feminists we read here chart their forms of struggle—politicization of violence against women, practices of gender self-determination, resistance to carcerality, and alliances with Black, Native, and Third World liberation movements—against this genocidal political order that made cis bodies on stolen land.

In the transatlantic slave trade that was used to convert Indigenous lands to settler property and capital, white settlers fashioned their genders in relation to Black and Native genders that they deemed aberrant. Spillers writes that, during the Middle Passage, the auction block and US slave law's accounting of Black lives as property were transmitted through the mother: "under these conditions, one is neither female, nor male, as both subjects are taken into 'account' as quantities."[11] For Spillers, while enslaved women were forced to reproduce enslaved children, gender specificity as reckoned in Euro-American settler norms—that is, sexual dimorphism, protected femininity, recognized motherhood and paternity—is denied to Black females, whose bodies could be invaded at any time by enslavers of either gender.[12] The color line marks cis genders as white.

If cis genders exist along the color line, the genealogy of transness shifts. Black life, as Che Gossett and Marquis Bey note, "obliterates" the cisgendered order.[13] C. Riley Snorton argues that "captive flesh figures a critical genealogy for modern transness, as chattel persons gave rise to an understanding of gender as mutable and as an amendable form of being."[14] That is, contemporary trans embodiments were made in relation to medical and cultural knowledge of Black flesh as alterable or mutable from gender through sexual and medical violence.[15] Snorton tracks Black gender embodiment as a form of fugitive freedom. As Black trans feminists in the 1970s lived and struggled in what Saidiya Hartman terms the "afterlives of slavery," Snorton reveals how modern trans enactments of gendered freedom depend on ungendered Blackness. That is, it is through the violence of medical experimentation and commoditization of Black flesh that Euro-Americans could know themselves as properly gendered (cis) or potentially trans.

Indigenous Two Spirit, queer, and trans organizing is rooted in languages, kinship, lands, roles, and political life rather than being a synonym for trans embodiment. The term *Two Spirit* (*niizh manido* in Anishnabemowin) emerged as a pan-Indigenous referent to these forms of embodiment, political life, and spiritual comportment at the 1990 Third Native American / First Nations Gay and Lesbian Conference in Winnipeg after it was proposed by elder Myra Laramee and Cree activist Albert McLeod.[16] Kwagiulth feminist Sarah Hunt argues that the very categories of colonial gender—man and woman—are the products of this violent colonial disciplining of desire, flesh, and comportments.[17] This was perpetrated through Spanish gendercide against Two Spirit Indigenous peoples in California, through the 1884 Dawes Act that allotted Indigenous lands to individual male household heads, and through missionization and Treaty negotiations where only "men" were authorized by the state to speak for Indigenous nations.[18] Billy-Ray Belcourt locates Canada's Residential Schools (and US Indian Boarding Schools) as sites where gender "was violently made and remade on the bodies" of Indigenous children through sexual violence by both priests and nuns, enforced attire, social separation, cutting the hair of "boys" and "girls," and gendered labor training.[19] Indian Boarding Schools were enforced and shared a violent imperative, and often physical location, with postslavery industrial schools.

Nehiyaw poet Arielle Twist's poem "Residential" moves from these sites of ungendering to affirm Indigenous trans femininity, expressing gratitude to her mother and kokum for her trans being, "for not letting the incendiary of womanhood / Be extinguished by this body."[20] From the scales of embodiment to and as political collectivity, Indigenous resistance has struggled against the making of cis polities on stolen land. Crow historian Joe Medicine Crow argues that when a US Indian agent incarcerated Crow *badé* in 1890, cutting their hair and forcing them to wear male clothing, "the people were so upset with this that Chief Pretty Eagle came into Crow Agency, and told [the agent] to leave the reservation."[21] Crow resistance and appeals to leadership illustrate how *badé* were recognized not only as having socially significant genders but also as carrying and embodying legitimate Crow political life.

These prohibitions on different modes of gendered life produced the New World as a state of enforced cisness. Black life breaches this injunction in its fugitive and transitive movements and, together with Indigenous decolonial refusal expressed through trans and Two Spirit organizing, interrupts the colonial partition of bodies according to assigned sex. Anticolonial resistance and Black liberation struggle are therefore a resistance to the making cis of North America. In reading texts by trans feminists that named themselves as part of trans feminist history, we want to make clear that trans feminine and gender-nonconforming people have always resisted settler colonialism and anti-Blackness through their political solidarities in resistance to the cis settler state. We are attentive to how white trans people have appropriated Indigeneity and Black gender variance as a transit for their becoming or as a signifier of their politics, while refusing to obligate themselves to struggle against colonialism and the settler state. We read trans feminist histories in East Coast metropolitan areas in the United States to foreground the ways that non-cis bodies are part of centuries-long insurgencies against the white cis order of American settler colonialism.

STAR: RIOTERS, MOTHERS

Marsha P. Johnson and Sylvia Rivera had already been involved in the Gay Liberation scene in New York when they founded Street Transvestites for Gay Power (later Street Transvestite Action Revolutionaries, or STAR) in 1970. They founded STAR following their participation in a student sit-in at Weinstein Hall at New York University (NYU). The sit-in protested the administration's resistance to a gay dance. Student activists at NYU favored breaking up the action after the arrival of the police. This reticence to defy the police underlined for the street revolutionaries the necessity of organizing separately because, as they wrote in a statement, "you people run if you want to. . . . We intend to fight."[22] It is here where we see the anticolonial trans feminist fissure within the broader field of Gay Liberation, explaining the fact that STAR first flew its banner at a Young Lords demonstration in Harlem in 1970. Sylvia recalls, "I met the Young Lords, I became one of them."[23] The fissures with white gay liberation moved STAR toward alignment with Third World liberation movements that shared its goals of collective care and liberation from the colonial state. Johnson and Rivera acted as Black and brown trans people who are always in the police department's crosshairs, both as trans feminine people and as people of color. When they chose to organize around the totality of this racialized and sexed reality, they asserted themselves against their Gay Liberation counterparts who had been conditioned collectively by history in an anti-Black settler colony to expect that capitulation to the police could win them desirable gains.

From this fissure came STAR House, a place for, in Rivera's memory, street homeless people and anybody that needed help at that time. . . . Marsha and I had always sneaked people into our hotel rooms. Marsha and I decided to get a building. [We] just decided it was time to help each other and help our other kids. We fed people and clothed people. We kept the building going. We went out and hustled the streets. We paid the rent. We didn't want the kids out in the streets hustling. They would go out and rip off food. There was always food in the house and everyone had fun. It lasted for two or three years.[24]

Johnson and Rivera were themselves trans feminine young people who experienced homelessness and relied on sex work for survival. Their autonomy built on the everyday help that queer and trans feminine youth offered one another.[25] STAR politicized care work and motherhood, crystallizing in Rivera describing STAR kids as her children. In naming them as such, Rivera enacted kinship outside the imperative of heteropatriarchy and its enforcement by the state. The practice of calling each other brothers and sisters was widespread in Gay and Trans Liberation milieus. STAR was a model for how to raise that affective connection to the level of an organized network of mutual care with the goal of maintaining the wellness of the collective.[26] Part of this practice was the strategic use of sex work as a means of generating resources for survival; in this way STAR politicized sex work.

Through this set of practices, STAR survived by building networks of care among groups of people whose kin structures had been shaped and confined by conditions of enslavement, forced migration, and bureaucratic enforcement of heteropatriarchy. STAR people took the spaces and forms of work that anti-Blackness and settler colonialism had relegated to Black and brown trans people and used them to make the everyday livable, for themselves, their sisters and siblings, and their children.[27]

In her 1973 address at Christopher Street Gay Liberation, Rivera succinctly outlined the work they did from STAR House. She demanded that the crowd recognize

your gay brothers and your gay sisters in jail . . . that write me every motherfucking week and ask for your help and you all don't do a goddamn thing for them. Have you ever been beaten up and raped in jail? They've had to spend much of their money in jail to get their silicone and try to get their sex change. The women have tried to fight . . . to become women of the women's liberation and they write STAR . . . because we're trying to do something for them. I have been raped by men. . . . If you all want to know about the people who are in jail and do not forget Bambie L'Amour, Dora Mark, and Kenny Messner and other gay people who are in jail come and see the people at STAR House on 12th Street . . . the people who are trying to do something for all of us and not the men and women who are part of a white, middle-class white club.[28]

Here, Rivera illuminates how the priorities of STAR—anticarcerality, prisoner support, politicizing sexual violence in prison, access to healthcare in prison, establishing networks of care and kinship extended into prisons— emerge from experiences resisting daily state violence.[29] STAR valued and affirmed women's rights to bodily self-determination and autonomous control of health care. While the women of Women's Liberation fought for abortion rights, women of color specifically fought both for abortion and against sterilization abuse, remediating through political struggle the violent seizure of bodily autonomy that colonial officials and chattel enslavers enacted. In the case of Black women, this is a political practice that remediates what European hegemonies did to Black flesh, to use Spillers's terms. Women of trans experience sought to aid each other in attaining silicone and hormones, making their own autonomous incursion on the European settler logic of cisness. When Rivera speaks about the strategies for putting trans feminine bodies in individual trans women's control through collective capacitation, she speaks precisely to this particular anticolonial political practice.

In a 1995 *New York Times* article, Sylvia remarked that "Marsha plugged in the light for me," as she described the older girl looking out for her when she arrived on 42nd Street at the age of eleven.[30] Their relationship is its own deeply trans feminist practice. Johnson and Rivera claim maternity and sorority where it was never sanctioned by any authority, but rather by their mutual care and common feeling. They sanctioned one another, fought and provided for each other in a mutual practice of survival. After the Tactical Patrol Force of the New York Police Department had broken up the first night of Stonewall rioting, Sylvia was so inspired that she roamed the streets till dawn "setting garbage cans on fire."[31] The following night Marsha joined Sylvia and the queer and trans people who came from all over New York after hearing about the previous night's events. Marsha "climbed a lamppost to drop a bag with something heavy in it on a [police] squad car parked below . . . shattering the windshield."[32] Johnson said that "STAR is a very revolutionary group. We believe in picking up the gun, starting a revolution if necessary."[33] Johnson's and Rivera's words and practices reflect the lessons of struggle, both moments of insurrection and projects of sustained care work.

At a different latitude of the lands claimed by the United States, Tatiana Kalaniopua Young writes that, simultaneous with the Stonewall uprisings, "māhū [Indigenous gendered 'oiwi] activists in Hawaii struggled alongside their brothers and sisters at the forefront of an indigenous land dispute in cities like Waianae and Waimanalo, Oahu, as the state of Hawaii began evicting dozens of Kanaka Maoli . . . families from their ancestral homelands."[34] Young describes how prior to this reclamation, *māhū* were made most vulnerable to houselessness and policing by a 1963 public ordinance dubiously termed by the courts as "deception under the law," or paragraph 175, which forced *māhū*, trans women, and street queens to wear a button that stated "I am a boy."[35] Young writes that Layla, a *māhū* organizer in the more recent Indigenous land reclamation at Puʻuhonua o Waiʻanae, "recalls having to wear these buttons every night in town, especially in the 1960s and '70s when Vietnam soldiers were making their way to Honolulu for redeployment and recreation. She recalls police beating up 'the queens' . . . who refused to wear the buttons and the sheer brutality forced upon the girls who did."[36] Layla and her comrades struggled in land reclamations against a cis settler order that had subjected them to the policing that STAR too resisted on the other side of the American empire. As with the street queens organized by STAR, *māhū* were vulnerable to daily police and state violence for existing. When they took a central role in these land reclamations at Waianae and Waimanalo, and the more recent tent cities at Waianae, *māhu* Kanaka Maoli nationalists, like STAR people, were at the forefront of resistance to US empire and its carceral enforcement of cisness and/as settlement. Indigenous land protection and/as trans revolt and care can unmake the carceral architecture of settlement and its enforcement of cisness.

Examining STAR's political work alongside Kanaka Maoli revolt demonstrates that valorizing moments of revolt can obscure the feminized tactics that reproduce resistance collectivities. STAR people, as well as *māhū* organizers in Hawaiian land struggles, understood that *rioter, land protector*, and/or *mother* are not mutually exclusive categories of women. In mothering each other, they refused the instrumentalization of motherhood by white heteropatriarchy and enacted the mother function as a capacitating practice for trans women of color.

Less than a year after Stonewall and only months prior to the NYU occupation, on March 16, 1970, thirty-eight Indigenous people from fourteen tribes re-occupied Ellis Island, in Lenapehoking.[37] Archival silences haunt the space between STAR and the Ellis Island occupation, an effect of the erasure of New York City as Lenni Lenape and Canarsie lands, a part of a broader dynamic of what Jean O'Brien has termed "firsting and lasting"—or the writing of Indigenous nations in the Northeast out of existence.[38]

Within the cracks of southeastern and West Coast trans feminist archives, we find a different narrative of Indigenous presence in trans feminist organizing. In a 1974 issue of the Transsexual Action Organization's publication *Mirage*, Monica, a Yaqui woman, was introduced as a TAO member.[39] Despite her active involvement in TAO's trans feminist organizing, her words did not appear as a reprinted correspondence but were filtered as "news" by TAO founder Angela Douglas. The passage reads: "TAO member Monica, a Yaqui Indian from Sonora, reports that police and public reaction to Mexican transsexuals is still very severe but she has also encountered extreme reaction in the United States. Monica says that sex change operations are being performed now in other Mexican cities besides Tijuana for around $4000."[40] Monica was hailed as part of separatist trans feminism, which in some way was clearly capacitating to her existence. However, this brief trace of her voice on paper is the only record of an Indigenous trans woman within TAO's publication history. Elsewhere in the publication, a communiqué from the Transvestite-Transsexual Action Organization (TACO) in Los Angeles, reprinted from the California-based newspaper *Gay Sunshine*, requested funds for the legal defense of Angela Douglas, a white trans woman who had been arrested in Miami for "cross-dressing."[41] TACO and its allies hoped that Douglas's case could spur the overturn of the many cross-dressing laws that kept low-income trans women and transvestites in a revolving door of incarceration. In Miami, Douglas's group (TAO) was a trans feminist group that restricted its membership to (in its terms) post-op trans women and trans women on hormones. They explained this choice as the desire to bar male heterosexual transvestites.[42] TAO's separatism centered daily violences against trans feminine people in an attempt to build a practice of organizing against cis normativity, centering work against policing and incarceration. Susana Peña illustrates that three of the six central organizers in TAO Miami were Latinx trans women, and that the images of trans Latinas dominated the pages of TAO, although it's unclear to what extent that Douglas retained editorial control over the content of their magazine *Mirage*, later renamed *Moonshadow*.[43] In organizing its politics exclusively around trans femininity, TAO effaced the nexus at which trans women of color existed, the particularities of anti-Blackness and settler colonialism.

Monica's refusal to remain constricted by the geopolitics of settlement not only marked the border as a nexus of racial violence in the North/South divide but enacted an ongoing Yaqui life that preceded and exceeded the colonial partition that inaugurated the United States and Mexico as settler and mestizo nations. Monica's Indigenous trans womanhood became a transit for TAO to actualize its trans politics, but TAO both denied her a direct voice and evaded accountability to the struggle against the colonial states that transect and divide Yaqui territories along the colonial border. In studying Mohawk political life across the US-Canada border, Audra Simpson moves away from a debate about a politics of recognition to "the productive ambit of refusal."[44] Simpson writes, "By refusing to agree to these terms and to be eliminated Mohawks are asserting actual histories and thus legislating interpretive possibilities in contestation—interpretations of treaty, possibilities of movement, electoral practices—not only individual selves."[45] Monica posited her existence across the borders of these states and so asserted Yaqui space over the settler geopolitics of the United States and Mexico. In doing so, she highlighted the violence that was the colonial mapping of space, a mapping Mishuana Goeman says works to "devour Native lands and bodies."[46] In this remapping, she finds not a discontinuity but an extension of state violence, that "police and public reaction to Mexican transsexuals is still very severe but she has also encountered extreme reaction in the United States."[47]

How are we to read Monica's movements as they are met by an editorial gesture that swallows her voice as ethnographic informant to non-Indigenous-led trans feminine organizing? This gesture has a long history within trans and gay rights organizing, notably surfacing in Mattachine Society and Radical Faerie founder Harry Hay's utilization of Indigenous non-cis bodies to ground the "roots" of gay male belonging in Indigenous genders and embodiments.[48] TAO claims Monica's trans femininity as the significance of her intervention. Thus, Monica's life was mobilized as a resource to capacitate white trans feminine existence without a reciprocal gesture toward Indigenous life. While TAO's separatism enacts the potentiality of trans bodies organizing without cis people, this separatism tended toward an implicit whiteness that

elided the foundation of cis normativity in racial slavery and settler colonization. Yet Monica's organizing and words remain resolutely present, radicalizing TAO's project by portending a trans feminism that might break the
borders of settler states and expose the colonial foundations of cisness.

In "Venus in Two Acts," Hartman reads the archives of women disappeared
into the ledgers and account books of racial slavery. She asks, "Is it possible to
construct a story from 'the locus of impossible speech' or resurrect lives from
the ruins?"[49] How do we read the refraction of Monica's voice in a way that
attends to the claim she had and made on trans femininity, on our present,
and on a decolonized future? Can we do so without repeating the gesture of
Douglas, that is, a theft of Monica's narrative for a trans feminism that elides
its own formation within whiteness? In the field of settler colonization, to
at once assert one's life as trans feminine and Indigenous is a locus of speech
barred twice from intelligibility from narrative to impossibility.

In her contributions to TAO, Monica highlights the continuity of cis-
normative violence across the borders of settler and mestizo states, and she
also practices a mobility that refuses to be contained by these states. Moving
across Yaqui and Tohono O'odham lands across the borders of settler states,
the passage illuminates Monica talking to and organizing with trans women
across the geopolitical divides of settlement, learning from trans sisters and
providing them with information on medical and surgical options. We might
imagine her helping sisters, friends, and members of her nation or trans community access hormones or medicine through this mobility, just as she offers
information on surgical options to the readers of *Moonshadow* at a moment
when barriers to trans surgery were severe and medical support was limited
to pathologizing and normalizing interventions. The brief report indicates
that as she moved across the militarized lines of settlement, she monitored
police, Border Patrol, and settler and mestizo violence against trans and/or
Indigenous kin. Perhaps she was strategizing to defend her and their lives
as the members of TAO Miami did when it organized patrols and support
against police harassment on the Miami Beach boardwalk. Monica's words
cut against Angela Douglas's xenophobic tirade in response to the song "Mar-
iposa" by a Miami Cuban band in which Douglas positions Cuba as back-
wardly homophobic, calling for the band to be deported because they "do
not understand the meaning" of "liberty and justice."[50] Monica's report, even
as it is filtered through Douglas's pen and typewriter, refutes Douglas's US
exceptionalism and settler notions of "liberty and justice" by asserting the
continuity of the carceral, state, and civic violence of colonial cisness across

borders. Against this continuity, Monica asserts Indigenous trans life across the borders of settler states. Her practices of refusal and care that the report indexes provide a ground for trans politics that radicalizes TAO's project, calling it away from a détente with the murderous settler colony and toward an obligation to Indigenous internationalism. In these traces of Monica's life and words, we trace not only a gesture of care to trans sisters across borders but also a horizon that positions trans politics against the colonial present.

RADICAL QUEENS: POLITICS OF THE NON-MAN

Tommi Avicolli Mecca and Cei Bell formed another autonomous Trans Liberation group in Philadelphia in 1972, which they called Radical Queens. The first issue of the group's journal, *The Radical Queen: The Magazine of the Non-man*, provides a short history of the organization, which began as a "small consciousness raising group" within the Philadelphia Gay Activists' Alliance and set out to produce a "radical feminist, gender-free revolution."[51] The group took the most emblematic political form of Women's Liberation, the consciousness-raising group, and formed when Cei and Tommi were lying around with their butch boyfriends and decided there was a power dynamic to these relationships that they had to work through together as femmes. In her remembrance of the group, Bell writes, "If Tommi and I had been pretty queens . . . who fit in, Radical Queens probably would never have happened. Pretty queens didn't spend Saturday nights writing manifestos."[52] The friends' experiences as outsider queens who felt devalued in their relationships with masculine men underwrote their analysis of gender as "the caste system by which male-dominated society designates women and effeminates as inferior."[53] Their practice and publication combined the perspective of lesbians, trans masculine people, and queens: a coalition of all those whom "machismo men loathe and fear" and who will therefore "storm their streets."[54] This was an organization of those that white, settler cis patriarchy had to make monstrous; these were the feminized, feminine "not-pretty," whose solidarity was built on their rejection of cis patriarchy.

Radical Queens' second manifesto resisted "straight-identified machismo gays" who had ostracized them as "tacky queens" motivating them to "[band] together as a union of radical queens" for "the right to be ourselves . . . including wearing makeup, doing drag, and other femme-identified activity that any queen decides expresses him or herself."[55] This collective trans feminine affirmation cut the relation between femininity and compulsory heterosexuality, enacting a kind of home for all women-identified and femme-identified people. Significantly the manifesto made space for femme-identified people who use either pronoun and those of cis and trans experience. Here, Radical Queens participated in the long trans feminine tradition of finding language to name, and thus it coordinated for calling together those trans feminine people whom standard American kinship terms have relegated to namelessness and isolation from one another.

These substantive practices of resistance to settler colonial orders of heteropatriarchy were complemented by the Radical Queens' direct anti-imperialist analysis. They observed that for straight male society "life is a battle to be fought in Vietnam . . . against the communist" and that even within the resistant formations movement men "still reduced the women in the movement to secretaries and typists," voicing a critique that was founda-tional to Women's Liberation's formation.[56] These observations led Radical Queens to articulate a political position as "non-men," allowing them to resist both "counter-revolutionary" masculinity and "the passivity, non-aggression and fragility" that their "sisters in the Women's Movement see as oppres-sive."[57] Radical Queens discussed violence that had both been inflicted and suffered, including taunting, physical abuse, and sexual assault. Speaking from those experiences, the queens affirmed that "sisters and sissies have broken the shackles."[58] Cei Bell evidenced the commonness of the experience of sexual assault among trans feminine people by both lovers and strangers. In fact, she missed the announcement of Radical Queens because she was drugged and raped by her partner. Tommi had also experienced being raped by a lover. They agreed that "in none of these situations was calling the po-lice a reasonable possibility."[59] Their critique exposed sexual assault in queer and non-cis pairings and, like STAR, affirmed the necessity of anticarceral responses, including queens' mutual care.

The fifth issue of the *Radical Queen* reprints "As to the Matter of Dress" from the *Uranian Mirror*, a paper out of Berkeley, California, which con-nected policing gender within the Gay Liberation movement to policing by the state and addressed male appropriation of feminist language in the movement:

> Queen-stomping comes guised in many styles—no less the enemy than the
> uniformed policeman. We've become accustomed to attacks on our com-
> munity culture from straight radicals and homosexual manliness activists

under such masks as "revolutionary discipline" and the butch defense that our blatancy threatened the P.R. image of the movement. The latest and most cleverly camouflaged strategy of this same anti-Gay offensive rips off from our sisters and sissies the anti-macho ideology, while being in fact the effort [to] deny our feelings the oppression and joy from which that feminist consciousness arises.[60]

This is crucial: cis gay and antiwar movement men enforced a masculinist "discipline" that equated femininity with mainstream values and appropriated feminist language to repackage their allergy to femininity as a feminist position. Radical Queens integrated an affirmation of the feminine with a feminism that decentered cis women. They spoke of "the destructive venom of masculinity [that] is everywhere" and spoke from the perspective of those who were coerced into masculinity that equated "manhood" with "the acquisition of property (car, house, woman)."[61] It was also a deft reading and deep indictment of the way masculinism and capitalism ground each other and, jointly, provide the condition for white supremacy as the maintenance of anti-Blackness and settler colonial dispossession.

CONCLUSION: TRACING TRANS FEMINIST FUTURES

In a 2015 performance at the Vancouver Arts Festival entitled *Death in the Shadow of the Umbrella*, the late Kanien'kehá (Mohawk) trans feminist artist and writer Aiyyanna Maracle stands on a red mat depicting a turtle's back.[62] She stands two feet in from a shadow cast by a suspended black umbrella with LGBT labels such as "gender variant," "gay," and "lesbian." She is naked with her body painted in red, facing her audience, adorned only with a fur headdress that covers her eyes. The turtle mat she stands on ties her trans existence to the role of Sky Woman in the creation of the world in Haudenosaunee (Iroquois) cosmology, in which Sky Woman, falling from heaven, is assisted by animals in creating land on top of a turtle's back.[63] Over the course of the performance, Maracle invites audience participants to come write words of care on her body. At the end, she moves in a circle, indexing the collective care that capacitates Indigenous trans life against the colonial present. In her writeup, she asks, "Why is it, that 20-some years after the imposition of this 'umbrella of inclusivity,' . . . that transsexual women are the only segment of society where it is largely socially acceptable to publicly, loudly, ridicule and humiliate us?"[64] Her writeup speaks of the general conditions of trans femininity, but the optics of her performance tie the possibility of trans life outside the umbrella of inclusivity to Indigenous political orders against the lethality of daily life. In this, Maracle's gesture takes up where Monica's work in TAO left off, elaborating this legacy through the order of Haudenosaunee politics and the centrality of trans femininity to a decolonized Turtle Island.

Monica's organizing in TAO, despite its attenuated representation in the archive, interrupts the work of settlement, illustrating how a trans feminine future must also be a decolonized future. Her labor and care against the cis-settler state, as part of separatist trans feminist organizing, dovetails with the legacy of the alliances of STAR and Radical Queens, illustrating how trans feminine people capacitate one another's flesh within—and against—the murderous space of the settler colony. As Indigenous, Black, and Third World trans women shaped and radicalized the terms of trans feminist struggle, the labor of *māhū* within Kanaka Maoli land reclamations demonstrates how decolonization necessitates the breaking of the cis order. Their work challenged the settler colonization of the Americas and its partition into settler nation-states. Trans feminist movements challenged the racism, classism, and misogyny within Gay Liberation, when they organized for trans freedom authorized by Black, Indigenous, and Puerto Rican liberation struggles.

STAR, Radical Queens, and TAO radicalize gay liberation with the grammars of half-sisters, queens, and non-men and the practices of care by which they made each other's bodies possible as the grounds of trans feminist liberation. Monica, Aiyyanna Maracle, Young, and *māhū* land reclaimers at Waianae offer a further radicalizing gesture, one that centers trans feminist organizing in obligation to Indigenous internationalism and the decolonization of the stolen ground of Turtle Island and Hawai'i—against the lethal capture offered by US empire as a gesture of "inclusion."

These observations also destabilize the persistence of colonizing imaginaries in the claim that settler recognition of trans life is a next "frontier" of the long liberalizing project of the so-called United States. Rather, the struggles that this essay has sought to celebrate and situate disengage from any triumphalist narrative of colonial progress and refuse equally any claim that trans freedom would require an impossible return to a precolonial time. Rather, these struggles form part of the living substance of survival against the impositions of coloniality and slavery's afterlife that has been passed down intergenerationally from the sixteenth century to the present. Such enlivening struggles will always, by necessity, travel along a genealogy outside of the view of state sovereignty because these two entities are deadly to one another.

NOTES

1 For an American Civil Liberties Union (ACLU) summary of the most prominent of these cases regarding students' rights, see *Grimm v. Gloucester County School Board*, accessed April 1, 2021, https://www.aclu.org/cases/grimm-v-gloucester -county-school-board. For the ACLU's summary of the most prominent of these cases regarding job discrimination, see *R. G. & G. R. Harris Funeral Home v. EEOC and Amy Stephens*, accessed April 1, 2021, https://www.aclu.org/cases/rg-gr -harris-funeral-homes-v-eeoc-aimee-stephens.

2 Bendery, "Joe Biden: Transgender Rights Is 'the Civil Rights Issue of Our Time'"; Steinmetz, "Transgender Tipping Point."

3 See Jules Gill-Peterson's and Joanna Wuest's contributions to this volume.

4 Duffy, "Failed by the System, Trans People Resort to Crowdfunding for Transitions." For information about bail funds, see the website for the LGBTQ Freedom Fund: https://www.lgbtqfund.org/.

5 See Patil, "How the March for Trans Lives Became a Huge Event."

6 While gay liberationists of color were enacting such politics, here we attempt to address those practices that were specific to trans feminine people and their conditions of life and forms of struggle. See "Third World Gay Revolution, What We Want, What We Believe," reprinted in *Pinko: A Journal of Gay Communism* 1, no. 1 (2019).

7 See Green, "Pocahontas Perplex"; and Lugones, "Heterosexualism and the Colonial/Modern Gender System."

8 Lugones, "Coloniality of Gender," 2.

9 Byrd, *Transit of Empire*. Tiffany Lethabo King's statement, in *The Black Shoals*, that "genocide and slavery do not have an edge" (x) is instructive here. For differential grammars of self-determination and the centrality of "gender self-determination," see Stanley, "Gender Self-Determination." For more on Indigenous political self-determination, see Coulthard, *Red Skin, White Masks*; and Trask, *From a Native Daughter*.

10 Spillers, "Mama's Baby, Papa's Maybe," 67.

11 Spillers, "Mama's Baby, Papa's Maybe," 72.

12 Spillers, "Mama's Baby, Papa's Maybe," 79.

13 Bey, *Anarcho-Blackness*, 81; Gossett, "Blackness and the Trouble of Trans Visibility."

14 Snorton, *Black on Both Sides*, 57.

15 Snorton, *Black on Both Sides*.

16 Driskill, *Asegi Stories*; Morgensen, *Spaces between Us*.

17 Hunt, "Witnessing the Colonialscape," 28.

18 Miranda, "Extermination of the Joyas," 259.

19 Belcourt, *History of My Brief Body*, 16–17.

20 Twist, *Disintegrate/Dissociate*, 35.

21 Joe Medicine Crow, in Morgensen, *Spaces between Us*, 82.

22 STAR, "Gay Power: When Do We Want It, or Do We?," 1.

23 STAR, "Gay Power: When Do We Want It, or Do We?," 1.

24 Sylvia Rivera, in Bell, "Sylvia Goes to College," 61.

25 The survival programs of the Black Panther Party (including free breakfast, liberation schools) were largely organized by Panther women and had politicized access to basic needs for women and children. The Welfare Rights Movement, a movement of poor women and women of color, supported women and families who accessed welfare. See Kornbluh, *Battle for Welfare Rights*.

26 There is evidence that this organizational model was built off larger trends and strategies of gay and trans mutual aid, the scope of which it is difficult to index. See, for instance, Buckminster Fuller, *Cosmography*.

27 STAR's work shares political strategies and objectives with a range of feminized political projects during the period. Housing was a central front of feminized political organizing. Rent strikes and tenants' rights and public housing organizing pushed back against deadbeat landlords and discriminatory housing policy since the early twentieth century, and these movements were largely populated by poor women, white ethnic women, and women of color. See Williams, *Politics of Public Housing*; and Feldman and Stall, *Dignity of Resistance*. The Battered Women's Movement organized the first domestic abuse shelters in the 1970s by pooling organizers' funds to rent houses and offer shelter, space, and time for women leaving abusive partnerships. Susan Schechter's *Women and Male Violence* tells the story of the movement in Chicago. There were many experiments in collective housing among radicals during the period. Just one example was the Black Panthers' houses. See Spencer, "Communalism and the Black Panther Party"; and Pulido, *Black, Brown, Yellow, and Left*.

28 This excerpt was transcribed from a video recording by the authors. To view the speech in its totality, go to Sylvia Rivera, "Y'all Better Quiet Down," Original Authorized Video by Love Tapes Collective, 1973 Gay Pride Rally, NYC, https://vimeo.com/234353103. All thanks and praise to the artist and filmmaker Tourmaline for finding this video in the New York Public Library archive and introducing it to wide audiences.

29 Because STAR politicizes incarceration, STAR's work bears a practice-based solidarity with the many 1970s gay and feminist antiprison and prisoner solidarity projects. An example is lesbians who worked for the abolition of the "daddy tank": the special cell that was reserved for women whom the cops read as masculine. In an article from the *Lesbian Tide* ("New Freedoms for Daddy-Tanked Lesbians"), Cordova describes the daddy tank as a tool to isolate lesbian and butch women in solitary and single them out for abuse. The article goes on to detail the deprivations of nutrition, reading material, and sunlight. The September 1974 issue

describes a Father's Day demonstration against the daddy tank outside a women's prison, the Sybil Brand Institute.

30 See Kaufman, "About New York; Still Here."

31 Rivera, interview with Leslie Feinberg, *Worker's World*, 204.

32 Rivera, interview with Leslie Feinberg, *Worker's World*, 204.

33 Johnson, "Rapping with a Street Transvestite Revolutionary."

34 Young, in Boellstorff et al., "Decolonizing Transgender," 430.

35 Young, "Home-Free and Nothing (. . .)-Less," 13.

36 Young, Home-Free and Nothing (. . .)-Less," 13.

37 Johnson, *American Indian Occupation of Alcatraz Island*, 30.

38 O'Brien, *Firsting and Lasting*.

39 Transsexual Action Organization, *Mirage* 1, no. 2 (1974): 4.

40 Transsexual Action Organization, *Mirage* 1, no. 2 (1974): 4.

41 "Arrest of Angela K Douglas," *Mirage* 1, no. 2 (1974); reprinted from *Gay Sunshine* (1974): 8.

42 Transsexual Action Organization, *Mirage* 1, no. 2 (1974): 1.

43 Peña, "Gender and Sexuality in Latina/o Miami"; Transsexual Action Organization, *Moonshadow* 1, no. 1 (August 1973): 1.

44 Simpson, *Mohawk Interruptus*, 197.

45 Simpson, *Mohawk Interruptus*, 13.

46 Goeman, *Mark My Words*, 50.

47 Transsexual Action Organization, *Mirage* 1, no. 2 (1974): 4.

48 Hay, as a founding member of an LA organization, the Mattachine Society, claimed to have been directly given a mandate for his spiritual revolutionary work by Pauite prophet and revolutionary Wovoka, founder of the Ghost Dance movement (this is both unlikely in terms of the story's veracity and in terms of Hay's birth and Wovoka's age). Hay would later go on to create the Radical Faeries as a back-to-the-land movement of urbane middle-class queers reconnecting with nature—although Mattachine did do some solidarity work with Indigenous liberation, and though Radical Faeries today have Indigenous and POC membership and caucuses, in the formulation of this organization, Indigenous genders became something for white gay men to claim as their heritage. See Povinelli, *Empire of Love*; Morgensen, *Spaces between Us*; and Cornum, "Desiring the Tribe."

49 Hartman, "Venus in Two Acts," 3.

50 Peña, "Gender and Sexuality in Latina/o Miami," 764.

51 Mecca, *Smash the Church, Smash the State*, 122.

52 Mecca, *Smash the Church, Smash the State*, 116.

53 Radical Queens, *The Radical Queen*, no. 1, 2.

54 Radical Queens, *The Radical Queen*, no. 1, 11.

55 Radical Queens, *The Radical Queen*, no. 1, 1.

56 Radical Queens, *The Radical Queen*, no. 1, 9.

57 Radical Queens, *The Radical Queen*, no. 1, 10.

58 Radical Queens, *The Radical Queen*, no. 1, 4.

59 Mecca, *Smash the Church, Smash the State*, 122.
60 "As to the Matter of Dress," *The Radical Queen*, no. 5, 15.
61 Radical Queens, *The Radical Queen*, no. 1, 8.
62 Aiyyanna Maracle, *Death in the Shadow of the Umbrella*, performance at the Vancouver Arts Festival, 2015, https://vimeo.com/137714829.
63 Brant, *Mohawk Trail*.
64 Maracle, "Death in the Shadow of the Umbrella."

BIBLIOGRAPHY

Belcourt, Billy-Ray. *A History of My Brief Body*. Columbus, OH: Two Dollar Radio, 2020.
Bell, Arthur. "Sylvia Goes to College." *Village Voice*, October 13, 1970, 61. Arthur Bell papers, New York Public Library [courtesy of Tourmaline].
Bendery, Jennifer. "Joe Biden: Transgender Rights Is 'the Civil Rights Issue of Our Time." *Huffington Post*, October 30, 2012. https://www.huffpost.com/entry/joe -biden-transgender-rights_n_204727.
Bey, Marquis. *Anarcho-Blackness: Notes toward a Black Anarchism*. Oakland, CA: AK Press, 2020.
Boellstorff, Tom, Mauro Cabral, Micha Cardenas, Trystan Cotton, Eric A. Stanley, T. Kalaniopua Young, and Aren Z. Aizura. "Decolonizing Transgender: A Roundtable Discussion." *TSQ* 1, no. 3 (2014): 419–39.
Brant, Beth. *Mohawk Trail*. Ithaca, NY: Firebrand Books, 1985.
Buckminster Fuller, R. *Cosmography: A Posthumous Scenario for the Future of Humanity*. Adjuvant: Kiyoshi Kuromiya. New York: MacMillan, 1992.
Byrd, Jodi. *The Transit of Empire: Indigenous Critiques of Colonialism*. Minneapolis: University of Minnesota Press, 2011.
Cordova, Jeanne. "New Freedoms for Daddy-Tanked Lesbians." *Lesbian Tide*, March/April 1977, 38.
Cornum, Lou. "Desiring the Tribe." *Pinko: A Journal of Gay Communism* 1, no. 1 (2019): 034–045.
Coulthard, Glen Sean. *Red Skin, White Masks: Rejecting the Colonial Politics of Recognition*. Minneapolis: University of Minnesota Press, 2014.
Driskill, Qwo-Li. *Asegi Stories*. Tucson: University of Arizona Press, 2016.
Duffy, Nick. "Failed by the System, Trans People Resort to Crowdfunding for Transitions." *Pink News*, January 25, 2019. https://www.pinknews.co.uk/2019/01/25 /transgender-crowdfunding-healthcare/.
Feldman, Roberta M., and Susan Stall. *The Dignity of Resistance: Women's Resident's Activism in Chicago Public Housing*. New York: Cambridge University Press, 2004.
Goeman, Mishuana. *Mark My Words: Native Women Mapping Our Nations*. Minneapolis: University of Minnesota Press, 2013.

Gossett, Che. "Blackness and the Trouble of Trans Visibility." In *Trap Door: Trans Cultural Production and the Politics of Visibility*, edited by Reina Gossett, Eric A. Stanley, and Johanna Burton, 183–90. Cambridge, MA: MIT Press, 2017.

Green, Rayna. "The Pocahontas Perplex: The Image of the Indian Woman in American Culture." *Massachusetts Review* 16, no. 4 (Autumn 1975): 698–714.

Hartman, Saidiya V. "Venus in Two Acts." *Small Axe* 12, no. 2 (2008): 1–14.

Hunt, Sarah. "Witnessing the Colonialscape: Lighting the Intimate Fires of Indigenous Legal Pluralism." PhD diss., Simon Fraser University, 2013.

Johnson, Marsha P. "Rapping with a Street Transvestite Revolutionary: An Interview with Marcia [*sic*] Johnson." In *Out of the Closets: Voices of Gay Liberation*, edited by Karla Jay and Allen Young, 112–19. New York: New York University Press, 1994.

Johnson, Troy R. *The American Indian Occupation of Alcatraz Island: Red Power and Self-Determination*. Lincoln: University of Nebraska Press, 2008.

Kaufman, Michael T. "About New York; Still Here: Sylvia, Who Survived Stonewall, Time and the River." *New York Times*, May 24, 1995.

King, Tiffany Lethabo. *The Black Shoals: Offshore Formations of Black and Native Studies*. Durham, NC: Duke University Press, 2019.

Kornbluh, Felicia. *The Battle for Welfare Rights*. Philadelphia: University of Pennsylvania Press, 2007.

Lugones, María. "The Coloniality of Gender." *Worlds and Knowledges Otherwise* 2, no. 2 (2008). https://globalstudies.trinity.duke.edu/projects/wko-gender.

Lugones, María. "Heterosexualism and the Colonial/Modern Gender System." *Hypatia* 22, no. 1 (2007): 186–209.

Malatino, Hil. *Trans Care*. Minneapolis: University of Minnesota Press, 2020.

Maracle, Aiyyanna. *Death in the Shadow of the Umbrella*. Video. Camera by Bradley A. West. Queer Arts Festival, Vancouver, BC, 2015. https://vimeo.com/137714829.

Mecca, Tommi Avicola, ed. *Smash the Church, Smash the State: The Early Years of Gay Liberation*. San Francisco: City Lights Books, 2009.

Miranda, Deborah. "The Elimination of the Joyas: Gendercide in Spanish California." *GLQ* 16, no. 1–2 (2010): 253–84.

Morgensen, Scott. "Settler Homonationalism: Theorizing Settler Colonialism in Queer Modernities." *GLQ* 16, no. 1–2 (2010): 105–31.

Morgensen, Scott. *Spaces between Us: Queer Settler Colonialism and Indigenous Decolonization*. Minneapolis: University of Minnesota Press, 2013.

O'Brien, Jean M. *Firsting and Lasting: Writing Indians Out of Existence in New England*. Minneapolis: University of Minnesota Press, 2010.

Oyěwùmi, Oyèrónké. *The Invention of Women: Making an African Sense of Western Gender Discourses*. Minneapolis: University of Minnesota Press, 1997.

Patil, Anushka. "How the March for Trans Lives Became a Huge Event." *New York Times*, June 15, 2020. https://www.nytimes.com/2020/06/15/nyregion/brooklyn-black-trans-parade.html.

Peña, Susana. "Gender and Sexuality in Latina/o Miami: Documenting Latina Trans-sexual Activists." *Gender and History* 22, no. 3 (2010): 763–64.

Povinelli, Elizabeth. *The Empire of Love: Toward a Theory of Intimacy, Genealogy, and Carnality*. Durham, NC: Duke University Press, 2006.

Pulido, Laura. *Black, Brown, Yellow, and Left: Radical Activism in Los Angeles*. Berkeley: University of California Press, 2006.

Radical Queens. *The Radical Queen: Magazine of the Non-man*, edited by Cei Bell and Tommi Avicoli Mecca, no. 1 (1976). Shared with the author by Tommi Avicoli Mecca.

Radical Queens. *The Radical Queen: Magazine of the Non-man*, edited by Cei Bell and Tommi Avicoli Mecca, no. 2 (1976). Shared with the author by Tommi Avicoli Mecca.

Radical Queens. *The Radical Queen: Magazine of the Non-man*, edited by Cei Bell and Tommi Avicoli Mecca, no. 3 (1977). Shared with the author by Tommi Avicoli Mecca.

Radical Queens. *The Radical Queen: Magazine of the Non-man*, edited by Cei Bell and Tommi Avicoli Mecca, no. 4 (1977). Shared with the author by Tommi Avicoli Mecca.

Radical Queens. *The Radical Queen: Magazine of the Non-man*, edited by Cei Bell and Tommi Avicoli Mecca, no. 5 (1977). Shared with the author by Tommi Avicoli Mecca.

Rivera, Sylvia. Interview with Leslie Feinberg. *Worker's World*, 2002, 203–6.

Schecter, Susan. *Women and Male Violence: The Visions and Struggles of the Battered Women's Movement*. Boston: South End Press, 1982.

Simpson, Audra. *Mohawk Interruptus: Political Life across the Borders of the Settler States*. Durham, NC: Duke University Press, 2014.

Snorton, C. Riley. *Black on Both Sides: A Racial History of Trans Identity*. Minneapolis: University of Minnesota Press, 2017.

Spade, Dean. *Mutual Aid: Building Solidarity during This Crisis (and the Next)*. New York: Verso Books, 2020.

Spencer, Robyn C. "Communalism and the Black Panther Party in Oakland, California." In *West of Eden: Communes and Utopia in Northern California*, edited by Iain Boal, Janferie Stone, Michael Watts, and Cal Winslow, 92–121. Oakland, CA: PM Press, 2012.

Spillers, Hortense. "Mama's Baby, Papa's Maybe: An American Grammar Book." *Diacritics* 17, no. 2 (1987): 64–81.

Stanley, Eric. "Gender Self-Determination." *TSQ* 1, no. 1–2 (2014): 89–91.

STAR. "Gay Power: When Do We Want It, or Do We?" 1970. Arthur Bell papers, New York Public Library [courtesy of Tourmaline].

Steinmetz, Katy. "The Transgender Tipping Point." *Time*, May 29, 2014. https://time.com/135480/transgender-tipping-point/.

Transsexual Action Organization. *Mirage* 1, no. 2 (1974). Published: Pages 15–16. Subject File collection, Coll2012-001, ONE National Gay & Lesbian Archives, Los Angeles, California, GEO: 34.0908559, -118.374658.

Transsexual Action Organization. *Moonshadow* 1, no. 1 (August 1973). Published: Print. Douglas, Angela Lynn, ONE Subject File collection, Coll2012-001, ONE National Gay & Lesbian Archives, Los Angeles, California, GEO: 34.0908559, -118.374658.

Trask, Haunani-Kay. *From a Native Daughter: Colonialism and Sovereignty in Hawaiʻi*. Honolulu: University of Hawaiʻi Press, 1999.

Twist, Arielle. *Disintegrate/Dissociate*. Vancouver: Arsenal Pulp Press, 2019.

Williams, Rhonda Y. *The Politics of Public Housing: Black Women's Struggles against Urban Inequality*. Oxford: Oxford University Press, 2004.

Young, Kalaniopua. "Home-Free and Nothing (…)-Less: A Queer Cosmology of Aloha ʻĀina." *Hūlili: Multidisciplinary Research on Hawaiian Well-Being* 11, no. 1 (2019): 9–21.

PART II
TRANS HISTORY

GRETA LAFLEUR

TRANS FEMININE HISTORIES,   3
PIECE BY PIECE, OR,
VERNACULAR PRINT AND
THE HISTORIES OF GENDER

In 1884, two Ohio newspapers, the *Cincinnati Commercial Tribune* and Cleveland's *Plain Dealer*, ran a brief report at the end of their short weekly edition, under the heading "CONDENSED TELEGRAMS." The report read: "Henry Maxwell, 50 years old, unmarried, a woodchopper, living four miles south of Sidney, O[hio], deliberately castrated himself with an ax, Monday."[1] Neither paper gives any additional details about the information purportedly contained in this "condensed telegram" that gives us the story of H. Maxwell. Yet this brief, economical sentence is riddled with provocations. Most notable to me, as a scholar of eighteenth- and nineteenth-century North America, is the mention of Maxwell being "unmarried," and second is the insertion of the word "deliberately," which removes any question of whether Maxwell, a woodchopper by trade, may have cut or corrected their genitals in error or by accident.

This small anecdote is not an outlier or a mere curiosity of the late nineteenth century, an era that today, historians of gender and sexuality associate with the rise, circulation, and popularization of the sexological sciences, alongside expanded interest in the role of hormones, the endocrine system, and the place of the human gonads within each of these.[2] Indeed, small records such as this one, reporting self-castrations, appear not infrequently in newspapers throughout the eighteenth and nineteenth centuries, but they rarely contain more information than that which is offered above. Consider the following, printed in the *New-England Courant* on December 11, 1721, more than a century and a half before, under the heading of "Extract of a Letter from a Gentleman at New London to his Friend in Boston, dated Nov. 24th, 1721": "The same Letter adds, That a certain Man at Stonington (who has a Wife and several Children) lately castrated himself; which has occasion'd abundance of Waggish Talk among the looser Sort of the Female Tribe, who are so incensed against him, that some of them talk hotly of throwing Stones at him, if he lives to come abroad again. He is very much swell'd, but seems rejoyc'd at what he has done."[3] Like the 1884 anecdote, this one also notes the marital status of this unnamed person living in Stonington; not only are they married, but the piece notes in an eye-catching parenthetical that they also have "several Children." Distinct from the anecdote cited above, the deliberation of the decision to castrate themselves is not explicit but implied in the person's apparent satisfaction at their decision. Despite the ire of some local women, supposedly of the "looser Sort," this person "seems rejoyc'd at what [they have] done."

Dozens, and possibly hundreds, of reports like these appear in eighteenth- and nineteenth-century newspapers in North America. I have a small file of such anecdotes, which I began collecting while researching the use of castration as a legal form of punishment in the eighteenth-century British North American colonies. Because being sentenced to castration, when mandated by a court, was infrequent enough in New England to merit being reported in newspapers, periodical research—examining newsletters, newspapers, pamphlets, and other ephemera—was a critical part of the development of that chapter. What I did not expect, in embarking on that research, was how many reports of *self*-castrations I would find, as well as the incredible variety of explanations or justifications for those bodily transformations that would attend them. Every time I came across a new report, I added it to my growing list of these anecdotes, and even after a fairly cursory survey of the newspapers available in digitized format in the *America's Historical Newspapers* database, I had a collection of almost two dozen similar notices. As a scholar whose research is almost entirely archivally based, I came away from that research with the sense that an even more careful and comprehensive research would likely yield dozens more of these anecdotes. But what to do with them?

This chapter takes this small, eclectic collection of newspaper reports as a point of departure for a meditation on the methods of trans feminist historical research, analysis, and narration. How might we—and how *should* we—read these anecdotes, dozens of which appear in local newspapers, between the eighteenth and twentieth centuries? What might they elucidate, and what might they foreclose about trans pasts and trans feminist approaches to making knowledge about these histories? This essay offers less a series of arguments than a set of what I hope will be productive speculations about embarking on this kind of research, much of which is, as scholars in Black studies and the histories of sexuality have long argued, a process that requires us to reckon with how trans histories of all kinds have been uniquely subject to erasure and how trans lives of centuries past frequently appear to us only through individuals' or communities' encounters with disciplinary power: the police, the prison, the law, the hospital. Indeed, one of the reasons that I reach for these short, elusive newspaper articles is that they are one of the only sites that I have encountered in eighteenth- and nineteenth-century print culture and recordkeeping in which coming into the crosshairs of the state is *not* the occasion for these wispy gestures at the lives of people who might have been trans or otherwise gender nonconforming. Yet, as I will detail in what follows, that their stories appear as sensationalized curiosities in cheap newspapers still does not relieve them of state capture. Accordingly, this chapter also builds on thinking from fields that have had to reckon with the constitutive violence of archives, including scholarship in Black studies, postcolonial studies, and queer studies. A trans feminist historiographic method, I argue, needs the work of scholars such as Saidiya Hartman and Michel-Rolph Trouillot to account for the multiplicity of silences that shape how trans histories—and trans feminist histories in particular—manifest in early archives.[4] And it needs a thick theorization of how to reckon with the question of violence, both violences enacted against early trans and gender-nonconforming people as well as forms of structural violence that gave rise to the conditions out of which modern trans experience in the United States came to speak itself, including the well-documented connections between slavery, eugenics, and the sexological sciences.[5]

Importantly, for the purposes of this chapter, the eighteenth- and nineteenth-century newspaper articles that I examine announce an increasing awareness of the effects of castration in humans. Indeed, this burgeoning vernacular understanding of the role of the testicles and the possible effects of their removal may have actually been what prompted some of the people in these articles—H. Maxwell, or the unnamed person from Stonington, whose brief stories opened this essay—to attempt these bodily modifications in the first place. Yet any understanding of the effects of the removal of the testicles on humans was in part derived from the violence of slavery, and both formal and noncodified laws that designated castration as a punishment for anything from accusations of sexual assault to mere "high spirits" in enslaved people.[6] As a tactic of racialized violence, it persisted into the Jim Crow era and beyond, and it became, as Crystal Feimster and Martha Hodes have detailed, a form of maiming that often went hand in hand with other forms of white supremacist violence, including lynching.[7] Castration was also deployed as a sexualized tactic of violence outside of the context of bondage; in the same newspapers that yielded the anecdotes that are the subject of this chapter, I found almost as many accounts of castrations performed in the course of random acts of violence against white people. I have explored these complicities elsewhere in my work, and I invoke them here as an elaboration of yet another tenet of what might make a trans feminist historiographic method: a clear-eyed refusal of historical innocence in favor of a careful anatomization of the imbrication of emergent understandings of gender as a morphological and experiential vector of human experience *and* state discipline. The small, gestural anecdotes that I explore here, whispering possibilities of trans feminine and trans feminist histories, are only visible as a result of these complicities.

TRANS FEMINIST HISTORIOGRAPHIES,
TRANS FEMININE HISTORIES

But what about these anecdotes makes them trans histories, and should we worry that a trans feminist historiographic method will, to put it bluntly, convert into transness experiences that likely were not?

While this collection of anecdotes, each so brief that no single one could be described as anything more substantive than merely "suggestive," gives us no definitive answers, I argue their suggestiveness is enough and that attending to the possibility they provoke, even or especially without confirmation or certainty, creates more space in historical research for both the presence of trans feminine actors and the kinds of reading and analytical skills that allow us to better imagine those presences. Put differently, I argue that despite the fact that this collection of tiny reports promises no certainty, they can and should have a place in the history of trans femininity, and a trans feminist historiographic method is what allows us to see this archive for its potential in the first place.

By a trans feminist historiographic method, I mean a couple of things: first, I mean abandoning any sense of confidence that we can know what a trans experience looked like in the eighteenth century, the nineteenth century, or even in the decades previous to our own moment (and perhaps even *in* our own moment!). I like to tell my students that while I do not always feel comfortable identifying historical personae, in the era prior to the emergence of the sexological sciences, as *trans*, many figures whom I have encountered in my archives are without question figures in trans history, and this broad collection of people and events can include both people who, had they lived in our own time, might have identified as trans, alongside people who might have identified as cisgender but who were ousted or abjected from the landscape of normative gender experience by virtue of race or class experience.[8] C. Riley Snorton and Omise'eke Natasha Tinsley, for example, have both explored what they argue is the constitutive transness of Black genders and the racial histories that have laid the foundation for the articulation of transgender experience.[9] Toby Beauchamp has also explained how racialized structures of surveillance in and of themselves contribute to the production of the experience of feeling gender nonnormative, suggesting that trans experience may be as entwined in the rhizomatic structures of state control as it is any individuated sense of self. But what all of these scholars share is an understanding of the promiscuous sources and manifestations of trans experience, many of which exceed simply understanding oneself as in some way at odds with normative gender. By jettisoning any assumptions about what trans experiences, people, or phenomena might have looked like, we open ourselves up to the possibilities of what they *could* have looked like.

By asserting the importance of trans feminist historiographic methods, I also mean an embrace of speculation as a necessary condition of scholarship. In this sense, I am building on Hartman's work, but I am also insisting on the importance of the fact that a wide range of historical objects, events, actors, and knowledges—none of which were, in the standard sense of the word as we use it today, *trans*—can and do serve as sites of imagination, inspiration, and modeling for trans people and movements in the present.[10] A historical phenomenon need not be trans to be a source of trans inspiration; this is one of the best and most exciting promises of a speculative relationship to history, which embraces creativity rather than rejecting it as lacking rigor, and which sees fiction as a valid source for unpredictable theorizations, identifications, and knowledge. Think, for example, of Sam Feder's recent documentary, *Disclosure* (2020), which tracks the filmic representation of trans people from the turn of the twentieth century into the beginning of the twenty-first. Feder interviews a number of trans actors, directors, and other industry workers in the film, and at one moment, he invites them to describe screen representations of trans people that felt, to them, like moments of possibility. Laverne Cox names Barbara Streisand's character in the 1983 film *Yentl* (Streisand plays the eponymous Yentl) as a major source of early inspiration and identification for her. Similarly, director Lilly Wachowski and historian and director Susan Stryker both name Bugs Bunny—a cartoon rabbit character who, especially in their early days, appeared in various scenes as both female and/or feminine and male and/or masculine—as a vision of trans feminine possibility. Was Yentl or Bugs Bunny trans? I would argue that rather than trying to articulate a definitive yes or no to that question, both Yentl and Bugs Bunny warrant a place in trans history precisely because of the speculative identifications they wrought in both trans and cis audiences. As Cox puts it in the documentary, "I'm a Black, trans girl from Alabama, and, like, I live for *Yentl*. I don't know if I'm the target audience for *Yentl* . . . it embodied so many of my longings to be seen for who I was, but needing to fit in in a traditional way to sort of get by at the time. . . . I connected to that because I was a girl that no one saw as a girl at the time." Wachowski and Stryker both describe something similar in their youthful encounters with Bugs Bunny: "There was something about Bugs Bunny that activated in my trans imagination this idea of transformation," Wachowski explains. Stryker describes Bugs Bunny's appeal as more singular: "The only, *only*, positive representation I saw of anything trans feminine was Bugs Bunny."[11] A trans feminist historiographic method takes seriously the evocative power of past events, imagery, and people for their identificatory, aesthetic, or otherwise political significance in the present moment, and embraces these resonances—attenuated or even, at times, problematic as they may be—for what they are able to do or incite in the here and now. Ultimately, this method requires understanding history as something produced in the service of the present, which is *not* to say that we need to understand the past and the present as an unbroken, continuous progression or that past ways of being or knowing must be subordinated to later or current ones, but rather to simply acknowledge the power of historical knowledge for the creation of meaning.

In practice, adopting a speculative stance means that we need to lean away from precisely the kinds of empiricisms that typically serve as the bread and butter of scholarly historical method. Reading for what *might* be there rather than for what is *demonstrably* there renders a different reading of people, events, structures, and phenomena. It allows us to indulge in forms of both skepticism and imagining that are typically foreclosed by some of the most cherished analytical approaches in both historical and literary studies. It allows us to hold in abeyance the assumption that because a text tells us that someone is a woman, or, as in the case here, a "man," that no text—including one that might be written by the person themselves!—is a necessarily trustworthy indicator of gendered experience. While first-person texts—diaries, speeches, letters, and so on—may indeed give us a more reliable sense of how a person thinks about their own experience of their body, their feelings and desires, their identifications and misidentifications and disidentifications, we are none of us, for better or for worse, entirely transparent to ourselves either. And because widespread, shared vocabularies for trans experience have only just begun to coalesce over the past seventy years or so (and there are still great divisions among people globally about how to describe gender-nonconforming experience, and great debates over the traction that *transgender* as a framework does or should have), there are also a host of traditional historical questions to be asked about how to recognize people who found themselves at odds with normative gender in an era before there was consensus on how to describe that experience. While vocabularies did, of course, exist—Jen Manion has written compellingly about the "female husband," my own work has explored the "exception in nature," Leah DeVun has elaborated early "nonbinary" figures, and scholars of the medieval and early modern periods have unearthed a dictionary's worth of terms to describe gendered experiences that do not fall easily into the semantic realm of "woman" or "man"—these vocabularies were often highly regionally, historically, culturally, and racially specific.[12] Because even a traditional approach to trans history requires a commitment to experimental methods, a curious and speculative relationship to the possibility of trans pasts is part of the bedrock of a trans feminist historiographic method. In other words, if a trans feminist historiography is a commitment to seeing trans feminine people and pasts that conventional historical methods would prefer to leave unseen, an analytic approach that deploys and trusts speculation is one important means by which that commitment can be materialized.

This is not, of course, to say that my argument about these little anecdotes is the equivalent of scholarly wishful thinking or just a pure willing of trans feminine presences into archival being. My interest in these little reports stems from a vast scaffolding of archival instances in which it is clear that residents of eighteenth- and nineteenth-century North America had a clear sense of what the effects of castration were, in both humans and nonhuman animals. The procedure was quite clearly understood to have a specific range of possible effects on the behavior and comportment of the organism subjected to it. Between veterinary treatises, manuals on animal husbandry, and vernacular discussions and debates over the ethics and effects of castration, eighteenth- and nineteenth-century newspapers reveal a wide range of engagement with castration as an idea and as a bodily reality. Because so many of these sources describe processes of what we might term *devirilization* or *feminization*, I argue that they provide an undeniable source for analyses of how the relationship between physical form and gendered expression was understood during this era, and that contemporary notions of this relationship were, in turn, drawn on for understanding the effects of castration on humans.

A note on terminology: I use *castration* with some trepidation here, and I do so without any commitment to the genital nomenclature it implies. I use it only because it is the word used in these eighteenth- and nineteenth-century newspaper reports, and I want to make clear that in almost *none* of these reports does the writer state specifically what *castration* means, as a bodily experience and self-inflicted surgical procedure. This was, in fact, one of the challenges in writing the chapter of my book that was the occasion for finding these newspaper reports in the first place; when *castration*, as a term, can refer to a wide range of procedures, from the removal of the testes themselves while leaving the testicular sac intact, to the removal of the entire testicles, to the removal of the penis, to the removal of both the testicles *and* the penis, *castration* is at best a hazy modifier of experience. Broadly, and almost entirely from context clues, it seems that most uses of the term *castration* use the term in the way that it appears most frequently in the print culture of the era. Similar to its use in animal husbandry manuals and farmer's almanacs, it seems that *castration* generally indicates the removal of the testes or the removal of the testicles as a whole, inclusive of the testes. I will continue to refer to the procedures discussed in these brief newspaper reports as *castrations*, but I will do so advisedly, for even historians skeptical about the use of speculative methods will agree with me that it would be reasonable to assume that when we come across stories of people who have intentionally removed part of all of their external genitalia, they have done so because they want them to appear or function differently or disappear entirely.

One of the most common sites for discussions of the effects of castration is articles about animal husbandry, which were sometimes drawn from farmer's almanacs or natural historical lectures and reprinted in local newspapers. These discussions address a range of possible effects of castration and/or spaying, from the behavior of castrated animals to the taste of their flesh when eaten. To offer a fairly common example of what these discussions looked like, consider this passage from an article titled "A Treatise on Agriculture," published in the *Albany Argus*, an Albany, New York–based newspaper, in 1820: "2d. *Castration*. The flesh of male[] [cattle] is hard, fibrous, and ill flavored, and that of females, not spayed, far inferior to the flesh of those which have undergone that operation. Where the testicles in the one, and the ovaria in the other, are early and completely removed, the animals become more docile, less restless, and fat with great facility."[13] This article offers a fairly typical concatenation of the kinds of ideas that appear in veterinary and agricultural discussions of castration; the only thing unusual, about this particular passage, is its concomitant attention to the spaying of "female" animals, which is addressed far less frequently than the castration of "male" animals in similar publications. Here we see an assessment of the effects of castration and spaying that spans from the taste of the meat, once slaughtered; the procedure itself; and the physiological effects of the procedure on the animals subjected to it, relative to fatness in particular. This sentiment is echoed in an 1854 article in the New York–based *American Artisan*, on the effects of castration on fish; the unnamed author explains that "above a hundred years ago, Mr. Tul, famed for his agricultural success, had fish ponds so full of fish that they had not room to grow to the desired size. He castrated numbers of them . . . and found these castrated fish to grow much larger than their natural size, were more fat and were always in season for the table."[14] This is not, of course, to say that any of these theories were necessarily correct, but rather to emphasize that agricultural consensus about the physiological effects of castration tended to cluster around particular ideas. This aggregation of theories of the effects of castration appeared in almost all of the veterinary treatises and animal husbandry discussions I came across and also appears, though far less frequently, in discussions of the effects of castration in humans.

Consider the passage above next to a short piece on an "odd character," published in the *Hartford Gazette* (based in Hartford, Connecticut) about thirty years earlier, about a person who was putatively a curate in Scotland, titled simply "Singular Character":

> Mr. Naughley never was married; but having once some thoughts of entering into that state, he was rejected by the fair one to whom he paid his addresses. Enraged at this disappointment, and to prevent the fair sex from having any further influence over him, he castrated himself, giving for his reason, "if thy right eye offend thee, &c." In consequence of this operation he grew prodigiously fat, and his voice, which was naturally good, improved very much, and continued during his life. He died April 30, 1756, and the age of 76, having served this curacy forty-seven years.[15]

While at first glance this story of Naughley might appear quite distinct from the discussion of the castrated and spayed cattle, there are a number of clear similarities. First, we have a thick explanation of the physiological effect of the castration on Naughley, one that includes some overlap in terms of what those effects are: namely, fatness. Whereas the spayed and castrated cattle in the first anecdote "become . . . fat with great facility," Naughley, upon castration, "grew prodigiously fat." Naughley's voice also changed, gesturing to one of the other common tropes that we find exclusively in assessments of the effect of castration on humans: changes in voice. Here, the article actually lauds this change, asserting that Naughley's voice, which was already "naturally good," "improved very much," an improvement that "continued during his life." Unlike the discussion of castration and spaying in animals, there is a durational component to the analysis of Naughley; we have a sense that the physiological effects of the castration continued and compounded over time until Naughley's death at the age of seventy-six (in 1756, seventy-six would have been quite old). In any case, there is a shared attention to the physiological effects of castration, and I argue that we should assume that this shared attention to these physiological changes is evidence of a shared, if also vernacular, understanding that castration could and often *did* effect those changes. This is not to direct any sort of comparison between humans and nonhuman animals, but rather to identify that theories about the effects of castration on humans were frequently derived from understandings of the effects of castration on nonhuman animals, typically those cultivated in agricultural contexts.

I will return to the story of Naughley momentarily, but it also bears mentioning that veterinary or otherwise agricultural treatises on the effects of castration on nonhuman animals are attentive not only to physiological changes but to behavioral changes as well. Importantly, descriptions of behavioral changes tend to lean on gendered or sexual tropes, and castration, in particular, is predictably associated with devirilization. In a December 1824 edition of a Baltimore, Maryland, publication, *American Farmer*, an unnamed author describes castrated dogs as "much more harmless than others: they are as useful and capable of instruction as those that are entire: they may be rendered as vigilant and even as fierce: they are equally ready for the gun or the chase,—are much less disposed to ramble from home,—and may generally be found within the hearing of the master's call."[16] Castration, in short, is one means of making animals behave in a more domesticated manner. Three years later, the same newspaper ran another short article on the uses of castration. The unnamed author of the 1827 article muses that "tranquility is an obvious requisite, for where the passions of brutes are called into action, by whatever means, their influence on their bodies is often as great as in the human species. Hence the use of castration, complete or partial separation, shading from too much light, protection from insects, dogs and other annoying animals, and from the too frequent intrusion of man."[17] Castration, this author argues, ensures "tranquility" in animals and, by analogy, in humans as well, for the influence of the passions of animals over their bodies "is often as great as in the human species." To return to the Naughley anecdote, featuring the castration of a human, we see a similar logic: after being spurned by a member of "the fair sex," and "enraged at this disappointment," Naughley "castrated himself" "to prevent the fair sex from having any further influence over him." Castration was also, as an 1832 article published in a Washington, DC, newspaper, the *United States' Telegraph*, argued, a means by which animals' aggressive or otherwise unmanageable dispositions might be brought into control; writing about bulls, the anonymous author states flatly that "these animals are in their prime at two years old, and should never be suffered to continue longer in a state of virility than to the fifth year; as, after that time, bulls which before were gentle and lay quiet in the cow pastures, are mostly apt to contract vicious dispositions, and become very unmanageable. Whenever this happens, they should be immediately castrated."[18]

By the beginning of the nineteenth century, veterinary and agricultural treatises on the usefulness of castrating animals begin to conflate the physiological and the behavioral, linking the devirilizing or feminizing effects of castration with a feminine *mien*. An 1829 article in the *Pennsylvania Intelligencer, and Farmers' and Mechanics' Journal*, based in Harrisburg, Pennsylvania, titled "Of Castration. Its Ends and Effects," explains that "the intention of this operation is to render the horse more gentle. Some advantages are gained in this respect; but horses lose much of their vigor by it. . . . Care should be taken not to perform the operation till the horse is three years old, as he remains in the same state ever afterwards: he has not then acquired all the strength of which he would have been susceptible; and his chest, not being developed, remains thin and slender."[19] "Thin and slender" were attributes typically associated with femininity in this era, including (and sometimes especially) femininity in men. This attention to the chest of the castrated animal shows up frequently in these discussions, and the size and breadth of the chest are at times specifically and explicitly linked to animal masculinity or as a means by which a "masculine appearance" in animals might be measured.

Lord Spencer (John Charles Spencer, Third Earl of Spencer), the first president of the Royal Agricultural Society, was a notable cattle breeder whose lectures had been published widely in farmer's almanacs and natural history journals in the early 1840s. By the early 1850s, however, those essays were being widely reprinted in North American veterinary and newspaper articles on animal husbandry, especially one article in particular: "On the Selection of Male Animals in the Breeding of Cattle and Sheep," which was frequently published under a range of other titles, including "How to Select Male Animals in Breeding" and "Lord Spencer's Rules for the Selection of Male Animals for Breeding." In even just a cursory keyword search, selections from this particular essay were reprinted in US newspapers at least three times in the 1850s—in Concord, New Hampshire; Manchester, New Hampshire; and Easton, Maryland—which speaks to the fact that a number of editors found it interesting enough to reprint; most of the articles I cite here enjoyed only a single run in a single newspaper, even as the sensationalized character of castration stories tended to make it more likely that they would be reprinted in multiple fora.[20]

Spencer writes,

> The first things to be considered in the selection of a male animal are the indications by which it may be possible to form a judgement as to his constitution. In all animals a wide chest indicates strength of constitution, and there can be no doubt that this is the point of shape to which it is most material for any breeder to look in the selection either of a bull or ram. . . . Another indication of what a good constitution is, that a male animal should have a masculine appearance; with this view a certain degree of coarseness is by no means objectionable, but this coarseness should not be such as would be likely to show itself in a castrated animal.[21]

Here we see an early and explicit linking of specific physiological effects (for example, the size of the chest of the bull) to a particular gendered aesthetics, that of masculinity. Importantly, we *also* see the author divorcing what he seems to understand as physiological maleness from masculinity in appearance or behavior; that "a male animal should have a masculine appearance" indicates a strong constitution, but from the article itself we can see that not every male animal *does* have a strong constitution, which is in turn understood through outward indicia of masculinity (such as chest size). I emphasize the somewhat syllogistic logic at work in this piece not to beleaguer the semantics of Spencer's essay but to call attention to what those semantics reveal: first, that outward masculinity is divorced from genital "maleness" and can be engineered by castration, and second, that a synthetic connection between maleness and masculinity indicates, for Spencer, a strong constitution.

I have dedicated such time to elaborating agricultural theories about the effects of castration on nonhuman animals for two reasons. First, these materials are offered to establish the great energy and interest that farmers, scientists, and laypeople poured into understanding castration as a procedure that could have far-flung physiological, behavioral, and constitutional effects. Far from being an obscure, random, or little-attended-to question, understanding the effects of castration on nonhuman animals was of great import and taken very seriously. These same elite and lay scientists, natural philosophers and farmers also only rarely limited these inquiries about the physiology and anatomy of organic life forms to *only* questions about castration or questions about animals; in many cases, those theorizing about the effects of castration were also reading and writing treatises on anatomy, physiology, natural philosophy, and, increasingly over the course of the nineteenth century, natural selection. In other words, these writers, readers, and thinkers were engaging with the fields that, as Beans Velocci, Jules Gill-Peterson, and Kadji Amin argue, *made* modern understandings of gender, including zoology, gynecology, sexology, endocrinology, and others.[22] In their efforts to theorize the effects of castration, we find a broad cultural and scientific account of the non-self-identicality of *sex* as a concept. In other words—and to speak to the organizing framework of this volume as a whole—these are not histories of what might today be termed *cisness*.

Second, animal anatomy and physiology—especially that of mammals— was frequently understood as broadly analogous to human anatomy and physiology, to the point that many eighteenth- and nineteenth-century doctors were trained in comparative anatomy and saw human and animal medicine as related.[23] An understanding of the workings of animal bodies was thus not only relevant to the study of human bodies, but for many doctors— and especially doctors who practiced in rural areas of the United States prior to the professionalization of medicine—definitively central. Consider one of the only treatises of the effects of castration on humans that I have been able to find, an article titled "Note on the Power of Procreating after Castration," published in 1837 by Robley Dunglison, who was Thomas Jefferson's personal physician, a professor at Jefferson Medical College in Philadelphia, and who to this day is sometimes referred to as "the father of American physiology." In making his argument that humans have a limited but clear window of time following a castration during which a castrated person may still successfully inseminate another, Dunglison cites the cases of a castrated man, a castrated horse, and a castrated boar, in quick succession.[24] This is not sloppy science by the standard of the day, but, rather, a common nineteenth-century approach, in which comparative anatomy becomes evidence of a hypothesis about human physiology. We find rumblings of this epistemological osmosis, the assumption that human and nonhuman animal bodies may both be understood by certain shared theories, in nonscientific contexts as well; an 1858 edition of the *Louisville Daily Courier,* for example, reported in December of that year that

the body of Victor Inderbeth, a German, aged about fifty years, was, by a boy, found dead, lying on his face, eight or ten rods north of the trestle-work of the Coal Company, and between forty and fifty rods south of the engine house of the Terre Haute and Alton Railroad. Upon examination of the body, it was found that he had been corded and castrated, and from blood being found in several places, it is presumed the act was perpetrated at some distance from where the body lay. No other marks of violence, except the wounds made by emasculation, were discernable [*sic*]. The probability is that the deceased removed the cord and died from loss of blood, and that the deed was perpetrated between 7 and 12 o'clock Sunday night.[25]

Animals were typically castrated by tying a rope or cord tightly around the testicles to cut off blood flow to the area. This cord was either simply left in place until the lack of blood to the testicles caused the testicles to simply die and fall off, or, after blood flow to the area was sufficiently cut off, the person administering the castration would cut open the testicles and remove the testes. In the latter case, the cord is necessary to prevent the animal from dying from loss of blood. Here, the quiet and unelaborated implication is that someone did something quite similar to Victor Inderbeth, and that he died not from the castration itself but from the blood loss that followed when he removed the cord around his testicles. While brutal, this anecdote provides an example of exactly the effect that I am describing: that certain procedures used on animals were often understood to work on humans too.

IF THINE RIGHT EYE OFFEND THEE

Not every anecdote describing self-castrations provokes obvious questions about that person's gendered experience. Self-castrations were often reported in connection with assessments of the actor's putative "insanity," suggesting a set of important possible connections between this archive and disability histories. But insofar as scholars working at the intersections of trans studies and disability studies have explored how dominant expectations around the organization of mind, self-expression, and comportment *also* voice a set of demands about gender, these stories of self-castrations performed in fits of "insanity" may nonetheless be trans histories as well. I include them here because a trans feminist historiography demands that we take into account histories of active efforts to discipline, invisibilize, and eradicate forms of gender experience and expression that transgressed social norms, and the medical industrial complex and psychiatric hospitalization were without question iterations of that police and disciplinary power.

Three extremely brief anecdotes from the late nineteenth century—arising out of Ohio, Boston, and California—allow us to explore these tensions. First, the Cleveland, Ohio–area *Plain Dealer* ran a brief piece that reads simply, "Philip Flieger, of New Salem, Fairfield County, a married German, in a fit of insanity, castrated himself on the 14th inet., with probably fatal results."[26] Just two weeks later, the *Boston Daily Advertiser* ran a similarly sketchy account describing that "John Gantly [sic?], forty years old, [unmarried], castrated himself in a house on Milk Street, on Tuesday afternoon, and was taken to an insane asylum."[27] Finally, in 1891, the *Morning Oregonian* ran an only slightly more detailed story, with the title "A Frightful Suicide," revealing that "the body of a horribly mutilated stranger, with a dark beard, roughly dressed and about 45 years of age, was discovered among some baled hay about noon today in the California [stables]. The act is supposed to have been done last night, as deceased was seen alive last evening about 7 o'clock. The man had castrated himself, then cut his throat from ear to ear, using a razor, which was found beside the body."[28] While these incredibly short reports, all of them lacking in detail or explanation, give us little to go on by way of producing some sort of retrospective understanding of what might have motivated these people, I cannot help but track the overlay between these self-castrations, on the one hand, and what we would today term mental health crises, on the other. As scholars such as Regina Kunzel have elaborated, contemporary understandings of what might constitute sanity, rationality, or mental health are as politically inflected and historically specific as any other normative regime and, in that sense, were easily deployable as forms of gendered discipline.[29] This is not to argue that any of the people described above who were reported to have castrated themselves did so out of a sense of discomfort with their genitals, but it is also not to argue that they did not. These stories feel evocative, thick with the unsaid; when considered alongside other accounts of self-castrations in which the gendered mien of the actor in question is scrutinized or invoked, they begin to look more of a kind than not.

Indeed, most reports of castrated individuals that I have encountered in these archives do introduce the gendered character of the actor into question. Consider, for example, discussions of *castrati,* individuals who underwent castration, either voluntarily, coercively, or by force, in order that they might be able to preserve the type of vocal range for operatic and other performances associated with boy children. Discussions of *castrati* appear frequently in eighteenth-century newspapers in particular; if we were to judge popular interest in the topic by the frequency with which it was addressed in ephemeral print during the last half of the eighteenth century, we would have to assume that it was a topic that garnered widespread public interest, indeed.[30] Gossip columns also charted the movement of famous *castrati,* reprinting articles from the society pages of European newspapers on the lives of the eighteenth- and nineteenth-century equivalent of the rich and famous. In an 1820 issue of Boston's *Columbian Centinel,* for example, the unnamed author offers some salacious news about Signor Pergami, a famous *castrato* performer, revealing conspiratorially that "it turns out that the *castrata* of the *Times,* who was to set all Europe to *laughing* at the charges against the Queen, turns out to be a proper Man—has a wife, and family, and a daughter who has been adopted by her Majesty. Signor Pergami remains in *Paris,* where he lives in elegant style, and dresses in the full *pink of the mode.*—In general, he appears with large drop diamond ear-rings."[31] Here, despite Pergami's castrated status and his penchant for "large drop diamond ear-rings," he turns out to be "a proper Man," a status evidenced by the fact that he is married and has children. Like the anecdotes about self-castrations with which I opened this essay—

remember H. Maxwell, the unmarried woodchopper who effected their own castration, and the person from Stonington with a parenthetical "wife and several Children," who "seems rejoyc'd at what he has done"—this one takes care to mention that Pergami has a wife and children, even as it clearly places into doubt whether or not Pergami was "a proper Man" by referring to him as the feminine form of the word: *castrata*. Differently put, despite the brevity of this report, it nonetheless engages extensively with Pergami's gender, implying that Pergami's status as a *castrato* brings into question his status as a man. I mention this not to emphasize the presence of what was likely *also* a cheap, misogynist joke, but to point to the fact that this little article indexes a quiet understanding that those who elected their own castration might not *be* men, not because a penis or testicles is a reliable metric for masculinity but because they risked their lives in opting for this bodily modification. Again, this is in no way to reify any notion that equates gender and genitals, but rather to acknowledge that such notions did and do exist, and have at times exerted great pressure on individuals' self-understanding. And all questions of trans identification aside, that someone may have elected to modify or correct their genitals already rendered them at odds with conventional gendered and sexual expression.

Let us return for one final pass to the story of the curate, Naughley. The 1794 story of his castration is explained as a response to the experience of being spurned by "the fair one to whom he paid his addresses." That article makes sure to state that Naughley "never was married" and describes his rage and disappointment at being spurned as propelling him to make the decision to castrate himself, suggesting that Naughley himself explained the decision by a reference to a biblical verse: "'if thy right eye offend thee,' &c."[32] Here, the article is quoting the Book of Matthew 5:29–30 from the New Testament of the Bible, which finds Jesus instructing his followers that "if thy right eye offend thee, pluck it out, and cast it from thee: for it is profitable for thee that one of thy members should perish, and not that thy whole body should be cast into hell. And if thy right hand offend thee, cut it off, and cast it from thee: for it is profitable for thee that one of thy members should perish, and not that thy whole body should be cast into hell." This passage is generally read as a statement about the seriousness of sin, that even putatively small sins are so significant that it is wiser to take radical, possibly self-transformative measures to eradicate them than it is to explain sin away as a small or partial element of the person or the body. This passage is frequently offered as a hermeneutic response to the problem (or sin) of lust in particular, and this is certainly one of the ways it is being used in the Naughley anecdote.[33] To stave off further disappointment in love, the report suggests, Naughley castrates himself; the piece quietly implies that to do so was Naughley's act of removing himself from any future possibility of love or marriage. The implication is that the penis, or testicles, or something that either the penis or testicles corrals—passion, lust, and so on—was the source of "the fair sex['s]" influence over Naughley, so that the problem was most efficiently solved by castrating himself.

But there is another way to read this short anecdote, as both a scholar of colonial North American print culture and of trans cultural politics in the present. What if we read the passage literally? While readers from 1794 would likely have been intimately familiar with the biblical passage being invoked in this short article, and would have likewise been familiar with the conventions of the exegetical use of the Bible to instruct audiences on its applicability to real-world situations in their lives, the slightly sensationalized tone in which the report is rendered suggests that it might read otherwise, still. A literal interpretation would perhaps be the simplest approach for the twenty-first-century reader, and it would likely go something like this: Naughley "castrated himself" because his genitals, in their previous configuration, offended him. To see them, to use them, to have his genitals be the part of his body that gave "the fair sex" influence over him was uncomfortable, offensive. So he castrated himself and lived the rest of his life as an unmarried Anglican priest with an increasingly beautiful voice.

This is not, of course, a particularly inspiring story. None of the brief, elusive anecdotes that appear, over and over again, in eighteenth- and nineteenth-century newspapers, and that I have collected under the auspices of what I am calling a speculative archive of trans feminine pasts, are. A trans feminist historiographic method can only serve to make trans histories more visible and possibly more usable, but cannot make history, itself, *better*. As a method that refuses the patriarchal historiographic prerogatives that would automatically and anachronistically project cisness back onto a significantly-more-heterogeneously-gendered past, a trans feminist historiographic can still do very little about histories of actual patriarchal violence. It must be noted that these stories are still nonetheless more promising than the much more proliferate appearance of accounts of *unwanted* castrations in this same archive of eighteenth- and nineteenth-century newspapers, which overwhelmingly represent the experiences of both enslaved and free Black men whose sexual autonomies, along with their physical bodies, were so often targeted by white supremacist violence. If these brief, truncated stories—and I should mention, without irony or humor, that eighteenth- and nineteenth-century editors frequently referred to choppy, overzealous editing or excerpting as the "castration" of a text—provide us with a vision of trans feminine possibility in the eighteenth-century North American colonies or nineteenth-century United States, it is a fairly bleak vision. It is also not a universalizing one, and I do not offer it here as such. Many trans and gender-nonconforming people, then and now, saw no need to physically modify their bodies or genitals, making beautiful and often very fun lives in the gender of their choice and identification with the help of clothing and community members, and often little else.

I also want to be very careful to note that a trans feminist historiographic method cannot make or *reveal* any historical figures as *trans* in the modern sense of the term, or perhaps in *any* sense of the term. But at the same time, we know that so many of the methods we have for making sense of historical personae who lived at odds with the gendered strictures of their time are insufficient; it is not enough to simply gather all gender nonconforming people under the catachrestic shorthand of *feminists* or *queers* or *trans people* or *rebels* or any of the wide range of other descriptors historians have reached for to make sense of these historical figures and the way that they lived their lives. What a trans feminist historiographic method *might* offer, however—and I elaborate this point in a recent essay on historiography, language, and the use of they/them pronouns for historical figures—is to highlight or make more visible the social, political, and otherwise material conditions that produce something that, to us today, looks like *gender*, or the effect thereof.[34] That the Curate Naughley or Maxwell the Wood Chopper or the Certain Man at Stonington are not necessarily even obviously gender nonconforming to our scholarly eyes today may in fact denaturalize the putatively predictable range of factors that, in our own moment, add up to something called *gender*: behavior, clothing, professions, and so on. That this names part of the configuration of gendered being in our own moment, however, may have absolutely nothing to do with the configuration of gender—if we are sure one existed in the way we mean it now!—in the past. In short, a trans feminist historiographic method may demand *not* that we start with the person, but rather that we start with the conditions—epistemological, racial, political, classed, labor-based, and so on—in which the person lived in order to understand what might have constituted our present-day sense of their gender, or gender nonconformity. Insofar as I, as a scholar, have been entirely engrossed with the question of the influence of external, rather than identitarian or individuated factors, on people's behavior and self-understanding in the eighteenth and early nineteenth centuries, I think it is not only promising but important to ask a related set of questions about what we today call *gender* insofar as leaning on entirely subjective accounts of experience is, to my mind, always going to be on some level insufficient, because none of us dress ourselves, use language, or move through the world in the vacuum.

On a less historiographical, and more simply historical, concluding note: if these anecdotes school us in the kinds of histories that might be put to use in service of the present, the best that might be said for them is that they offer a vision of some of the earliest iterations of what Jules Gill-Peterson has termed "trans DIY," or trans people's experimental development of practices of what would today be termed gender-affirming medicine and care.[35] History is frequently unredeemable, but these tiny, uninspiring moments nonetheless have the possibly redeeming effect of pointing us to moments of the affirmative articulation of trans lives past. These are complicated, not painless pasts, but hopefully are histories we can recount in the same cheery, ambivalent idiom of the nameless person from Stonington, whose self-castration left them "very much swell'd, but . . . rejoyc'd at what [they have] done."

NOTES

1   See the *Cincinnati Commercial Tribune*, January 22, 1884, 3; and the *Plain Dealer* (Cleveland, OH), January 23, 1884, [1].

2   See Schuller, *Biopolitics of Feeling*; and Amin, "Glands, Eugenics, and Rejuvenation."

3   *New-England Courant*, from Monday, December 4, to Monday, December 11, 1721, 2, right-most column, near the bottom, couched in a letter.

4   See Hartman, "Venus in Two Acts"; and Trouillot, *Silencing the Past*.

5   I am indebted to Jules Gill-Peterson and my student Beans Velocci for this understanding. See Gill-Peterson, *Histories of the Transgender Child*; and Velocci, "Binary Logic."

6   See Diane Sommerville's *Rape and Race in the Nineteenth-Century South*, 76. See also *Mathews v. Sims* 2 Mill. 103 (May 1818) and *Reports of Judicial Decisions in the Constitutional Court of South Carolina*. Also see Genovese, *Roll, Jordan, Roll*, 67–68.

7   See Feimster, *Southern Horrors*; and Hodes, *White Women, Black Men*, 26, 58, 152–55.

8   See Spillers, "Mama's Baby, Papa's Maybe." Regarding why I do not generally describe eighteenth- and nineteenth-century people as *trans*: I elaborate on this question in both the cowritten introduction to LaFleur, Kłosowska, and Raskol-

nikov, *Trans Historical*, and my single-authored conclusion in that same edited collection. Ultimately, I worry that to refer to people who lived prior to the twentieth century or so as trans risks foreclosing or occluding relevant (and important) vocabularies for the diversity of gendered experiences and presentations that existed in their own time, even as I would always include these figures as parts of trans history.

9 See Snorton, *Black on Both Sides*; and Tinsley, *Ezili's Mirrors*.

10 Hartman addresses the ethics of speculation as a method of engaging the history of slavery, as well as archival absences in Black histories more generally, in both "Venus in Two Acts," where she asks, "Is it possible to exceed or negotiate the constitutive limits of the archive? By advancing a series of speculative arguments and exploiting the capacities of the subjunctive (a grammatical mood that expresses doubts, wishes, and possibilities), in fashioning a narrative, which is based upon archival research, and by that I mean a critical reading of the archive that mimes the figurative dimensions of history, I intended both to tell an impossible story and to amplify the impossibility of its telling" (11). Hartman further theorizes this tension while also putting this method into practice in her monograph *Wayward Lives, Beautiful Experiments*.

11 *Disclosure*, dir. Sam Feder (Netflix, 2020).

12 On historical vocabularies for trans experience, see Stryker, *Transgender History*; LaFleur, "Sex and Unsex"; LaFleur, *Natural History of Sexuality in Early America*, chap. 4; Manion, *Female Husbands*; Bychowski and Kim, "Visions of Medieval Trans Feminism"; Chess, Gordon, and Fisher, "Early Modern Trans Studies"; DeVun, *Shape of Sex*; Gutt and Spencer-Hall, *Trans and Genderqueer Subjects in Medieval Historiography*; and LaFleur, Kłosowska, and Raskolnikov, *Trans Historical*.

13 "A Treatise on Agriculture," 2.

14 *American Artisan* (New York), March 4, 1854, 6.

15 "Singular Character," 4.

16 *American Farmer* (Baltimore, MD), December 10, 1824, 6.

17 *American Farmer* (Baltimore, MD), April 20, 1827, 1.

18 "AGRICULTURAL. Management of Cows Kept for The Dairy," 2.

19 "*Complete Treatise on Horses*," 1.

20 See "How to Select Male Animals in Breeding," 4; also printed as "Lord Spencer's Rules for the Selection of Male Animals for Breeding," in the *Granite Farmer* (Manchester, NH), October 29, 1851, 2; also reprinted in the *Easton Star* (Easton, MD), August 9, 1853, 1.

21 See "How to Select Male Animals in Breeding," 4.

22 See Gill-Peterson, *Histories of the Transgender Child*; Velocci, "Binary Logic"; and Amin, "Glands, Eugenics, and Rejuvenation." While each of these scholars works on a slightly later period than the focus of this chapter, each names the fields I am discussing here as contributing influences on the fields that each of them engages in their work on later periods.

23 Schmitt, "Studies on Animals."

24 Dunglison, "ART. X."

25 "ANOTHER ILLINOISTOWN HORROR—BRUTAL AND TERRIBLE MURDER," I.

26 *Plain Dealer* (Cleveland, OH), July 17, 1874, 2; reprinted in the *Cincinnati Commercial Gazette*, January 22, 1884, 3, and then again in the *Plain Dealer* in 1884.

27 *Boston Daily Advertiser*, July 30, 1874, [4].

28 "A Frightful Suicide," 2.

29 See Kunzel, "Queer History."

30 While some of the fascination with *castrati* seems to constellate around its association with Rome, and, by association, with Catholicism in particular, in 1798 a spate of newspaper articles celebrated the ratification of the new constitution of the extremely short-lived Roman republic (e.g., the French République Romaine) and explicitly explained that the new constitution outlawed the castration of young people. An article celebrates that "the horrible practice of *castration* of the human species is also prohibited. . . . [Before the revolution this shocking practice was carried to such an extent, that the barber's sign boards in the streets of Rome were seen inscribed with the words—'*qui si castrame I puti maravigliosamente*'—that is—Here boys are castrated with wonderful dexterity!!]" (2). See "Philadelphia, Nov. 1," [3].

31 See "London, July 14," 2.

32 "Singular Character," 4. It is not clear whether there was any firsthand information from Naughley himself, although this seems unlikely, given that the article was published in 1794 but says that Naughley died in 1756, almost forty years earlier. The article *does* state that Naughley "g[ave] for his reason, 'if thy right eye offend thee,' &c." The entire story may be apocryphal, but even if it is not, it is unlikely that the printer had any firsthand knowledge of Naughley's explanation for his decision to castrate himself.

33 The use of this biblical verse to gloss the problem of lust also appears in a passage from Friedrich Nietzsche reprinted by Moses Harman in a 1900 edition of his newspaper *Lucifer, the Light Bearer*:

> All passions have a time when they are fatal only, when, with the weight of their folly, they drag their victim down; and they have a later, very much later period, when they wed with spirit, when they are "spiritualised." Formerly, people waged war against passion itself, on account of the folly involved in it, they conspire[d] for its annihilation,—an old morality monsters are unanimous on this point: "*il faut tuer les passions*." The most notable formula for that view stands in the New Testament, in the Sermon on the Mount, where, let us say in passing, things are not at all regarded *from an elevated point of view*. For example, it is there said with application to sexuality. "If thine eye offend thee, pluck it out." Fortunately no Christian acts according to this precept. To *annihilate* passions and desires merely in order to obviate their folly and its unpleasant results appears to us at present simply as an acute form of folly. We

no longer admire the dentist who *pulls out* teeth, that they may no longer cause pain. It may be acknowledged, on the other hand, with some reasonableness that, on the soil out of which Christianity has grown, the notion of a "*spiritualisation*" of passion could not at all be conceived.

The primitive church, as it well known, battled *against* the 'intelligent' in favor of the "poor in spirit": how could we expect from it an intelligent war against passion?—The Church fights against passion with excision in every sense; its practice, its "cure," is *castration*. It never asks, "How to spiritualise, beautify, and deify a desire?"—it has, at all times, laid all the emphasis of discipline upon extermination (of sensuality, of pride, of ambition, of avarice, of revenge).—But to attack the passions at the root means to attack life itself at the root; the praxis of the Church is *inimical to life*. (134)

34 See LaFleur, "What's in a Name?"
35 See Jules Gill-Peterson's website with a description of her current book project, "Gender Underground: A History of Trans DIY," which is currently in progress: https://www.jgillpeterson.com/.

BIBLIOGRAPHY

"AGRICULTURAL. Management of Cows Kept for the Dairy." *United States' Telegraph* (Washington, DC). September 10, 1832, 2.
Amin, Kadji. "Glands, Eugenics, and Rejuvenation in *Man into Woman*: A Biopolitical Genealogy of Transsexuality." *TSQ* 5, no. 4 (2018): 589–605.
"ANOTHER ILLINOISTOWN HORROR—BRUTAL AND TERRIBLE MURDER." *Louisville Daily Courier* (Louisville, KY), December 11, 1858, 1.
Bychowski, M. W., and Dorothy Kim. "Visions of Medieval Trans Feminism: An Introduction." *Medieval Feminist Forum: A Journal of Gender and Sexuality* 55, no. 1 (2019): 6–41.
Chess, Simone, Colby Gordon, and Will Fisher, eds. "Early Modern Trans Studies." Special issue, *Journal for Early Modern Cultural Studies* 19, no. 4 (Fall 2019).
"*Complete Treatise on Horses*. By an old officer of the French Cavalry. Translated from the French, for the American Farmer. Chapter XVIII. *Different Ages of the Horse*." *Pennsylvania Intelligencer, and Farmers' and Mechanics' Journal* (Harrisburg, PA), October 20, 1829, 1.
DeVun, Leah. *The Shape of Sex: Nonbinary Gender from Genesis to the Renaissance*. New York: Columbia University Press, 2021.
Dunglison, Robley. "ART. X.—NOTE ON THE POWER OF PROCREATING AFTER CASTRATION. BY THE EDITOR." *American Medical Library and Intelligencer*, edited by Professor Dunglison, no. 8, July 15, 1837.
Feimster, Crystal. *Southern Horrors: Women and the Politics of Rape and Lynching*. Cambridge, MA: Harvard University Press, 2009.

"A Frightful Suicide." *Morning Oregonian* (Portland, OR), March 6, 1891, 2. Also printed in the *Riverside Morning Enterprise*, March 6, 1891, 1.

Genovese, Eugene. *Roll, Jordan, Roll: The World the Slaves Made.* New York: Random House, 1975.

Gill-Peterson, Jules. *Histories of the Transgender Child.* Minneapolis: University of Minnesota Press, 2018.

Gutt, Blake, and Alicia Spencer-Hall. *Trans and Genderqueer Subjects in Medieval Historiography.* Amsterdam: Amsterdam University Press, 2021.

Harman, Moses. "Spiritualization vs. Annihilation." *Lucifer, the Light Bearer* (Chicago, IL), May 4, 1900, 134.

Hartman, Saidiya. "Venus in Two Acts." *Small Axe* 12, no. 2 (2008): 1–14.

Hartman, Saidiya. *Wayward Lives, Beautiful Experiments.* New York: W. W. Norton, 2019.

Hodes, Martha. *White Women, Black Men.* New Haven, CT: Yale University Press, 1999.

"How to Select Male Animals in Breeding." *Independent Democrat* (Concord, NH), October 30, 1851, 4.

Kunzel, Regina. "Queer History, Mad History, and the Politics of Health." *American Quarterly* 69, no. 2 (2017): 315–19.

LaFleur, Greta. *The Natural History of Sexuality in Early America.* Baltimore, MD: Johns Hopkins University Press, 2018.

LaFleur, Greta. "Sex and Unsex: Histories of Gender Trouble in Eighteenth-Century North America." *Early American Studies* 12, no. 3 (2014): 469–99.

LaFleur, Greta. "'What's in a Name?': They/Them." *Journal of the Early Republic* 43, no. 1 (2023): 109–19.

LaFleur, Greta, Anna Kłosowska, and Masha Raskolnikov, eds. *Trans Historical: Gender Plurality before the Modern.* Ithaca, NY: Cornell University Press, 2021.

Larson, Scott. "Laid Open." In *Trans Historical: Gender Plurality before the Modern,* ed. Greta LaFleur, Anna Kłosowska, and Masha Raskolnikov, 350–65. Ithaca, NY: Cornell University Press, 2021.

"London, July 14." *Columbian Centinel* (Boston), August 30, 1820, 2.

Manion, Jen. *Female Husbands: A Trans History.* Cambridge: Cambridge University Press, 2020.

"Philadelphia, Nov. 1: Constitution of the Roman Republic." *Philadelphia General Advertiser*, November 1, 1798, [3]. Also reprinted in *The Herald of Liberty* (Washington, PA), November 19, 1798.

Reports of Judicial Decisions in the Constitutional Court of South Carolina, Held at Charleston and Columbia in 1817, 1818. Volume 2. Charleston, SC: John Mill, 1819.

Schmitt, Stéphane. "Studies on Animals and the Rise of Comparative Anatomy at and around the Parisian Royal Academy of Sciences in the Eighteenth Century." *Science in Context* 29, no. 1 (2016): 11–54.

Schuller, Kyla. *The Biopolitics of Feeling: Race, Sex, and Science in the Nineteenth Century.* Durham, NC: Duke University Press, 2018.

"Singular Character." *Hartford Gazette* (Hartford, CT), December 15, 1794, 4.

Snorton, C. Riley. *Black on Both Sides: A Racial History of Trans Identity*. Minneapolis: University of Minnesota Press, 2018.

Sommerville, Diane. *Rape and Race in the Nineteenth-Century South*. Chapel Hill: University of North Carolina Press, 2004.

Spillers, Hortense. "Mama's Baby, Papa's Maybe: An American Grammar Book." *Diacritics* 17, no. 2 (1987): 65–81.

Stryker, Susan. *Transgender History: The Roots of Today's Revolution*. New York: Seal Press, 2008.

Tinsley, Omise'eke Natasha. *Ezili's Mirrors: Imagining Black Queer Genders*. Durham, NC: Duke University Press, 2018.

"A Treatise on Agriculture." *Albany Argus*, June 16, 1820, 2.

Trouillot, Michel-Rolph. *Silencing the Past: Power and the Production of History*. Boston: Beacon Press, 1995.

Velocci, Beans. "Binary Logic: Race, Expertise, and the Persistence of Uncertainty in American Sex Research." PhD diss., Yale University, 2022.

DENATURING CISNESS, OR,   4
TOWARD TRANS HISTORY
AS METHOD

Say it with me, everyone: trans people have been here for a long time. Great. I'm so glad you agree. Now that we've gotten that out of the way, I would like to also say, with the utmost respect and gratitude to my colleagues who have laid the groundwork for me to make this claim, that *this is no longer a politically useful way to talk about the past.* We are spending too much time being defensive about the existence of trans people, playing nice with the disciplinary norms of hetero- and cis-normative historical practice, and being generally careful. Anti-trans violence doesn't care. It does not give half a shit about our carefully crafted arguments and delicate treatment of evidence. On the contrary, it is mobilizing the appearance of historicization to do more violence. It is literally deploying our work to do more violence.

The situation is this: the way that we're currently doing trans history is aligned with right-wing and trans-exclusionary radical feminist (TERF) interests in framing transness as a new minority population in need of careful verification. Case in point is the dissent of noted antifeminist and amateur historian Samuel Alito in his *Bostock v. Clayton County* dissent (remember when a good thing happened at the Supreme Court? I barely do). "It defies belief," he wrote, "to suggest that the public meaning of discrimination because of sex in 1964 encompassed discrimination on the basis of a concept that was essentially unknown to the public at that time."[1] The concept, of course, was transness. In *Bostock v. Clayton County,* which included a plaintiff who had been fired after informing her employer that she would begin presenting as a woman at work, the United States Supreme Court decided that Title VII of the Civil Rights Act of 1964 offers protection from employment discrimination on the basis of sexual orientation or gender identity, trans status included.[2] While Alito admitted that "it is likely true that there have always been individuals who experience what is now termed 'gender dysphoria,'" transness, he claimed, had only begun to emerge as a concept in the 1960s. People who experienced dysphoria or moved to a gender other than the one they had been assigned at birth, Alito implied, would not have been understood as *trans* specifically before the 1960s, and thus the legislators who wrote Title VII could not possibly have meant to offer them legal protection.[3] In fact, he argued, "terms like ['transgender status' and 'gender identity'] would have left people at the time scratching their heads."[4] (This affinity for historical reasoning toward fascist ends also features in Alito's decision in *Dobbs v. Jackson*, where he sagely reminds us that "the right to an abortion is not deeply rooted in the Nation's history and tradition."[5] My offense as a historian almost overwhelms my rage as a person invested in bodily autonomy.)

Historians also soberly claim that transness as a named identity is a post–World War II subject position. The consensus among historians is that, although people have been crossing gender lines at least since the Dionysian cults of antiquity routinely cross-dressed to worship their sex-transforming god, the category "trans" is a twentieth-century invention. Therefore we can't call people in the more distant past trans because that's not how people understood their own identity.[6] In fact, Alito cited Joanne Meyerowitz's *How Sex Changed,* the book on trans history that defined the field, which argues that understandings of sex fundamentally shifted in the twentieth century, beginning in the century's early decades and culminating after World War II, to make imagining transness possible. Alito apparently did a rather poor job of reading Meyerowitz, who literally opens with an anecdote about the 1952 *New York Times* headline that announced Christine Jorgenson's transition to the American masses over a decade before the crafting of Title VII. The Supreme Court Justice's sloppy engagement with scholarship reveals, though, that his claim did not hinge on specific dates so much as an insistence that trans people were unthinkable in the past and remain so in the present, with a vague gesture toward the expertise of history to back him up. Given that a Justice of the United States Supreme Court argued against protecting trans people on the basis that transness as a category is new, it appears that the close attention to accurately historicizing the emergence of trans identity is actively being used to undermine the rights and protections trans people are fighting for today. We may want to rethink our strategy here.

Here's why it matters: this isn't just about Alito's history fetish. Trans history is also being used against trans youth. The state of Texas is using Emily Bazelon's Transition Care Is Such a New Debate That We Should Be Super Careful About It hit-piece to argue that trans teens shouldn't be allowed to access puberty blockers or hormones.[7] Bazelon cited me (indeed, the only trans history or trans studies scholar cited in the piece) to give the article a whiff of trans expertise, a little historical framing of the World Professional Institute Association for Transgender Health (WPATH) *Standards of Care* as a treat. Never mind that the historical work I did makes it clear that conversations about transition care are *not* new; never mind that we had a long conversation about the 1950s construction of transness as highly uncertain through narratives of risk and regret. Did Bazelon use my article to enact precisely the thing I demonstrate, with a *plethora* of footnotes, has limited access to trans care? Sure did! So, forgive me for being salty, but the time for measured precision about who counts as trans in the past is over. Our good-faith historical methodologies are being used against us. It's time to go on the offensive. Say it again: trans people have been here a long time. You know who haven't? Cis people.

TRANS PASTS

Arguments like Alito's, which basically say that trans people are not protected by precedent-bound laws because we are literally unprecedented, are not new. To counter them, trans people and academic historians have worked to demonstrate that even if named categories have shifted over time, people who might be considered trans today have a long history that needs to be recovered. "I couldn't find *myself* in history. . . . No one like me seemed to have ever existed," Leslie Feinberg explained as hir reason to write *Transgender Warriors*, which highlights people who crossed the boundaries of gender norms from antiquity to the then-present of the 1990s and was one of the first books to insist that trans people had a history.[8] Feinberg's research showed that people like hir *had* existed for thousands of years.[9] This style of recovering the stories of pre-1950s figures stands to solve one problem, by refuting a version of history in which trans people did not exist in the past. Yet there is a misapprehension of history that it can't address: namely, the idea that trans people have always existed as a small minority, few and far between, while most people's sex and gender just happen to coincide. I propose another, complementary approach to trans history: dismantling cisness as a natural, majority category, with trans history deployed as method, rather than as subject.

Refuting the notion that contemporary transness is unprecedented, and therefore illegitimate as a way of being, continues to be a central goal of recent work in trans history. This history aims to provide representation and to document both the oppression and ability to thrive that trans people experienced in the past. *True Sex* author Emily Skidmore pointed out in a 2018 interview that much contemporary animosity toward and anxiety about trans people are based in narratives that transness is totally novel. Because of that, Skidmore said, trans history "can have incredible power because it suggests that trans people are not new; they've been around for a long time."[10] Jules Gill-Peterson emphasized in *Histories of the Transgender Child* the way that ideas about transness being new cause harm. In particular, Gill-Peterson demonstrates that children continue to be denied the agency to define their gender for themselves in large part *because* of arguments that it's only the most recent generation of kids who express a desire to transition. Documenting over a century of trans children serves as one way to undercut that narrative.[11] Trans history, then, from one of its earliest instantiations to the most cutting edge of the field, is a political project, one that is fully aware of the ways that history translates to legitimacy in the present.

This kind of history has been crucial. As someone who realized they were trans because of a history of sexuality class, I fully appreciate that the kinds of work I've just described push back against the ways trans people have been rendered invisible and against the ways history often masquerades as an authority to be used against us. Clearly, if powerful people are trying to tell us that we were invented too recently for protective laws to have any bearing on our lives, except potentially to protect people *from* us in bathrooms, then it remains a necessary part of trans history to tell trans stories. It's also not enough and, on its own, wielded by anti-trans actors, has the capacity to do significant damage.

The model of uncovering the historical figures that today would be called trans hides the process by which people who *aren't* trans came to be understood as categorically natural—as having not been invented at all. At the same time that historians have fruitfully told trans stories to activist ends, we have unintentionally reproduced a cis/trans binary that is imagined to persist on its own over time. Trans histories focused on illuminating a small minority of trans people and methods used to write about trans people before the category "trans" existed both make it seem like most people naturally fit quite neatly into the sex and gender categories they were assigned at birth. Most people, in the current trans history model, are cis. But, as this chapter will argue, the task of the historian is to notice that cisness is not a natural state— instead, the idea that most people fit into binary sex and gender categories took a tremendous amount of work to construct and takes a tremendous amount of work to maintain.

Trans history and historical work in trans studies offer a promise of another way: both have shown the multitudinous possibilities of gender that have existed throughout history and also expanded the very bounds of transness itself to encompass analyses of racial formation, the nonhuman, and opaque figures who resist easy sorting into a modern trans category.[12] The past is a very trans place. These insights regarding the pervasive existence of gendered lives and beings in the past lay the groundwork for a critique of the illogics of cisness. What is required next is another fundamental model of trans history, one that focuses on the systemic absurdity of static and binary gender and sex classification. Such an approach addresses the history of structures that have produced cisness and occluded trans life, thus producing transness as rare and individual exceptions to a general rule. This trans history is a methodology with an alternative logic of how sex and gender function, which complements but also exceeds trans history as an archive of particular, recognizable objects. This trans history refuses Alito's terms that trans people must be present in history and found using the same terms in order to expect protection from employment discrimination. Instead of responding to accusations of newness with assertions that we've always been here, this chapter offers the provocation that if you want to talk about newfangled subject positions, let's talk about cis people.

HISTORY OF SEXUALITY AND THE SEARCH
FOR THE TRANS SUBJECT

A cis/trans binary emerged in trans history by way of Foucauldian disciplinary norms in its parent field, history of sexuality. Thanks in large part to Michel Foucault's assertion that the "homosexual" did not come to exist in the minds of European doctors or sexual deviants until 1870 at the earliest, historians of sexuality are extremely careful about tightly historicizing sexual categories.[13] In the history of sexuality framework, it would be inaccurate to describe, for example, a seventeenth-century man who has sex with other men as "homosexual" because the category had not been invented yet, and that's not how people at the time would have conceptualized their own sexual behavior or desire—indeed, sexual behavior and desire wouldn't have been seen as constituting an individual sense of identity or subjectivity at all before the late nineteenth century. Historians have increasingly questioned aspects of this Foucauldian approach, since clearly people *did* recognize themselves and other members of their community as having and sometimes even sharing a distinctive sense of sexual self.[14] Even so, the rule about terminology remains firmly in place among academic historians: you may not use a term for people who lived before the invention of that particular identity category.

Because trans history emerged as a subset of the history of sexuality, those studying transness in the past have largely followed the same norms regarding the use of contemporary categories to describe historical actors.[15] Roughly speaking, "transvestite" came into use in the 1910s, "transsexual" emerged in the 1950s and 1960s, and "transgender," while coined in the 1960s, only came into widespread use in the 1990s.[16] While there's certainly debate about the precise use of these terms, and even more debate about whether pre-1950s figures like the "invert," "fairy," and "passing woman" should be considered trans, the foundational idea that categories need to be narrowly historicized remains.[17] Hewing closely to this disciplinary norm is one way that trans history has legitimized itself. The academic subfield has had to struggle against the exclusion of transness from history in the abstract as well as from the field of History as it has been defined in institutions, and insist on both the recognition of its objects of analysis and its own existence as worth spending time and tenure lines on. This struggle is especially fraught for historians who are, as trans people themselves, navigating calcified, trans-exclusive, or at the very least trans-disinterested universities. In this context, there's a particular premium on performing disciplinary expertise by reassuring everyone that we can follow the rules, not to mention a high burden of proof when it comes to naming anyone as any kind of queer in the past.[18]

In the process of establishing legitimacy through acceptable sorting practices, though, trans history runs up against the problem of defining "who counts" as a subject of trans history, and it has faced the considerable challenge of identifying its subject. This is particularly an issue when writing about people who lived before the invention of trans as a category. After all, you can't just run a keyword search for "transgender" in a nineteenth-century newspaper database.[19] Uncertainty in this regard manifests in the way that every single book of trans history that has been published thus far contains at least a paragraph, sometimes pages, explaining its use of terminology and how the author decided who to count, or not count, as trans. If you read through these paragraphs in quick succession, it becomes clear that although trans historians express anxiety about this issue, they are actually pretty much in agreement about who counts.

In the history of sexuality model, scholars often turn to familiar behavioral signals that make it into the historical record, like sodomy convictions when they want to do "gay history" when gay identity isn't quite present yet. Trans historians, building on this precedent, often look for something that looks behaviorally like what they know transness to be in order to find historical actors to write about. Processes of crossing and movement are key. The subject of trans history that emerges from this approach, especially in the pre-twentieth-century context, is someone who engages in "various forms and degrees of crossgender practices and identifications," or who persists in a gender presentation other than the one they were assigned at birth, one that is, again, "cross-gender."[20] In *True Sex*, for example, Skidmore has argued that her turn-of-the-twentieth-century subjects can rightfully be called "trans men," because they "transitioned from the gender assigned to them at birth to the one with which they identified."[21] In *Female Husbands*, Jen Manion proposes that the figure of the female husband was "effectively a trans position," citing Susan Stryker's definition of transgender as referring to "people who move away from the gender they were assigned at birth."[22]

The practices that constitute this movement also align across texts and are markers of transness that make sense within a contemporary understanding of what transness is. Trans history tends to be populated by people who were arrested for cross-dressing, who turn up in sensational accounts about "female husbands" or "women masquerading as men" or, in later periods, who sought to make inhabiting their bodies more comfortable with hormonal and surgical interventions.[23] These are often people who have changed their names and pronouns, work a job that matches the gender they transitioned to within strictly gender-segmented labor markets, and have what would probably be considered in a hetero/homo binary "heterosexual" romantic and sexual relationships (i.e., they were revealed to be "masquerading as a man" while being married to a woman).[24] Often they make it into the historical record because they were somehow outed, frequently through some kind of interaction with carceral regimes and medical or psychiatric institutions, or while being prepared for burial after they died.[25]

The move to historicize transness is, by the current standards of the history of sexuality, good history. Yet the focus on searching for a type of person who engages in certain behaviors unexpected for their assigned sex requires the formulation of and adherence to a classification system for identifying transness. Foundational work in the study of classification by Geoffrey Bowker and Susan Leigh Star argues that every classification system "valorizes some point of view and silences another."[26] That is, classification systems aren't just neutral ways of describing the world. They limit what it's possible to imagine and to do. They have far-reaching ethical implications, from the literal privileging of some groups over others (and whom those groups contain), to decisions that states make about populations, to questions of who receives medical treatment and how. Most importantly, classification systems are *made*, and they are made by people and institutions with their own interests and investments about the outcome of who counts as what. Classification systems rarely fit everyone. When people come into contact with classification systems, especially people who don't easily fit into the available categories, disjunctures between the system and the person generally result in harm as lives are twisted to fit categories that can never encompass the full range and complexity of existence. Classifying, then, is a high-stakes enterprise.

The classification practices of trans history do just what Bowker and Star warn against. The traits that scholars use to find trans people in archival documents work only because they're supposed to be distinctive. The implication is that people who are not trans fit reasonably well into their assigned gender norms, and if they do cross-dress or work unexpectedly gendered jobs, these are anomalies with little to no bearing on how sex as a system works. As a result, the reliance on the apparent distinction of the traits I mentioned above produces a view of the past in which some small number of people transgress gender to such a degree that they leave the category they were assigned at birth, but most people don't. Or to put it another way, as Stryker does in *Transgender History*, "Being transgendered is like being gay—some people are just 'that way,' though most people aren't."[27]

This is a specific point of view on how sex and gender operate, and it's a point of view that obscures the way that cis people had to be made into cis people just as trans people had to be made into trans people. It's a point of view that assumes a perpetual, normalized alignment between most sexed bodies and their gender identities. In trying to work through the problem of who counts as trans, scholars have implicitly framed trans history as being concerned with a numerically minority population who can be identified by the extremity of their gender transgression, because most people simply aren't trans. Trans people become visible in archives because of behaviors that are supposed to be exceptional, and everyone else is presumed to be cis. If most people in the past are categorized as not-trans, and trans people are a numerically small minority that need to be carefully searched for, then it makes it look as though a cis/trans distinction has basically been around forever. It hides the way that cisness had to be constructed as a privileged way of being.

Of course, no one is outright saying in those words that everyone else has always been cis. After all, cisness only became a named concept in the mid-1990s and only began to see broader circulation in the early 2000s.[28] So as with the category "trans," good historians do not call people in the past "cis." But that's rather the point: you don't even have to bother saying anyone *wasn't* trans. "Cis," as Finn Enke has succinctly put it, "never needs to prove itself."[29] The classification practices of trans history silence a more complex view of how sex and gender categories function because they create a version of the past in which most people just happen to fit the gender category they were assigned at birth. Herein lies the key to a central contention of a trans history against cisness. Most people *don't* just happen to fit the category they were assigned. There's a whole apparatus that has churned along in the background, willfully ignored, to make it *look* like they do. The power of cis normativity comes precisely from this hiding of its own invention, and it is there that trans history can intervene.

HISTORIANS AGAINST CISNESS, OR, ANOTHER WAY

A wide array of gender nonconformities *don't* cohere into a diagnostic or legal or otherwise identitarian figure adjacent to transness, and nor are they particularly recognizable in their cross-dressing, name-changing, or pronoun-switching. These figures could be the basis of another version of trans history that is a gadfly to cisness and attuned to the many ambiguous states that somehow become reclaimed and declawed as not-trans. Historians and trans studies scholars have already created a path toward this more expansive model. Take, for example, the celebrated Fall 2019 "Early Modern Trans Studies" special issue of the *Journal for Early Modern Cultural Studies*, which made waves in the realm of historical trans scholarship precisely because it pointed to the possibility of "interpretation that does not turn on identity."[30] Indeed, as the thirteen essays in the special issue so clearly demonstrate, the early modern period was filled with a cast of characters who cannot be easily categorized as trans or not but are certainly indicative of an extensive range of gender variance before the development of modern categories.[31] We know, then, that history is more trans than we have been led to believe. I offer a corollary: history is far less cis than one might anticipate. I propose a trans historical methodology that interrogates subjects who do not seem trans at all, that reveals the way that their genders and sexes required constant management to make it seem as though they simply fit.

A subset of scholars writing trans histories and historical works in trans studies is increasingly moving away from an outright distinction between trans and cis people in their analysis. Emma Heaney, for example, argues that modern womanhood itself is always constructed through and around trans femininity, suggesting that "woman" as a category cannot be neatly split into cis and trans types.[32] Scott Larson has emphasized the importance of "engaging in historical work from a transgender perspective," which "take[s] seriously the possibility of imagining gender outside binary categories."[33] Scholars taking this approach have begun to outline how putting trans analysis together with questions of race, species, and age all throw the notion of well-constructed cis/trans *and* male/female binaries into disarray. These orienting questions can be expanded in historical practice to produce a research agenda invested in deconstructing cisness, whether its archival subjects seem trans or not, which in turn sidesteps the illusion of a perpetual cisgender majority.

Paying attention to race in this context immediately shows the mental gymnastics required to get a cis/trans binary to seem even remotely plausible—indeed, it reveals the intractable whiteness of cisness itself.[34] As Kyla Schuller has argued, binary sexes emerged as specifically racial categories when nineteenth- and early twentieth-century scientists claimed that true sexual dimorphism existed only at the pinnacle of evolutionary advancement (that is, among white humans). Everyone else, according to these scientists, exhibited far less distinction between men and women.[35] C. Riley Snorton likewise attends to histories of how the racial unsexing and degendering of Black people, especially Black women, helped pave the way for the invention of transness to begin with. These histories led Snorton to "eschew binaristic logic that might reify a distinction between transgender and cisgender" in his analysis.[36] Thus, while Snorton engages with historical actors legible as trans or trans adjacent in a contemporary sense (for example, Mary Jones, who took on the identity Peter Sewally to escape slavery, and Lucy Hicks Anderson, whose transness was criminalized in nationally reported trials as "impersonating a woman" in the 1940s), he also attends to J. Marion Sims's gynecological experiments on Betsey, Anarcha, and Lucey—all enslaved women who demonstrated none of the traits of transness that trans history tends to gravitate around. By pairing legible trans-ish figures with those who would not be imagined as trans at all by most historians, Snorton demonstrates how the forced degendering of Blackness contributed to possibilities for imagining trans bodily mutability in the separation of the body from its social being. The sexed body could be uncategorized by race. Thinking with Schuller and Snorton, as well as the many other scholars who have interrogated the ways that racialization outside of whiteness interrupts full membership in male or female categories, a set of questions emerges for a renewed trans history: What does it mean for a history of cis/trans and male/female binaries if we take seriously the notion that one can be pushed out of a normative sex or gender category on the basis of race?[37] How did sex and gender come to be seen as nonracial categories, such that all of the people who in the nineteenth century were excluded from sexual normativity were folded, at least partially, back into it?

Another way forward: looking to how animals have been classified by sex further emphasizes that an extensive amount of sexual variation has been repeatedly plastered over in the service of either maintaining the idea that clear sexual distinctions are natural or positioning humanity itself as relying on having an obvious binary sex.[38] Kadji Amin's work on glandular science, for example, describes the high hopes of early twentieth-century medical men who grafted segments of nonhuman ovaries and testicles into human bodies—sometimes across sex lines, but usually for the purpose of restoring or "rejuvenating" normative masculinity and femininity.[39] As Amin convincingly argues, this hybridizing of human and animal at the site of gonadal tissue aided in materializing a racial logic in which whiteness and sexual dimorphism went hand in hand. The things we might recognize in the present as trans (e.g., physically reorganizing a body's sex characteristics by medical means) worked *against* expansive possibilities for gendered lives in the past. Other enactments of that process are sites for further trans history inquiry.

While much of the scholarship at the nexus of transness and the nonhuman so far has been organized around the concept of plasticity in specific bodies, there is also much to be explored where taxonomies themselves must either flex or collapse under their own weight.[40] In my own work, I have looked to the nonhuman as a space where scientists consistently grapple with and disagree about what counts as maleness or femaleness and even what constitutes sex itself. Nineteenth-century debates over what sex classifications and pronouns to use for worker bees (Third neuter sex? Nonreproductive females? Anatomically female but socially a third sex?) indicate a whirlwind of possibility that had to be tamed over decades into an insistence that worker bees were really female. Early twentieth-century studies of reproduction in fungi posited wildly different criteria for sex designation than those scientists' colleagues were using down the campus lane to conduct sex research in pigeons.[41] Though I persistently joke about bees as trans icons, this turn to the nonhuman highlights the benefit of pursuing in the archive life forms that are not remotely trans. They enable one to track how multiplicitous possibilities of sex became ensnared in a system that demanded only two and then pretended that there had been only two sexes all along that science had merely gotten better at identifying.

Age also provides a possible means of exploring how an experience that applies to everyone, not only trans people, has the capacity to torque sex and gender classifications that are then realigned with the normative. While not a trans studies text as such, Kathryn Bond Stockton's *The Queer Child* opens with a provocation of far-reaching implications: "If you scratch a child, you will find a queer."[42] That is to say, there is something about the malleability of childhood itself that requires careful molding of strangely oriented children into normative adult women and men. Jules Gill-Peterson further illuminates the intricacies of the problems that childhood itself caused for sex and gender in the twentieth century: as medical discourse and practice increasingly coalesced around a model of childhood plasticity where children's sex could be reassigned as doctors deemed necessary, a binary model of sex began to fray around the edges.[43] And what of old age? While childhood has so far been the primary point of departure for studies of age and sex, the power of the latter stages of the life course to unsettle sex and gender categories is increasingly apparent. Amin's attention to glandular medicine in the service of rejuvenation, for example, suggests the threat senescence poses toward full masculinity and femininity. There is, I think, exceptional promise here for ongoing investigation.

Trans history, in these lines of thought and many others, has the potential to make it abundantly clear that "non-trans" people's sex and gender are just as constructed as trans people's. Scholars are rapidly pushing trans history in new directions, and the various components necessary to dismantle a cis-normative historical imaginary are there. At the same time, these histories continue to focus primarily on people recognizable to a present eye as trans or trans adjacent. So, for example, Larson's analysis of the transcendence of gender categories by the "Publick Universal Friend" of eighteenth-century Rhode Island is a fantastic example of the possibilities for using trans history as a method of analysis for people for whom the modern category "transgender" would not apply. But the Publick Universal Friend was, in Larson's description, someone who performed many different signifiers of gender, sometimes masculine, sometimes feminine, actively disavowing the stability of the gender categories of the period in question—someone, that is, who clearly shows signs of some kind of gender deviance. The essays in Simone Chess, Colby Gordon, and Will Fisher's "Early Modern Trans Studies" special issue take a similar focus. Or, from another angle, Joanne Meyerowitz and Gill-Peterson both make compelling arguments about how sex and gender functioned in the twentieth century, but they do so *through* the clearly legible trans subject. Trans people, or people who behave very similarly to trans people, remain the exemplar for exceeding the bounds of gender categories assigned at birth.

I want us to tell more stories about trans and trans-adjacent people, yes, but I also want trans history to make bold claims about how trans people are not the only ones who crack open sex and gender categories. People who don't experience themselves as gender nonconforming, who know themselves, as soon as the category emerges, as cis, break the rules just as much as we do, but they are often forgiven for it and are either welcomed or forcefully yanked back into neat binary categories. Trans history already has the tools to ask why this is and to demand a reckoning around cis normativity's successful masking of its own invention. In the 1980s and early 1990s, scholars argued that by looking at the history of transness, we can see how binary gender classification systems are made and how they kind of unravel under scrutiny. In 1987, for example, Sandy Stone articulated this framing as she rebutted Janice Raymond's *The Transsexual Empire*, which had argued that transsexualism reinforced patriarchal gender stereotypes. Stone's retort, "The *Empire* Strikes Back," argued that it was doctors who insisted that trans people fit stereotypical definitions of gender, with the incitement to "pass" being something forced *onto* trans people. But this was not merely about trans people. "The origin of gender dysphoria clinics," Stone said of the institutionalization of requirements that trans people do gender "correctly" in order to access hormones and surgery, "is a microcosmic look at the construction of criteria for gender."[44] Historicizing how trans women, especially, were assessed for femininity makes clear the borders of normative gender, and that's about everyone, not just trans people.

Stryker built on this in a 1994 performance-piece-turned-academic-article, "My Words to Victor Frankenstein above the Village of Chamounix." Like Stone, Stryker took aim against medico-scientific efforts to subsume trans experience back into normativity: American medical science of the mid- to late twentieth century had deigned to allow transition if and only if trans people hid their own experience and performed and identified as normal men and women, declawing in the process the threats to the gender and sexual order that movement away from one's assigned sex and gender could otherwise pose. Calling on Frankenstein's monster for inspiration, Stryker spoke back to her medical "creators" in the piece, cautioning that she had become much more than her doctors' attempts to produce normative womanhood through scientific expertise had anticipated. Indeed, when unmasked and embraced, and when rejecting incitements to normativity, transness can show that *all* sex and gender is created. "I offer you this warning: the Nature you bedevil me with is a lie," Stryker wrote, referring to the supposed "unnaturalness" of trans bodies. "Do not trust it to protect you from what I represent, for it is a fabrication that cloaks the groundlessness of the privilege you seek to maintain for yourself at my expense. You are as constructed as me.... Heed my words, and you may well discover the seams and sutures in yourself."[45] *You are as constructed as me. The seams and sutures in yourself.* This is the promise of trans history: to trouble the line between "natural" cisness and "unnatural" transness and to use trans experience to inform critical academic work. I want to reengage this scholarly tradition, which has, since the early 1990s, often been overshadowed by a drive for political legibility that favors a minoritizing trans history model.

Contrary to the model of trans history that defines transness through movement away from an initial gender assignment, gender categories aren't merely out there, waiting to be crossed or not. There's not a specific point at which someone becomes trans. In fact, people who have tried to come up with diagnostic tools for assessing whether or not people are trans generally fail to develop any metric that does anything other than restrict trans people's access to transition-related medical care.[46] In the 1960s, as the category "transsexual" was becoming increasingly institutionalized within American medicine and psychiatry, Harry Benjamin developed a classification system for differing degrees by which someone's gender matched or didn't match their sexed body.[47]

But decisions regarding who could access surgery and hormones often took years for Benjamin and allied doctors to make because even with this system, they didn't actually have a way to determine who was "really trans"—because it turns out it's not actually that simple.[48] As clinicians further developed what came to be known as the *Standards of Care* for assessing who qualified for surgery, the rigorous gatekeeping built into those standards based on ensuring people "prove" they were "really" trans so they wouldn't regret their transition only made accessing care extremely difficult.[49] Who, then, is "really" cis?

Shifting the gaze of trans history away from the recognizable trans or trans-adjacent subject will, I propose, help show that most people only remain in the category they were assigned at birth because the ways that those categories don't actually match up with the bodies or behaviors of those contained within them have been rendered invisible. Trans historians need to find the seams and sutures, to use Stryker's language, in cisness. Focusing on a minoritized trans subject forces us to make classificatory choices, but a trans history that assumes all sex and gender, *especially* the cis kinds, to be constructed and constantly managed rather than inherent allows us to ask different questions. How did we end up with a gender system that foists its category troubles off onto a handful of "exceptions," while ignoring the countless inconsistencies within its normative categories? How do the deviances of those who supposedly stay put in contrast to the motion of the trans subject get reclaimed as normal rather than casting doubt on the system they provide evidence against? What happens if we assume that the distinction between trans and not has very little to do with inherent classifiability of identities or bodies and instead has everything to do with the power to classify?

Let me be clear that this is not an either/or proposition—I don't want to replace histories of recognizable trans or trans-adjacent people, which have tremendous political utility in emphasizing that trans people are not some newfangled invention and in telling stories that have been overwhelmingly left out of most historical narratives. But we can both argue for the importance of writing histories of trans people *and* refuse a cis/trans binary model. As Eve Sedgwick put it, we need a "multi-pronged movement . . . whose minority-model and universalist model strategies proceed in parallel without any high premium placed on ideological rationalization between them."[50] Sedgwick discussed this coexistence of minoritizing and universalizing models of sexuality in terms of a fixed, distinct minority of homosexual individuals, on one hand, and a much more expansive model, on the other, in which bits and pieces of queerness attach themselves to a wider and more nebulous range of people of all kinds of identities. But the same dynamic applies to simultaneously being able to talk about both trans people and a broad systemic sorting of sex and gender that applies to everyone. A universalizing position that maintains a healthy degree of skepticism about the idea that most people are cis shows how one of the primary ways that gendered power operates is by sorting most people into normative categories even though they don't remotely fit that norm and then pretending that sorting hasn't happened.

If being a good historian of sexuality requires carefully bounding one's subject categories, let us extend the same analysis to all forms of sex and gender. As Afsaneh Najmabadi wrote in an article titled "Beyond the Americas: Are Gender and Sexuality Useful Categories of Historical Analysis?," we need to ask not only whether there were, for example, any lesbians in medieval Europe, but also whether there were any women. "That we ask the first question [about lesbians] with comfort," Najmabadi continues, "and presume the ease of the answer to the second (well, of course there were women, but defined differently) works on the presumption of naturalness of woman; that there have always been women."[51] The approach to trans history has been much the same: of course, there were trans people but defined differently. Of course, there were cis people but defined differently. What could it mean if there had not always been cis people? Scholars writing on the expansive range of sexed and gendered experiences in the past have already begun to chip away at the notion that splitting people into groups of trans and not-trans is an easy or useful thing to do. Just imagine if trans historians were as suspicious of the existence of cis people in the past as everyone else seems to be about the existence of trans people in the past. Trans history could be a method, an entire framework for thinking about gender. Instead of being featured in a single week on a syllabus or as the object of a still-marginalized subfield, transness would become a critical site of engagement in all histories of gender and sex. I want to reframe the conversation such that it's not only "there are more trans people in the past than we thought," but also "there are fewer cis people than we thought, and perhaps none at all."

The insistence on trans people always having been here is an ironic one, given that the whole point of transness is that your past doesn't have to dictate your future. Legitimacy doesn't come from having always been one thing. If transness is movement, as Stryker first articulated, then trans history needs a way to account for change and a way to privilege self-determination when articulating contemporary uses of trans history.[52] The politics of trans history cannot stop at claiming that we were always here even if we were called something else. The politics of trans history needs to include leaving the past behind and starting over, a subject that isn't legible, a challenge to the idea that any category is coherent. Stability isn't the thing that makes trans lives worth protecting, just as much as stability isn't the thing that makes cisness somehow better than transness. Samuel Alito wants trans people out of public life because he wants trans people out of public life, not because the word "transsexual" wasn't yet coined in 1789. Which is to say, sure, "trans" is a historically contingent, invented category—but so what? The relevant corollary point is: so is cis. Every sex and gender is a historically contingent, invented category. It's time to start treating them *all* that way.

NOTES

1 *Bostock v. Clayton County, Georgia* 590 U.S. ___ (2020) (Alito dissenting opinion), 34, https://www.supremecourt.gov/opinions/19pdf/17–1618_hfci.pdf. To illustrate the relative novelty of the concept of transness, Alito used as his examples Robert Stoller's 1964 article "A Contribution to the Study of Gender Identity," which was one of the first scholarly efforts to separate gender from sex and a key text in midcentury trans medicine, and the addition of transsexualism to the *DSM-III* at the comparatively late date of 1980.

2 *Bostock v. Clayton County*'s decision covered three cases all decided under the heading of the *Bostock* name. The case regarding trans protections specifically was *R. G. & G. R. Harris Funeral Homes Inc. v. Equal Employment Opportunity Commission*.

3 *Bostock*, 35.

4 *Bostock*, 34.

5 *Dobbs v. Jackson Women's Health Organization*, No. 19-1392, 597 U.S. ___ (2022).

6 See especially Meyerowitz, *How Sex Changed*; and Stryker, *Transgender History*. While recent work has emphasized the existence of pre- to mid-twentieth-century people who crossed gender lines to live as something other than the sex they were assigned at birth, authors like Emily Skidmore in *True Sex* and Jen Manion in *Female Husbands* are careful to distinguish between *trans* as a contemporary descriptor that historians can use to show a linkage between experience in past and present, and *transgender* or *transsexual* as actors' categories. Indeed, Stryker, Meyerowitz, Skidmore, Manion, Gill-Peterson, Boag, and Sears all include notes regarding trans terminology and its specific twentieth-century origins. See Skidmore, *True Sex*; Manion, *Female Husbands*; Gill-Peterson, *Histories of the Transgender Child*; Boag, *Re-dressing America's Frontier Past*; and Sears, *Arresting Dress*. On transness in antiquity, see Campanile, Carlà-Uhink, and Facella, *TransAntiquity*. These authors are certainly not the first to point to antiquity for evidence of the long history of gender-crossing: an appendix to Harry Benjamin's

Transsexual Phenomenon, one of the texts that popularized the category of the transsexual in the 1960s, cites several examples of "sex change" in Greek and Roman myth to illustrate transsexualism's deep historical origins.

7　O'Connell, "There Is No Legitimate 'Debate.'"

8　Feinberg, *Transgender Warriors*, 11.

9　Feinberg, *Transgender Warriors*, xii–xiii.

10　Agarwal, "What Is Trans History?"

11　Gill-Peterson, *Histories of the Transgender Child*.

12　I distinguish between trans history and historical work in trans studies to draw attention to somewhat divergent methods and especially divergent levels of institutional support. While the past few years have seen the publication of several new monographs on trans history, more trans history and trans studies courses, and a small handful of job ads for history and gender studies positions that mention trans history and/or studies as a preferred specialty for applicants, it should be noted that there is far greater enthusiasm for trans studies *outside* of history departments than within them. I suspect also that nonhistorians writing trans histories are perhaps less beholden to historical disciplinary norms of demonstrating expertise via evidentiary standards that implicitly reject expansive uses of contemporary sexual categories. See, for example, several of the most recent works on the history of transness published by scholars working outside of history departments: Snorton, *Black on Both Sides* (now English, previously Africana Studies); Gill-Peterson, *Histories of the Transgender Child* (English, when the book was published); Heaney, *The New Woman* (English); and Chess, Gordon, and Fisher, introduction to "Early Modern Trans Studies" (all English). This is not to say there is *no* trans history coming out of history departments in recent years. There certainly is: Emily Skidmore, Jen Manion, and Howard Chiang are all publishing on trans history from history departments. Gill-Peterson and I traded places, maintaining the numbers despite my ascension to the tenure track: she is now based in a history department, while I initially wrote this piece from a history department and have since landed in a stand-alone History and Sociology of Science department. Regardless of the details, it is striking to see how many of the most influential voices in trans history right now are working external to disciplinary history, and it is perhaps worth future study how this path of field formation has influenced what kinds of trans histories are being written. For a brief discussion of trans approaches being pushed out of disciplinary history, see Stryker, "Transgender History," 153–55.

13　Foucault, *History of Sexuality, Volume One*. On the invention of homosexuality, see also Halperin, "How to Do the History of Male Homosexuality"; Terry, *American Obsession*; D'Emilio, *Sexual Politics, Sexual Communities*; and Chauncey, *Gay New York*, among many others. While not all these scholars agree with Foucault wholesale—D'Emilio and Chauncey, for example, put far more stock in communities' understandings of themselves than in medical discourse as the driving force of the development of modern sexual categories—they all nonetheless take as axiomatic the idea that sexual categories at the end of the nineteenth century are fundamentally different from earlier understandings of sexual behavior and its relationship to identity.

14 See, for example, Chauncey, *Gay New York*, as well as Godbeer, *Sexual Revolution in Early America*; and Cleves, *Charity and Sylvia*, among others.

15 While outside the scope of this chapter, this does raise the question of whether homosexuality and transness can be seen as historically comparable categories. On one hand, it seems suspect that they should be conflated and thus require the same methodology. On the other hand, the *splitting* of transness and homosexuality into separate categories of "sexual orientation" and "gender identity" masks their shared origins and the ways that trans people and other queer people who violate gender norms have historically been thrown under the bus to make gender-normative queer people seem more respectable. See Stryker, *Transgender History*, 151–52, as well as Stryker, "Transgender History"; and Valentine, *Imagining Transgender.*

16 Stryker, *Transgender History*, 16, 18, 123.

17 This means that books like *Transgender Warriors* are not considered rigorous history.

18 So much so that there are Instagram memes and a subreddit mocking the propensity among historians to label as "friends" people who lived and shared a bed with, expressed sexual desire for, and are shown in photos kissing ostensibly same-gender people.

19 Authors writing about the twentieth century seem less concerned with bounding the category "trans." Jules Gill-Peterson, for example, says merely that "trans is invoked throughout in an expansive sense" and that she favors the precision of words like "transsexual" and "sexual inversion" when talking specifically about those constructions in historical context (*Histories of the Transgender Child*, 8–9). I suspect also that nonhistorians writing trans histories are perhaps less beholden to disciplinary norms of demonstrating expertise via precise historicization of categories.

20 Meyerowitz, *How Sex Changed*, 5; Boag, *Re-dressing America's Frontier Past*, 52; Sears, *Arresting Dress*, 9.

21 Skidmore, *True Sex*, 10.

22 Manion, *Female Husbands*, 10. Stryker's definition comes from *Transgender History*, 1.

23 For cross-dressing, see Boag, *Re-dressing America's Frontier Past*; and Sears, *Arresting Dress*. For female husbands, see Manion, *Female Husbands*. For passing or masquerading, see LaFleur, "Precipitous Sensations." For hormones and surgery, see Meyerowitz, *How Sex Changed*; and Gill-Peterson, *Histories of the Transgender Child*.

24 These are patterns in the literature, not explicitly stated criteria for classification as trans. In a representative example, in the opening of *True Sex*, Skidmore recounts the stories of Harry Gorman and Frank Dubois, two trans men who both

changed their names, married women, frequented saloons, and earned respect for their hard work as men (1–3). While it is the movement from one gender to another that constitutes transness, these other traits are illustrative evidence that movement has taken place.

25 See, for example, the story of Joseph Lobdell's encounters with state institutions in Manion, "The Queer History of Passing"; or the mysteriously named Mrs. Nash's outing when a friend changed the deceased Mrs. Nash's clothing for her burial in Boag, *Re-dressing America's Frontier Past*, 130–38. On the ways that a heterosexual/homosexual binary relies on stable sex and gender categories, see Stryker, "Transgender History."

26 Bowker and Star, *Sorting Things Out*, 5.

27 Stryker, *Transgender History*, 4. This is, however, Stryker writing for an audience needing Trans 101, and her other work, as in "My Words to Victor Frankenstein," takes aim on the idea that transness is the unnatural move away from natural cisness. Nonetheless, this turn of phrase captures the minoritizing tendency of contemporary mainstream understandings of transness.

28 Enke, "The Education of Little Cis," 60.

29 Enke, "The Education of Little Cis," 76. Enke critiques the entire category of "cisgender" for ascribing a fixity to gender categories that ultimately goes against queer and feminist efforts to trouble stability, even though it was intended to refuse the othering tendencies of the prefix *trans* (i.e., the construction of trans man versus just plain old normative man without any markers). While I am not willing to throw the proverbial cis baby out with the bathwater—there *is* certainly something to be said for the way that people who aren't identified as trans experience the world differently from those who are—I do think it's necessary to remember that a differential cis or trans experience comes from the existence of a state, medical, and social attachment to coherently sexed and gendered subjects, not a fundamental difference in types of person.

30 Chess, Gordon, and Fisher, introduction to "Early Modern Trans Studies," 6. Other recent examples of this expansive framing include many of the essays in LaFleur, Raskolnikov, and Kłosowska, *Trans Historical*. I suspect the pre- and early modernists with literary inclinations are on to something!

31 Chess, Gordon, and Fisher, introduction to "Early Modern Trans Studies," 11.

32 Heaney, *The New Woman*.

33 Larson, "'Indescribable Being,'" 582.

34 For reflections on the inadequacy of cisness to account for black (de)gendering in a contemporary frame, see Bey, *Cistem Failure*.

35 Schuller, *Biopolitics of Feeling*.

36 Snorton, *Black on Both Sides*, 7.

37 This line of thought follows a robust collection of scholarship, which is itself indebted to Black feminist thought. See, for but a few wide-ranging examples, Spillers, "Mama's Baby, Papa's Maybe"; Gilman, *Difference and Pathology*; Somerville, "Scientific Racism"; and Rosen, *Terror in the Heart of Freedom*.

38 See Bagemihl, *Biological Exuberance*; and Roughgarden, *Evolution's Rainbow*, for an extensive range of examples of sexual variety across species. On the relationship between humanity and binary sex, see Luciano and Chen, "Has the Queer Ever Been Human?," 182–207; and Hayward and Weinstein, "Tranimalities."

39 Amin, "Trans* Plasticity."

40 On plasticity, see Schuller and Gill-Peterson, "Biopolitics of Plasticity."

41 Velocci, "Binary Logic."

42 Stockton, *The Queer Child*, 1.

43 Gill-Peterson, *Histories of the Transgender Child*, especially chapter 3.

44 Stone, "The *Empire* Strikes Back," 227.

45 Stryker, "My Words to Victor Frankenstein," 240–41.

46 See, for example, shuster, "Uncertain Expertise."

47 Benjamin, *Transsexual Phenomenon*.

48 Indeed, in the early days of trans medicine, clinicians did not even bother that much with such ontological designations and instead focused on which patients they thought would be least likely to regret their transitions and sue. Velocci, "Standards of Care."

49 Harry Benjamin International Gender Dysphoria Association, "Standards of Care." For the contemporary standards from the same organization with an updated name, see World Professional Association for Transgender Health, *Standards of Care*.

50 Sedgwick, *Epistemology of the Closet*, 13.

51 Najmabadi, "Beyond the Americas," 18.

52 On transness as movement, see Stryker, *Transgender History*, 1.

BIBLIOGRAPHY

Agarwal, Kritika. "What Is Trans History?" *Perspectives on History*, May 1, 2018. https://www.historians.org/publications-and-directories/perspectives-on -history/may-2018/what-is-trans-history-from-activist-and-academic-roots-a -field-takes-shape.

Amin, Kadji. "Trans* Plasticity and the Ontology of Race and Species." *Social Text* 38, no. 2 (2020): 49–71.

Bagemihl, Bruce. *Biological Exuberance: Animal Homosexuality and Natural Diversity.* New York: St. Martin's Press, 1999.

Benjamin, Harry. *The Transsexual Phenomenon.* New York: Julian Press, 1966.

Bey, Marquis. *Cistem Failure.* Durham, NC: Duke University Press, 2022.

Boag, Peter. *Re-dressing America's Frontier Past.* Berkeley: University of California Press, 2011.

Bostock v. Clayton County, Georgia, 590 U.S. ___ (2020).

Bowker, Geoffrey C., and Susan Leigh Star. *Sorting Things Out: Classification and Its Consequences.* Cambridge, MA: MIT Press, 1999.

Campanile, Domitilla, Filippo Carlà-Uhink, and Margherita Facella, eds. *TransAntiquity: Cross-Dressing and Transgender Dynamics in the Ancient World*. New York: Routledge, 2017.

Chauncey, George. *Gay New York: Gender, Urban Culture, and the Making of the Gay Male World, 1890–1940*. New York: Basic Books, 1994.

Chess, Simone, Colby Gordon, and Will Fisher, eds. "Early Modern Trans Studies." Special issue, *Journal for Early Modern Cultural Studies* 19, no. 4 (Fall 2019).

Cleves, Rachel Hope. *Charity and Sylvia: A Same-Sex Marriage in Early America*. New York: Oxford University Press, 2014.

D'Emilio, John. *Sexual Politics, Sexual Communities: The Making of a Homosexual Minority in the United States, 1940–1970*. Chicago: University of Chicago Press, 1983.

Dobbs v. Jackson Women's Health Organization, No. 19-1392, 597 U.S. ___ (2022).

Enke, A. Finn. "The Education of Little Cis: Cisgender and the Discipline of Opposing Bodies." In *The Transgender Studies Reader 2*, edited by Susan Stryker and Aren Z. Aizura, 234–47. New York: Routledge, 2013.

Feinberg, Leslie. *Transgender Warriors: Making History from Joan of Arc to Dennis Rodman*. Boston: Beacon Press, 1996.

Foucault, Michel. *The History of Sexuality, Volume One: An Introduction*. Translated by Robert Hurley. New York: Vintage Books, 1990.

Gill-Peterson, Jules. *Histories of the Transgender Child*. Minneapolis: University of Minnesota Press, 2018.

Gilman, Sander L. *Difference and Pathology: Stereotypes of Sexuality, Race, and Madness*. Ithaca, NY: Cornell University Press, 1985.

Godbeer, Richard. *Sexual Revolution in Early America*. Baltimore, MD: Johns Hopkins University Press, 2002.

Halperin, David M. "How to Do the History of Male Homosexuality." *GLQ* 6, no. 1 (2000): 87–124.

Harry Benjamin International Gender Dysphoria Association. "Standards of Care: The Hormonal and Surgical Sex Reassignment of Gender Dysphoric Persons." Unpublished manuscript, February 1979, Series VIC, Box 25, Folder 19, Harry Benjamin Collection, Kinsey Institute.

Hayward, Eva, and Jami Weinstein, eds. "Tranimalities." Special issue, *TSQ* 2, no. 2 (May 2015).

Heaney, Emma. *The New Woman: Literary Modernism, Queer Theory, and the Feminine Allegory*. Evanston, IL: Northwestern University Press, 2017.

LaFleur, Greta. "Precipitous Sensations: Herman Mann's *The Female Review* (1797), Botanical Sexuality, and the Challenge of Queer Historiography." *Early American Literature* 48, no. 1 (2013): 93–123.

LaFleur, Greta, Masha Raskolnikov, and Anna Kłosowska, eds. *Trans Historical: Gender Plurality before the Modern*. Ithaca, NY: Cornell University Press, 2021.

Larson, Scott. "'Indescribable Being': Theological Performances of Genderlessness in the Society of the Publick Universal Friend, 1776–1819." *Early American Studies: An Interdisciplinary Journal* 12, no. 3 (2014): 576–600.

Luciano, Dana, and Mel Y. Chen, eds. "Queer Inhumanisms." Special issue, *GLQ* 21, no. 2–3 (2015).

Manion, Jen. *Female Husbands: A Trans History*. Cambridge: Cambridge University Press, 2020.

Manion, Jen. "The Queer History of Passing as a Man in Early Pennsylvania." *Pennsylvania Legacies* 16, no. 1 (Spring 2016): 6–11.

Meyerowitz, Joanne. *How Sex Changed: A History of Transsexuality in the United States*. Cambridge, MA: Harvard University Press, 2002.

Najmabadi, Afsaneh. "Beyond the Americas: Are Gender and Sexuality Useful Categories of Historical Analysis?" *Journal of Women's History* 18, no. 1 (Spring 2006): 11–21.

O'Connell, Kit. "There Is No Legitimate 'Debate' over Gender-Affirming Healthcare." *Texas Observer*, July 22, 2022.

Rosen, Hannah. *Terror in the Heart of Freedom: Citizenship, Sexual Violence, and the Meaning of Race in the Postemancipation South*. Chapel Hill: University of North Carolina Press, 2009.

Roughgarden, Joan. *Evolution's Rainbow: Diversity, Gender, and Sexuality in Nature and People*. Berkeley: University of California Press, 2004.

Schuller, Kyla. *The Biopolitics of Feeling: Race, Sex, and Science in the Nineteenth Century*. Durham, NC: Duke University Press, 2017.

Schuller, Kyla, and Jules Gill-Peterson, eds. "The Biopolitics of Plasticity." Special issue, *Social Text* 38, no. 2 (2020).

Sears, Clare. *Arresting Dress: Cross-Dressing, Law, and Fascination in Nineteenth-Century San Francisco*. Durham, NC: Duke University Press, 2015.

Sedgwick, Eve Kosofsky. *Epistemology of the Closet*. Berkeley: University of California Press, 1990.

shuster, stef. "Uncertain Expertise and the Limitations of Clinical Guidelines in Transgender Healthcare." *Journal of Health and Social Behavior* 57, no. 3 (2016): 319–32.

Skidmore, Emily. *True Sex: The Lives of Trans Men at the Turn of the 20th Century*. New York: New York University Press, 2017.

Snorton, C. Riley. *Black on Both Sides: A Racial History of Trans Identity*. Minneapolis: University of Minnesota Press, 2017.

Somerville, Siobhan. "Scientific Racism and the Emergence of the Homosexual Body." *Journal of the History of Sexuality* 5, no. 2 (October 1994): 243–66.

Spillers, Hortense J. "Mama's Baby, Papa's Maybe: An American Grammar Book." *Diacritics* 17, no. 2 (Summer 1987): 64–81.

Stockton, Kathryn Bond. *The Queer Child, or Growing Sideways in the Twentieth Century*. Durham, NC: Duke University Press, 2009.

Stoller, Robert. "A Contribution to the Study of Gender Identity." *International Journal of Psychoanalysis* 45 (1964): 220–26.

Stone, Sandy. "The *Empire* Strikes Back: A Posttransexual Manifesto." In *The Transgender Studies Reader*, edited by Susan Stryker and Stephen Whittle, 221–35. New York: Routledge, 2006.

Stryker, Susan. "My Words to Victor Frankenstein above the Village of Chamounix: Performing Transgender Rage." *GLQ* 1, no. 3 (1994): 237–54.

Stryker, Susan. *Transgender History.* Berkeley, CA: Seal Press, 2008.

Stryker, Susan. "Transgender History, Homonormativity, and Disciplinarity." *Radical History Review* 100 (Winter 2008): 145–57.

Terry, Jennifer. *An American Obsession: Science, Medicine, and Homosexuality in Modern Society.* Chicago: University of Chicago Press, 2002.

Valentine, David. *Imagining Transgender: An Ethnography of a Category.* Durham, NC: Duke University Press, 2007.

Velocci, Beans. "Binary Logic: Race, Expertise, and the Persistence of Uncertainty in American Sex Research." PhD diss., Yale University, 2021.

Velocci, Beans. "Standards of Care: Uncertainty and Risk in Harry Benjamin's Transsexual Classifications." *TSQ* 8, no. 4 (2021): 462–80.

World Professional Association for Transgender Health. *Standards of Care for the Health of Transgender and Gender Diverse People.* 8th version. 2022. https://www.wpath.org/publications/soc.

PART III
TRANS THEORY

TWO SENSES OF GENDER ABOLITION

5

Gender as Accumulation Strategy

In one of her Revolutionary Letters, Diane Di Prima instructs: "Remember you can have what you ask for, ask for / everything."[1] Di Prima ushers possibility into the space cleared and composed by the demand. Her drastic line break puts "everything" in a space of its own, right where it's possible to grasp.

I want to open here, on the terrain of creative opposition, where we discover in our needs and desires something more than equal to the creative destruction of the capitalist lifeworld. Call it the potential of a collective, an enthusiastic mutuality. The strength of this mutual derives precisely from its proximity to addressing our needs as we understand them, in a full and anti-ascetic conceptualization of their possible extent. Where the crises of the present seem to foreshorten the future, and to force us to settle for something, so to speak, "less than a nightmare," our first strength is our ability to conceive of demands equal to our ambition. Their common object must be nothing other than a life worth living for everyone.

What contribution does the struggle for trans liberation make to this communist horizon? To pose this question immediately raises the vexed relationship between class struggle and so-called identity politics. In this chapter it'll be my aim to understand the totalizing, rather than particularizing, force of political movement from one or another standpoint of social identity. Hungarian philosopher Georg Lukács introduced *standpoint* as a category in order to think the differential perspectives onto capitalist totality that class positions enable. In a Lukácsian attempt to account for the capitalist production of sexual identity, Kevin Floyd in *The Reification of Desire* argues that this production of identity—a reification in the sense of the freezing and solidification of a stable position out of a historical process—enables a particular, historically situated, and critical knowledge of capitalist totality: "To think sexuality in reification's terms is to begin to see the way in which reification refers to a social dynamic that opens critical vantages on the totality of capital as much as it closes them down."[2] Here I'll pursue an analogous argument from a specifically transsexual perspective. I say transsexual, versus trans or transgender, in order to foreground the sphere of embodiment that transsexuality bears on. My object here overall is the body—not the body as a dead empirical fact, as something given or unchanging, but the body as a site of agency, constraint, and social signification—subject to dispossession, wrung for its resources, and the object of immense and intensive social struggle.

In the chapter that follows, I claim first that, for capital, gender as an ideological regime functions as an accumulation strategy, an instrument by which capital manages and intensifies the process of the accumulation of value.[3] Second, I argue that the project of trans liberation looks to the aesthetic and sensuous qualities of gender as a dimension of bodily autonomy, an intensive dimension of disalienation, and that this in turn discloses its totalizing relationship to class struggle. The object of gender abolition must therefore be not gender itself in the sense of the collective and social signification of sexual difference but rather the instrumentalization of this difference in the relations that produce and reproduce capital. The social struggle over the body and its capacities is a fight that transsexual people have a particular, but by no means exclusive, stake in. In foregrounding the role of disalienation in the intensive struggle over the body and its relationship to social signification, the project of trans liberation clarifies the stakes, terms, and directions of "gender abolition": the abolition of the capital relation and its use of gender as an accumulation strategy, that is, rather than gender itself.

These formulations sketch the concerns of my approach. On the one hand, this chapter attends to the force of abjection that capital develops, reproduces, and instrumentalizes in the process of the accumulation of value; on the other, I attend to a series of high-stakes desires and pleasures, pertaining to and dependent on forms of embodiment, and I argue that these have a central role in present forms of class struggle. I mean abjection in the sense proposed by Rosemary Hennessy: "In devaluing some bodies abjection helps to produce subjects who are worth less—that is, subjects who forfeit more of themselves in the labor relations that produce capital."[4] On the other hand, my focus on pleasure will probably raise some eyebrows: according to a certain strain of "Left puritanism," pleasure appears already as a suspect dimension of experience, and not without reason.[5] The main form of appearance of pleasure in a consumer society dominated by the tyranny of the commodity-form is the promise of satisfaction that capital parasitizes in order to circulate goods and realize profit. In that regard, the relationship of pleasure to class struggle is at best obscure.

Meanwhile, relating pleasure to the projects of gender liberation risks either a willful false consciousness or shilling for the kind of aesthetic experience available only to the materially secure. To speak of gender at all invokes at minimum a system of social differentiation whose form of appearance is primarily abjection, in the sense described above, unevenly racialized and variously distributed, and whose function for capital is the enabling and maintenance of an unequal division of labor. When the Endnotes collective, for instance, names gender as a "misfortune" and a "powerful constraint," they correctly identify in this form of differentiation both its deployment by capital and its imprint as a species of immiseration.[6] The uneven subjection of different gender configurations to forms of un- or low-waged labor; the "double shift" of waged labor and reproductive labor; underemployment or unemployability; vulnerability to sexual violence and femicide; exclusion from the protections of labor laws; surveillance by the death-making institutions of the state from border patrols to municipal police to the military; external control over reproductive capacities, whether in the form of refused abortion access or forced sterilization; and/or modulations of official or unofficial forms of racial apartheid—these modes of exploitation and social deprivation all name the complex and simultaneous strategies by which capital pursues a particular and intensive form of what David Harvey has called "accumulation by dispossession."[7]

On the other hand, the desire for a disalienated lifeworld—as envisioned in the old socialist slogan "bread and roses"—is, if nothing else, the demand for everyone to enjoy the kinds of aesthetic contingency that capital cordons off for the wealthy. As a result any genuine revolutionary politics will orient itself toward a radically pleasurable future. As Fredric Jameson argues, this orientation necessarily recenters the body and its mediations: "Pleasure is finally the consent of life in the body, the reconciliation—momentary as it may be—with the necessity of physical existence in a physical world."[8] The minimal demand of trans people, then, to exercise autonomy to the fullest possible extent over our own relationships to the signification of sexual difference foregrounds pleasure as a critical dimension of social movement.[9] The point of this politics is to attend to the body as a site of struggle over the intensive disalienation of mental and manual labor. This thesis, meanwhile, discloses a certain determinate ambit to an abolitionist politics: the abolition of gendered abjection, not—at least, not in the abstract—gendered *signification*. The orientation of a trans politics toward autonomy over the body and its social significations and its capacities designate the proper object of abolition: the capital relation and its murderous instrumentalization of difference in the unequal division of labor, resources, and access to life.

GENDER AS ACCUMULATION STRATEGY

At a moment marked by the vigorous alignment between repressive state apparatuses and crypto-right-wing feminists, many of whom focus their efforts on the elimination of sex workers and trans people, it has become especially critical to identify the object of a liberatory gender politics.[10] This means making some claims about gender as a dimension of both social and subjective experience. Consider the following theses:

(1) Gender belongs to the sphere of ideology—not in the pejorative sense of false consciousness but in the descriptive sense of the conceptual representation of social relations.

(2) As such, gender names the subjective imprint of the symbolization of sexual difference—a formulation that provisionally captures both a subjective valence of desire and identification together with the objective determinations of the structural, systemic, and historical formations that enable these desires and identifications in the first place.

(3) The secondary signifiers of gender, together with other social codes, inflect social relations at every turn. In its capacity as an axis of difference, then, gender serves as one of the instruments by which capital unevenly compels and exploits labor.

The partial list I've advanced here responds to the critical mandate of Marxist feminism to think simultaneously the social dimensions of oppression and exploitation—of group-differentiated social degradations and uneven access to means of life on the one hand and of the differential production of surplus value through the labor process on the other. It takes a cue from queer theory, to the degree that the theses above displace any would-be ontological ground of the operations of gender in favor of an account of its social origins. But this purely social phenomenon nonetheless doesn't admit any voluntarist attempt to simply "undo" its determinative force. By way of analogy, the value-form too is only a "product of the human brain" but cannot simply be undone by force of will.[11] The challenge is then to theorize the gendered contours of immiseration and violence without the clumsy wish fulfillment of opting out of the totalizing and abstract force of ideology—or indeed supplanting the project of a materialist transformation of the social with ideology-critique.

To name the techniques by which gender contours labor and vice versa, to confront gender as a mediating term of class and property relations—this account sounds a basically consonant note with the analytic of social reproduction theory (SRT). This theory works outward from Lise Vogel's critical insight that the social oppression of women derives primarily from the outsized burden—maintained through the historically contingent institution of the family—of reproducing labor-*power*, which Marx defines as the sum of the manual and intellectual capacities of human beings.[12] Tithi Bhattacharya writes, "Simply put, while labor puts the system of capitalist production in motion, SRT points out that labor power itself is the *sole* commodity—'the unique commodity,' as Marx calls it—that is produced outside of the circuit of commodity production."[13] The theory steps forward as an attempt to wrestle with this unique commodity—to comprehend "the processes necessary for the reproduction of the workforce, both biologically and as compliant wage workers."[14] This initiates a step into what Jordy Rosenberg has named capital's "hiddener abode."[15] Marx famously describes the production of surplus value in the labor process as the "hidden abode" of capital; Rosenberg varies this description to look toward the sites and institutions—from households to schools to prisons—that reproduce an exploitable labor force.[16]

Social reproduction theory updates an insight of 1970s autonomist feminism: the feminized category of reproductive labor, occulted in its capacity *as* labor, aids capitalist accumulation by reproducing the worker. In her classic pamphlet on the wages for housework movement, Silvia Federici argued that "just to want wages for housework means to refuse that work as the expression of our nature, and therefore to refuse precisely the female role that capital has invented for us."[17] Federici's "us," of course, splits on the racial unevenness of the category of "women": the drive of racial capitalism to identify group difference according to which it can normalize the unequal division of labor and resources has in various situations split the category of women according to widely varying relationships to labor, property, and possession. Capital invents and differentiates multiple and simultaneous "roles" for the objects of gendered abjection. Similarly, the sphere of reproductive labor is scarcely entirely or even mostly unwaged: the work of social reproduction—from nannying to surrogacy to sanitation to education—straddles the line between waged and unwaged work. Such work is therefore not delimited by the boundaries of the home and the family—more or less the force of Angela Davis's critique that "Black women . . . have . . . carried the double burden of wage labor and housework."[18] But the kernel of Federici's claim—that capital has "invented roles" for the social categories it abjects, and that it uses these as a lever of exploitation—enables a fourth thesis in addition to the three advanced above:

(4) *Gender for capital assumes the form of an accumulation strategy*, an ideological scaffolding that sustains an unequal division of labor, contours practices of dispossession and predation, and conditions particular forms of exploitation, including and especially in the form of un- and low-waged reproductive labor.

My formulation here riffs on Neil Smith's claim that nature, the sphere that capitalist society secretes as ideologically other than itself, functions for capital as an accumulation strategy.[19] Smith's thesis itself derives from Donna Haraway's provocation that the *body* functions as an accumulation strategy in light of the advent of biocapital.[20] The point in pushing this polemical formulation is then less to proliferate an ultimately empirical list of the diverse tactics of the production of value—tactics that are, anyways, widely recognized and elsewhere recorded—than to highlight a commonality among these various strategies: the exploitative repurposing of the *residual*, of preexisting ideological structures and social practices, which capitalism tightly aggregates to itself as co-extensors of its operations. This strategy of repurposing the residual generates a theoretical challenge for Marxists: to think capital's instrumentalization of gender without reducing the latter to the former as epiphenomenon or, indeed, a handmaiden.

One consequence of this thesis is that the forms of gendered exploitation and dispossession *cannot* be captured by reference solely—liberally—to the distinction between women and men or, for that matter, cis and trans identity.

Understanding gender as an accumulation strategy therefore aligns with an approach sensitive to the strategies of the dispossession and reinscription of gender through colonialism. María Lugones, in the mode of a postcolonial analysis, claims that the category of gender itself is a colonial imposition by the dominant European states of the sixteenth through twentieth centuries over the territories and peoples they suppressed, dispossessed, enslaved, and compelled into labor; Lugones observes the introduction of "gender differentials . . . where there were none" as a violent reordering of social and political life in the places of European expansion and extraction.[21] If, following Lugones, we historicize contemporary and widespread gender categories to the period of European military and economic dominance over much of the globe, then the historical role of gender as an accumulation strategy in the spaces of peripheral capital comes more sharply into view. Or, as Jordy Rosenberg puts it, "Gender does not mean the same thing in every context. Some genderings we fight for, stake our lives on. Some 'gender' is a missile sent by the metropole."[22]

In that capacity, the simultaneous imposition and racialization of European gender norms has historically enabled primitive accumulation, the violent compulsion of colonized peoples into labor, waged or not. In that regard, Hortense Spillers's thesis of the "ungendering" of the transatlantic slave trade proceeds in a contrary but complementary mode to Lugones's thesis of the colonial "introduction" of gender. Spillers argues that the commodification of African people through the chattel slavery system assumed the form of an "ungendering" whereby "one is neither female, nor male, as both subjects are taken into 'account' as *quantities*"—that is to say, quantities of a commodity.[23] Here, a gendering episteme takes the form of dispossession through commodifying and attempting to realize value from human life—not through the imposition of gender but through its forced withdrawal. The shared term that relates the violent removal of gendered categories for some people to the violent introduction of gendered categories for others is the relentless creative destruction of the capital relation, and its relentless use of gender as a lever of accumulation even in contradictory forms.

IDEOLOGY AND ITS ANTONYMS

Consider the transphobic canard—repeated by such politically distinct figures as anti-trans feminists, right-wing shills for the ruling class, and queer theory darlings—that transsexuals shore up the oppressive operations of gender via the biomedical interventions into the body that travel under the category of "transition."[24] A secret moralism lurks in these various attacks, which target transsexual desires—to have a certain embodied relationship to the signification of sexual difference, and to assert autonomy over that relationship—as misguided, regressive, or disgusting. The left-wing version of this moralism might go something like this: after the operations of gender in reproducing an immiserated world are disclosed, what could gender transition accomplish if not an entrenchment of the processes of accumulation that sustain capitalist gender relations in the first place? According to the arch bad faith of this accusation, transsexual desires assume the cast of false consciousness in the extreme, a particular susceptibility to the ideological allure of a commodified gender persona in apparently willful ignorance of the violence and precarity that gender asymmetrically distributes—as if transsexuals weren't variously and violently subject to these effects. This wildly misplaced moralism scapegoats transsexuals to disguise its own failure to come to terms with the roots of gendered oppression in the present, grounded in the capitalist production of value.

Meanwhile, the other side of this bad-faith accusation appears in the contrary assertion that transition actually destabilizes or denaturalizes or undoes this ideological force, just like that. That's more or less the thesis of Paul B. Preciado's *Testo Junkie*. Preciado writes, "I'm not taking testosterone to change myself into a man or as a physical strategy of transsexualism; I take it to foil what society wanted to make of me"—words penned, somewhat infamously, before the author's transition.[25] Preciado's spin on the voluntarist thesis simply bears out in its most naked form a tendency of queer theory to treat gender as something whose social dictates are as possible to denature as eggs in a pan. Preciado transvalues a moralistic code of values until transition appears as politically good rather than politically bad—but the common term this thesis shares with the moralism it rejects is its commitment to the malleability of ideology, and the determination of ideology over the subject.

In effect, the debate splits into two contraries: either transition sustains gendered abjection, and per Janice Raymond should be "mandated out of existence,"[26] or transition subverts gendered abjection and should be pursued as an attack on normative modes of possible subjectivity. Not coincidentally, this antagonism recalls the contrary positions of feminisms, sex-negative or -positive: either women's sexual desires are a kind of ideological coercion from without and deserve suspicion, or feminized sexual pleasure is an ideologically foreclosed aspect of human life and deserves embracing. Both contradictions are, effectively, homologues of each other, historically situated in second-wave feminist debates on trans identity, pornography, and sex work from the 1970s and 1980s. Both ignore the enabling of bodily autonomy as a critical dimension of social life and political struggle, opting instead to prescribe the correct positions to take toward ideological dictates. Both are moralisms, and both are equally useless.

Let's start instead from an antimoralistic premise: transition pertains to something entirely other than holding a politically virtuous or vicious position within or toward the signification of sexual difference. In a widely read intervention for *n+1*, Andrea Long Chu asserts that "transition expresses not the truth of an identity but the force of a desire."[27] Articulating a theory of subject formation, Chu offers a basically psychoanalytic thesis, if not explicitly in psychoanalytic terms. But at a certain Lacanian level of abstraction, the opposition between "the truth of an identity and the force of a desire" turns into identical formulations, united in the priority of desire over the subject: desires mediate between a psychic ideal and the unrepresentable Real of sexual and embodied experience, the tether that allows the development of subject formation at all. Consider, for instance, Oren Gozlan's antipathologizing attempt to align gender with "fantasy and imagination": "The body in psychoanalysis is a sexual one and therefore a relational body that interacts with and is affected by other bodies, that takes other bodies as its own and that finds its own corporal experience through its relation to others. . . . Considered in this way, gender can function as a transitional object or as fetish. Like the fetish, gender cannot be given up; however, like a transitional object, it provides an intermediate area of experience between discovery and creation, between subjective and shared experience."[28] Gender, in other words, is "a fantasy object that mediates between the drives and social reality, . . . a construction that links, through fantasy, subject and object."[29]

So transsexuals aren't unique in bearing a desiring relationship toward their own embodied relationship to gender and sexuality—just the opposite. Gozlan writes, "Every gender disposition carries a kernel of helplessness, anxiety and guilt, and therefore is vulnerable to dissociation, splitting and idealization."[30] Nontranssexuals too are hailed into subjectivity by the ideological operations of gender; *non*-transition expresses the force of a desire also. The pathologization of specifically transsexual desires marks out, and resexualizes, only these configurations of gender according to the normative force of the history of the clinic.[31] Therefore, the Althusserian chestnut that "being in ideology only applies to others, never to oneself."[32]

In short: gender on the scale of the subject names a desire that mediates between drives and the real—between idea and actuality. The point isn't a defense of libertinage, of an antisocial indulgence in the ethically suspect or politically quietistic. Transsexual desires aren't either good or bad: they're *real*. Ideology has no antonym, and the ultimately aesthetic decisions that mark conformity to or departure from the dictates of gender norms are, in every possible sense, immaterial. The critical question is then not whether transsexual desires are appropriately counter-ideological but *what is to be done given that they have the desires they do*. What demands do these place on the structure of the world as it stands? And how do they relate to and oppose the instrumentalization of gender in the service of accumulation? When a trans politics steps outside the tug-of-war over the political virtue of our desires into the material world of the forces that precaritize our lives and those of others, what resources can be found for both liberation and solidarity?

TRANSSEXUALS IN THE HIDDENER ABODE

Any provisional answer to these questions needs to emerge out of an encounter with trans life as it's actually, materially lived. How does the asymmetrical abjection of transsexuals square with capital's deployment of gender as an accumulation strategy? Hennessy draws our attention to the role of abjection in deepening the exploitation of the labor process, but the force of her insight doesn't stop there. Hennessy argues for understanding social identity as a "second skin"; the secondary signifiers of that identity inflect social relations according to the intangible and frequently unconscious maneuvers of ideology writ large.[33] Abjection in this sense seeps beyond the wage-labor relationship (manifest, say, in lower pay, longer work, poorer conditions, and so on) to the precarity of not being able to get or hold on to a job in the first place or secure access to other means of subsistence—housing, healthcare, education.[34]

Abjection contours not just what you do for a wage, then, but un- and underemployment, and the social precarity that follows. Trish Salah emphasizes the "crisis of classification wherein a suspicion as to the ontological (sexed) status of the trans subject may preclude the assignment of value; certainly, non-passing trans people's difficulty in accessing paid employment within the legal economy is directly tied to transphobic repudiation of not only trans people's sex of identification, but of their value as people within the sex of assignment."[35] Salah's attention to the relationship between wage labor and passing divulges the critical insight that vulnerability to phobic abjection tracks the disclosure, discovery, and/or legibility of trans status—the point in a social encounter when the "second skin" of identity becomes perceptible.

This impact of phobic abjection extends beyond the wage relationship into the reproductive sphere, variously constraining the ability of transsexuals to reproduce ourselves. Considering the critical role of the family in regulating social reproduction—a role that, following Salar Mohandesi and Emma Teitelman, has only expanded in the "crisis of social reproduction" in the post-1980s Global North—the uneven alienation of trans people from the family unit further exacerbates our social precarity.[36] As Kate Doyle Griffiths writes, "In the interstices of increased rights, the elaboration of family networks and a right-wing backlash, queers serve as a category of 'last hired, first fired' with respect to the family . . . an optional category of reserve reproductive labor for a working class increasingly pressed in our efforts to self-reproduce."[37] Doyle Griffiths's remarks pertain with particular force to transsexuals, who by and large cannot avoid disclosing trans status to family members.

Call this an inconsistent downward mobility, highly racialized in practical terms.[38] It's this downward mobility that contours the historical alignment between transsexuals and the underground economy, sex work above all. This isn't to repeat the stigmatizing myth that sex work is, as Nihils Rev and Fiona Mae Geist dispute, a "labour of last resort."[39] Rather, barriers to legal employment together with the ideological coding of legibly transsexual bodies as sexual commodities—if anything, the private and illicit face of the public abjection of trans embodiments—enable the trans sex industry, a field characterized by unequal criminalization and vulnerability to harm that nonetheless "offer[s] greater autonomy and financial stability compared to more traditional workplaces, with few barriers to entry."[40] Monica Forrester, Jamie-Lee Hamilton, Mirha-Soleil Ross, and Viviane Namaste argue that "a history of transsexuality is a history of prostitution," contending that the social enclaves that have historically enabled trans communities are predicated on the political struggles of trans sex workers, a category largely made up of women of color.[41]

The thesis that a history of transsexuality is a history of sex work helps point toward two critical insights: first, in transsexuals capital discovers a reserve category of disposable reproductive labor in the form of sex work. Hennessy registers the effect of "feminization" on the sale and purchase of labor-power: "All subjects who transgress this prescribed distribution of gendered bodies are feminized, whether they are men or women. . . . To be feminized is to bear on your embodied second skin the mark of (de)valuation, which is indeed quite valuable to capital."[42] Sex work is then the primary form that feminized labor has historically taken for transsexuals—albeit differently, depending on race, geographic location, trans masculine or trans feminine status, and other sociological factors. But second, and from the standpoint of labor, trans sex work has been the grounding condition for the emergence of politically mobilized and culturally active trans communities, capable of determining what we need and identifying pressure points of solidarity with other social and political movements.

To ground a liberatory trans politics in its historical configuration along-side and emergent from sex work skirts both (1) the epistemology of the clinic and its attention to the appropriateness or authenticity of transsexual desires and (2) an emerging trans-inflected homonationalism focusing narrowly on rights and representation centered on easing the lives of white bourgeois subjects of the imperial core. C. Riley Snorton and Jin Haritaworn argue that this trans-inflected homonationalism "produces a transnormative subject, whose universalized trajectory of coming out/transition, visibility, recognition, protection and self-actualization largely remains uninterrogated in its complicities and converges with biomedical, neoliberal, racist and imperialist projects."[43] This particular liberal project of demanding rights and recognitions for trans people as possible bearers of equal property rights largely aligns in focus, method, and class composition with the bourgeois feminisms that sometimes and increasingly target trans individuals as the object of feminist critique; although sometimes antagonistic toward each other, these movements equally fail to address the forms of abjection, exploitation, and dispossession that racial capitalism maintains and reproduces through the logic of gender. The point for those of us who intend, by contrast, to change everything is to frame our politics from the side of those with only their labor-power to sell—to determine, from the standpoint of labor, the coordinates where the needs and demands of a trans politics inflect and are inflected by class struggle.

HEDONISMS, UTOPIAN AND SCIENTIFIC

What are these demands? Let's start with a provisional list: decriminalization of sex work, to start, together with the abolition of prisons and borders, free and comprehensive healthcare, universal housing, the routinized affirmation of the autonomy and development of children and adolescents, and the socialization of reproductive care, including care for the elderly.[44]

I want to urge that transsexual demands to exercise autonomy, however enabled by social or medical interventions, over configurations of embodiment and sexuality pertain to a category of high-stakes desires and pleasures, whose utopian core is the demand for the body to be a site of affirmation over and against routine abjection. Designating pleasure as a site of political struggle recognizes, with Jameson, the inevitability of sensuous life in a material world. Being hungry, or tired, in chronic pain or constant grief, routinely fearful or simply bored—these textures of everyday life matter politically, if only because they name the miseries that one class inflicts on another in order to access nourishment, rest, health, safety, company, or aesthetically engaging experience. Opting for an ascetic stance toward these dimensions of experience isn't good enough; why *shouldn't* the object of our revolutionary dreaming include a world where everyone can sustain a full, disalienated life—fishing in the afternoon, criticizing after dinner?[45] But a transsexual hedonism designates more than sensuousness. "Transsexuality frightens / us," the poet Stephen Ira writes. "It confesses how much beauty matters / to life."[46] A transsexual hedonism recognizes that the signification of sexual difference mediates every relationship between people in the social world, including one's relation to oneself; it insists on embodiment as both the mediator of that social world and the enabling of agency toward and autonomy over desiring interventions into that process of mediation. Finally, against the prurient interest in spectacles of trans suffering that the culture industry has ruthlessly capitalized on for a buck since the so-called tipping point, such a politically interested hedonism suggests in the opposite direction that the subjects of trans liberation are *not* passive victims of our own supposed pathologies but rather political agents who more or less know exactly what we need and have every intention of securing our access to it, in solidarity with each other and in broader left movement.[47]

As discussed, my emphasis on the political valence of pleasure will probably upset a left conscience that sees in sexual difference *only* the differential strategies for the extraction of surplus value. But the ground of this scandal arises in part through the residue of previously dominant, and surprisingly hardy, transphobias: the feminisms that have emphasized the pornographic and supposedly revolting image of transsexuals taking pleasure in our bodies, or the objectifications of Ray Blanchard's debunked category of the autogynephilic trans woman who derives sexual satisfaction only from her own feminization.

In their own way, these phantasms combine with the left puritanism Jameson described in 1983 to produce a deep-seated suspicion of pleasure—as, say, the mental silt of a late-capitalistic civic imperative to consume and enjoy that consumption. Jameson's reply to the double-bind of an insensate asceticism on the one hand and a nonpolitics of bourgeois leisure on the other is to insist on the allegorical function of pleasure, its capacity to suggest the dimensions of a transformed social world: "The right to a specific pleasure, to a specific enjoyment of the potentialities of the material body—if it is not to remain only that, if it is to become genuinely political . . . —must always in one way or another also be able to stand as a figure for the transformation of social relations as a whole."[48]

Taken as an imperative over consumption, Jameson's claim sets the bar a little high. But I think the force of reframing pleasure in terms of its allegorical function—what Jameson names as the ability of pleasure to figure the total and emancipatory transformation of social relations—consists instead in restoring pleasure to the revolutionary project that Kristin Ross more recently has called "communal luxury." For Ross, the slogan of communal luxury opposes a bourgeois luxury of consumer goods in imagining a world "where everyone would have his or her share of the best."[49] In Jameson's approach, pleasure has at least the potential to body forth the force of this slogan in the image of a world thought otherwise. The ideal of communal luxury recenters the aesthetic and pleasurable dimensions of social and political life and sensory experience in the ongoing projects of revolutionary movement.

From this perspective, the aesthetic gains a valence altogether different from the tug-of-war over ideological versus counterideological configurations of the body and its sensations. For transsexuals this aesthetic project is basically an embodied one—which is to say it's social, but irreducibly mediated by the body. The minimal demand to assert autonomy over one's own sexed disposition bears down on the capacity of the body to be a source of continuous pleasure over and against routine alienation. Needless to say, the liberatory horizon of a pleasurable, disalienated life matters to cis and trans people both. A specifically transsexual standpoint then discloses for a liberatory gender politics the critical insight that the body, *including its capacities within the signification of sexual difference*, is an indispensable site of struggle over the creation of a disalienated lifeworld available to all. Where Bhattacharya urges that the "demand by [working-class] communities to extend their sphere of pleasure is a vital class demand," the foregrounding of the body as a mediation between desire and the social appears as the intensive side of this extensive demand.[50]

The desire of any revolutionary left politics must be for a world where these politics are no longer necessary—where all the tools at our disposal for understanding capital and colonial relations no longer have an object to understand. In a word, the theoretical end of any Marxism is its own *Aufhebung*, its abolition and overcoming. So when I suggest that the aesthetic edge of trans liberation *both* discloses certain coordinates for political struggle in the present—full access to trans-related medical care for people of all ages, for instance—*and* orients itself toward a radically pleasurable future, I also mean that the horizon of such a hedonism would necessarily belong to a world where the aesthetic would not be distinguishable from life as such. That accords with the horizon identified by the Endnotes collective, "a life in which all separate spheres of activity have been abolished."[51]

In a sense my project here has been to identify the operations of gender at two different scales—the subjective scale of interpersonal relations and the scale of political economy—and to urge that one scale offers a way to think about the determinations of the other as well as the dimensions of liberatory struggles in both. To that degree, this project accords with gender abolition at the vanishing point of a world where, as the Xenofeminist manifesto states, "traits currently assembled under the rubric of gender no longer furnish a grid for the operations of power."[52] At the furthest utopian point of the world we're fighting over, we can imagine that the signification of sexual difference would matter only on the level of contingency. If we understand abolition in the sense of an *Aufhebung*, not an evacuation, we begin to grasp the project of trans liberation in the Lukácsian sense of a "movement of mediations proceeding from the present to the future."[53]

I want here, however, to suggest a departure from the understanding of abolition as theorized in the Endnotes' "Logic of Gender" essay, and to do so on the basis of the arguments I've furnished here. I've argued that on the scale of subjective relations, gender names the imprint of the symbolization of sexual difference, a desire that mediates between the drives and actuality, and therefore discloses an aesthetic orientation toward the world that on the scale of political struggle helps to determine *some* of the coordinates for liberation. If we are attentive to the collective liberation of people to lead livable, disalienated lives, then equally we need to attend to the ability of people to act on their desires for living in certain embodied ways, in relation to themselves and each other. The understanding of these desires simply as so many distractions or forms of false consciousness ignores ultimately desire itself as a material force in the world, with the capacity to shape people, movements, practices, and social relations.

Endnotes offers a somewhat different, if not entirely competing, formulation: that gender just names "a separation between [social] spheres" as a mediation of the production of value. They distinguish the sphere of directly and indirectly market-mediated activities, DMM and IMM for short. Gender then names the "anchoring of a certain group of individuals in a specific sphere of social activities. The result of this anchoring process is at the same time the continuous reproduction of two separate genders."[54] In this capacity, gender turns out to be, in strict terms, a Marxian real abstraction on analogy to the value-form, in which the sex of the material body occupies the position of a use-value. The analogy generates an imperative of abolition, "just as exchange-value and use-value will both have to be abolished in the process of communisation."[55] Trading on Judith Butler's idiom, Endnotes advances an essentially Hegelian claim that the denaturalization of gender enables a form of consciousness about its operations: "The process of de-naturalization creates the possibility of gender appearing as an *external constraint*. This is not to say that the constraint of gender is less powerful than before, but that it can now be seen as a constraint, that is, as something outside oneself that it is possible to abolish."[56]

In a comradely vein, and sensitive to the clear-eyed realism about the miseries of the present that Endnotes sustains, I object that to synonymize gender with the production of value obviates the subject, or rather the entire subjective scale. Endnotes enables us to grasp capital's instrumentalization of gender as an accumulation strategy but makes the critical error I urged against above: comprehending gender as merely epiphenomenal of and accessory to capitalist political economy. This account raises a number of problems, both analytic and political. Analytically, it fails to account for the subjective moment either as an irreducible dimension of experience or as the site of politically inflected desires. It also operates on a presentist conception of gender, which poses a problem for both an accounting of history and the imagination of a future politics: to identify gender just as a function of the value-form offers us few resources for thinking about gender anterior to and outside of the global domination of the capital and colonial relations. Further, if gender is only an instrument for the production of value, and therefore shares in its fate absolutely, then maintaining or acting on a desiring relationship toward gendered difference can only take the form of false consciousness, the politically misguided embrace of an "external constraint."

As discussed, the diagnosis of false consciousness tends toward, at best, a sympathetic misrecognition of transsexual desires, and at worst, an antipathetic accusation that trans people, insufficiently critical of gendered abjection, are "more royalist than the king." My claim is less that the collective has forwarded a hostile argument than that their account of gendered abjection is insufficiently attentive to, and flexes away from, the stakes of bodily autonomy that trans liberation foregrounds and insists on.

In effect, Endnotes correctly identifies *that* and *how* capital instrumentalizes gender but derives a mistaken conclusion: capital uses gender to exploit people, and therefore the object of abolition would be not that exploitative instrumentalization but gender itself. (In personal correspondence, the writer Cam Scott identifies this argumentative move as a reverse syllogism and analogizes it to an accelerationist misprision: capital's bad for people, let's get rid of *them*.) Ultimately, I submit that the reflexive attention to gender purely in terms of abjection testifies to something like a failure of imagination about a liberatory reworking of sexual and gender relations, coextensive with any revolutionary project worth fighting for.

Consider a different staging of abolition. Jules Joanne Gleeson helpfully identifies the roots of contemporary abolitionisms in gay liberation–era thinkers including Mario Mieli and Monique Wittig.[57] Mieli's *Homosexuality and Liberation: Elements of a Gay Critique* advances an idiomatic "trans-sexuality" as the name for the reclaiming of wide-ranging capacities under the mode of a polymorphous perversity.[58] Some of his formulations may embarrass—think of Mieli's comrade Guy Hocquenghem on the anticapitalist universality of anal eroticism. But Mieli instructively attends to a hedonistic utopianism at every turn, defining the "revolutionary homosexual moment" through its "particular pleasures."[59] He further apprehends pleasure taking place not just through the liberation of sexuality—though he clearly regards the decriminalized ability to exercise eroticism in public as a demand of gay liberation—but also through the proscribed transgressions of drag, a further "dimension of pleasure covered by a taboo."[60] *Elements of a Gay Critique* sustains the argument I urge here: a revolutionary politics of gender and sexuality will foreground the autonomy over the capacities of the body within the signification of sexual difference as elements of the struggle over intensive disalienation. He says as much:

> The achievement of trans-sexuality can only follow from the work of the
> women's movement and the complete liberation of homoeroticism, as well
> as the other components of human erotic polymorphism; nor must the

utopian ideal of trans-sexuality, if it is to serve as a "concrete utopia," be divorced from the concrete dialectic presently underway between the sexes and between the different sexual tendencies. . . . If trans-sexuality is the inherent goal, it can only be achieved when women have defeated the male "power" based on the sexual polarity and homosexuals have abolished the Norm that prohibits homosexuality. Besides, given the very important functional role for the perpetuation of capitalism of the subordination of women and the sublimation of certain "perverse" erotic tendencies in labour, the (re)conquest of trans-sexuality will coincide with the fall of capitalism and the rejection of alienated and alienating labour: the struggle of homosexuals and women is essential to the communist revolution.[61]

Mieli thinks mediation in articulating a politics grounded in the now and turned toward the future. This is just the point—to throw us back into the here and now of foreclosed configurations of human life and the struggle over their liberation. We can't narrow the horizon of this struggle to the exclusive terms of trans liberation, which could only result in the racist and imperialist allegiances of a trans-inflected homonationalism—but equally we can't ignore it. In view of a politically urgent hedonism, the question becomes: What does it mean for gender to function as a source of disalienated pleasure rather than an accumulation strategy?—a question that helps us to engage the world at every relevant scale.

Mobilized in practice, this principle could help forge a real solidarity of trans and cis feminists against both an anti-trans moral panic and the liberal feminism that centers exclusively on a political struggle over individual women as possible bearers of a relation to property. Centered on the demands for universal bodily autonomy, for an end to exploitation, for a world no longer contoured by incarceration and policing, for open borders and ecological justice, for the self-determination of people and states against the capital and colonial relations, such a movement could produce a universalism worth the name.

NOTES

1   Di Prima, *Revolutionary Letters*, 32.
2   Floyd, *Reification of Desire*, 20.
3   See Smith, "Nature as Accumulation Strategy."
4   Hennessy, *Fires on the Border*, 131: "These values and the affective charge that accompanies the abjection or recognition of embodied subjects of different sorts are embedded in the capacities that produce surplus value during the working day."

5 As named by Jameson in "Pleasure," 377.

6 Gonzalez and Neton, "Logic of Gender."

7 Harvey, "'New' Imperialism." Harvey names an *extensive* regime of accumulation by dispossession in the form of global pillaging of assets, enclosing of the commons, and environmental degradation.

8 Jameson, "Pleasure," 381.

9 See, for instance, the Edinburgh Action for Trans Health's manifesto, which forcefully demands the intentional enabling of trans bodily autonomy together with the freeing of trans prisoners, decriminalization of sex work, fully socialized reproduction, and exhilaratingly more: "Trans Health Manifesto," https://edinburghath .tumblr.com/post/163521055802/trans-health-manifesto.

10 See Gira Grant, "Beyond Strange Bedfellows"; and Lewis, "Julie Bindel and the Wrong School of Abolitionism."

11 Marx, *Capital, Vol. 1*, 165.

12 Vogel, *Marxism and the Oppression of Women*, 141–56, 270.

13 Bhattacharya, "Introduction," 3.

14 Ben Fine and Alfredo Saad-Filho, *Marx's "Capital,"* 6th ed. (London: Pluto Press, 2017), 60, quoted in Bhattacharya, "Introduction," 8.

15 Rosenberg, "Becoming Hole (The Hiddener Abode)."

16 Marx, *Capital, Vol. 1*, 279.

17 Federici, *Wages against Housework*, 4.

18 Davis, *Women, Race and Class*, 260.

19 Smith, "Nature as Accumulation Strategy."

20 Haraway, *Modest_Witness*.

21 Lugones, "Heterosexualism," 196.

22 Rosenberg, *Confessions of the Fox*, 296.

23 Spillers, "Mama's Baby, Papa's Maybe," 72 (emphasis in original).

24 For the queer theory darlings, see Dean, *Beyond Sexuality*, 61–93. For the other list of villains, check Twitter.

25 Preciado, *Testo Junkie*, 11.

26 Raymond, *Transsexual Empire*, 178.

27 Chu, "On Liking Women."

28 Gozlan, *Transsexuality*, 41.

29 Gozlan, *Transsexuality*, 103.

30 Gozlan, *Transsexuality*, 13.

31 Routed, as Trish Salah has forcefully argued, through the vexed history of the Freudian and post-Freudian interpretation of the memoirs of Daniel Paul Schreber; see, e.g., her "To Return to Schreber." See also Griffin Hansbury's claim in "Unthinkable Anxieties" that the pathologization of transsexual desires and embodiments develops out of the analyst's transphobic countertransference— specifically, the anxiety of being brought into proximity with homosexuality.

32 Althusser, *Essays on Ideology*, 49.

33 See Hennessy, *Fires on the Border*, 125–50.

34 All these forms of precarity, at least in the United States, are well documented in the 2015 US Transgender Survey. See the executive summary: https://transequality.org/sites/default/files/docs/usts/USTS-Executive-Summary-Dec17.pdf.
35 Salah, "Notes towards Thinking Trans Institutional Poetics," 178.
36 Mohandesi and Teitelman, "Without Reserves," 62.
37 Doyle Griffiths, "Only Way Out Is Through."
38 As the National Center for Transgender Equality demonstrates, rampant poverty among trans people in the United States cleaves heavily along racial lines.
39 Rev and Geist, "Staging the Trans Sex Worker," 118.
40 Fitzgerald et al., *Meaningful Work*, 7.
41 Forrester et al., "Statement for Social Services Agencies," 105. The results of the National Center for Transgender Equality survey show that 20 percent of respondents who had done sex work in their lifetimes were trans men and a further 23 percent of respondents were nonbinary with female marked on their original birth certificate.
42 Hennessy, *Fires on the Border*, 130.
43 Snorton and Haritaworn, "Trans Necropolitics," 66.
44 For an ambitious description of the socialization of reproductive care, see especially Lewis's *Full Surrogacy Now*.
45 For the sake of intellectual honesty, I admit that these formulations derive from a kind of humanism, in the sense that they presuppose certain limits to the possible and historically situated dimensions of human experience. I don't have the space here to defend any given conception of humanism, so I'll just say that humanism is less wedded to a static and therefore reactionary concept of the human than its detractors allow—while the conceptually available and currently popular antihumanisms, from the so-called new materialisms to accelerationism, basically suck. As Nicholas Brown suggests, the proper response to the unhappy contraries would be to determine an anti-antihumanism sufficient for understanding both determination and the subject.
46 Ira, *Chasers*, 4.
47 On this point, see Tourmaline, Stanley, and Burton, "Introduction."
48 Jameson, "Pleasure," 384–85.
49 Ross, *Communal Luxury*, 100.
50 Bhattacharya, "How Not to Skip Class," 92.
51 Once again from Gonzalez and Neton, "Logic of Gender."
52 Laboria Cuboniks, *Xenofeminism: A Politics for Alienation*.
53 Lukács, "Reification and the Consciousness of the Proletariat," in *History and Class Consciousness*, 179.
54 Gonzalez and Neton, "Logic of Gender."
55 Gonzalez and Neton, "Logic of Gender."
56 Gonzalez and Neton, "Logic of Gender."
57 See Gleeson, "Call for Abolition."

58 Mieli, *Towards a Gay Communism*. "Trans-sexuality" is not to be confused with actual transsexuals, whom Mieli also addresses: "These reactionary homosexuals (homo-cops) make out that outrageous queens and transvestites ruin the gay scene and spoil the image of homosexuality. . . . [T]here is no harm in us queens having our bit of fantasy" (Mieli, *Towards a Gay Communism*, 194).
59 Mieli, *Towards a Gay Communism*, 204.
60 Mieli, *Towards a Gay Communism*, 194: "Even today we can't make love freely wherever we like it, on the buses or in the streets."
61 Mieli, *Towards a Gay Communism*, 38.

BIBLIOGRAPHY

Althusser, Louis. *Essays on Ideology*. New York: Verso, 1984.
Bhattacharya, Tithi. "How Not to Skip Class: Social Reproduction of Labor and the Global Working Class." In *Social Reproduction: Remapping Class, Recentering Oppression*, edited by Tithi Bhattacharya, 68–93. London: Pluto Press, 2017.
Bhattacharya, Tithi. "Introduction: Mapping Social Reproduction Theory." In *Social Reproduction: Remapping Class, Recentering Oppression*, edited by Tithi Bhattacharya, 1–20. London: Pluto Press, 2017.
Chu, Andrea Long. "On Liking Women." *n+1*, Winter 2018. https://nplusonemag .com/issue-30/essays/on-liking-women/.
Davis, Angela. *Women, Race and Class*. New York: Vintage, 1983.
Dean, Tim. *Beyond Sexuality*. Chicago: University of Chicago Press, 2000.
di Prima, Diane. *Revolutionary Letters*. San Francisco: Last Gasp of San Francisco, 2005.
Doyle Griffiths, Kade. "The Only Way Out Is Through: A Reply to Melinda Cooper." Verso blog, March 26, 2018. https://www.versobooks.com/blogs/3709-the-only -way-out-is-through-a-reply-to-melinda-cooper.
Federici, Silvia. *Wages against Housework*. Bristol, UK: Power of Women Collective and Falling Wall Press, 1975.
Fitzgerald, Erin, Sarah Elspeth, Darby Hickey, Cherno Biko, and Harper Tobin. *Meaningful Work: Transgender Experiences in the Sex Trade*. Washington, DC: National Center for Transgender Equality, 2015.
Floyd, Kevin. *The Reification of Desire*. Minneapolis: University of Minnesota Press, 2009.
Forrester, Monica, Jamie-Lee Hamilton, Mirha-Soleil Ross, and Viviane Namaste. "Statement for Social Services Agencies and Transsexual/Transgender Organizations on Service Delivery to Transsexual and Transvestite Prostitutes." In *Sex Change, Social Change: Reflections on Identity, Institutions, and Imperialism*, edited by Viviane Namaste, 82–85. Toronto: Women's Press, 2011.
Gira Grant, Melissa, "Beyond Strange Bedfellows: How the 'War on Trafficking' Was Made to Unite Left and Right." *Public Eye*, August 6, 2018. http://feature .politicalresearch.org/beyond-strange-bedfellows.

Gleeson, Jules. "The Call for Abolition: From Materialist Lesbianism to Gay Communism." *Blindfield Journal*, July 31, 2017. https://blindfieldjournal.com/2017/07/31/the-call-for-gender-abolition-from-materialist-lesbianism-to-gay-communism/.

Gonzalez, Maya Andrea, and Jeanne Neton. "The Logic of Gender: On the Separation of Spheres and the Process of Abjection." *Endnotes* 3 (2013). https://endnotes.org.uk/issues/3/en/endnotes-the-logic-of-gender.

Gozlan, Oren. *Transsexuality and the Art of Transitioning: A Lacanian Approach.* New York: Routledge, 2015.

Hansbury, Griffin. "Unthinkable Anxieties: Reading Transphobic Countertransference in a Century of Psychoanalytic Writing." *TSQ* 4, nos. 3–4 (2017): 384–404.

Haraway, Donna. *Modest_Witness@Second_Millennium.Female_Meets_OncoMouse™.* New York: Routledge, 1997.

Hennessy, Rosemary. *Fires on the Border: The Passionate Politics of Labor Organizing on the Mexican Frontera.* Minneapolis: University of Minnesota Press, 2013.

Ira, Stephen. *Chasers.* Tucson: New Michigan Press, 2022.

Jameson, Fredric. "Pleasure: A Political Issue." In *Ideologies of Theory*, 372–85. New York: Verso, 2009.

Laboria Cuboniks. *Xenofeminism: A Politics for Alienation.* New York: Verso, 2018.

Lewis, Sophie. *Full Surrogacy Now.* New York: Verso, 2019.

Lewis, Sophie. "Julie Bindel and the Wrong School of Abolitionism." Verso blog, May 24, 2018. https://www.versobooks.com/blogs/news/3845-not-a-workplace-julie-bindel-and-the-school-of-wrong-abolitionism.

Lugones, Maria. "Heterosexualism and the Colonial/Modern Gender System." *Hypatia* 22, no. 1 (2007): 186–209.

Lukács, Georg. *History and Class Consciousness: Studies in Marxist Dialectics.* Translated by Rodney Livingstone. Cambridge, MA: MIT Press, 1972.

Marx, Karl. *Capital, Vol. 1.* Translated by Ben Fowkes. London: Penguin and Verso, 1976.

Mieli, Mario. *Towards a Gay Communism.* Translated by David Fernbach and Evan Calder Williams. London: Pluto Press, 2018.

Mohandesi, Salar, and Emma Teitelman. "Without Reserves." In *Social Reproduction Theory: Remapping Class, Recentering Oppression*, edited by Tithi Bhattacharya, 62–67. London: Pluto Press, 2017.

Preciado, Paul B. *Testo Junkie: Sex, Drugs, and Biopolitics in the Pharmacopornographic Era.* New York: Feminist Press, 2013.

Raymond, Janice. *The Transsexual Empire: The Making of the She-Male.* New York: Teachers College, 1994.

Rev, Nihils, and Fiona Mae Geist. "Staging the Trans Sex Worker." *TSQ* 4, no. 1 (February 2017): 112–27.

Rosenberg, Jordy. "Becoming Hole (The Hiddener Abode)." *World Picture Journal* 11 (2016). http://worldpicturejournal.com/WP_11/Rosenberg_11.html.

Rosenberg, Jordy. *Confessions of the Fox.* New York: One World, 2018.

Ross, Kristin. *Communal Luxury: The Political Imagination of the Paris Commune.* New York: Verso, 2015.

Salah, Trish. "Notes towards Thinking Trans Institutional Poetics." In *Trans/acting Culture, Writing, and Memory: Essays in Honour of Barbara Godard,* edited by Eva Karpinski, Jennifer Henderson, Ian Sowton, and Ray Ellenwood, 167–89. Toronto: Wilfrid Laurier University Press, 2013.

Salah, Trish. "To Return to Schreber: Trans Literatures as Psychoanalysis." In *Current Debates in the Field of Transsexual Studies,* edited by Oren Gozlan, 169–80. New York: Routledge, 2018.

Smith, Neil. "Nature as Accumulation Strategy." *Socialist Register* 43 (2007): 16–36.

Snorton, C. Riley, and Jin Haritaworn. "Trans Necropolitics: A Transnational Reflection on Violence, Death, and the Trans of Color Afterlife." In *The Transgender Studies Reader 2,* edited by Susan Stryker and Aren Aizura, 65–76. New York: Routledge: 2013.

Spillers, Hortense. "Mama's Baby, Papa's Maybe: An American Grammar Book." *Diacritics* 17, no. 2 (1987): 65–81.

Tourmaline, Eric A. Stanley, and Johanna Burton. "Introduction." In *Trap Door: Trans Cultural Production and the Politics of Visibility,* xv–xxvi. Cambridge, MA: MIT Press, 2017.

Vogel, Lise. *Marxism and the Oppression of Women: Towards a Unitary Theory.* 1983. Chicago: Haymarket, 2013.

FACELESS   6

Nonconfessions of a Gender

> Then can there ever be a true confession,
> not extracted under torture?
> —DENISE RILEY, *THE WORDS OF SELVES:*
> *IDENTIFICATION, SOLIDARITY, IRONY*

It is by now a bit cliché to open a scholarly meditation with a Foucault quote, but I risk the cliché with hopes that it pays off. Foucault writes, "I am no doubt not the only one who writes in order to have no face."[1] That is what I want, and that is the kind of gendered subjectivity I yearn for: a facelessness. I know that my body, read as cis too often, read as Black nearly always, and rarely understood as what that impossible nexus entails, is made to confess certain things. Indeed, Foucault says elsewhere that sociality is structured by the demand to confess oneself, to give a "veridiction of self," as a way to coerce "truth" from deviant criminality.[2] What concerns me here, and perhaps always, is not only the demand to tell the truth of oneself but also the criteria by which others deem a truth, indeed, truthful. I am concerned with how the assertion of a legible gender at times acts as a coerced capitulation that forecloses a radical alternative possibility of subjectivity in the refusal of gender, of gender abolition, in favor of requisites that one must "fess up"—

to their privileges, to their physicality—as an ethical gesture. It is held here that, inasmuch as gender abolition is part of a general radical movement and revolutionary politic, gender must be abolished on the way to the actualization of such a radicality, not after. This then means that gender abolition is a vector through which revolution happens, or a notch in the chain toward revolution precisely because it "is part of the totality of relations that daily reproduce the capitalist mode of production." In short, as Maya Andrea Gonzalez concludes cogently, radical and revolutionary politics—what Gonzalez expresses under the heading of communization—"must destroy gender *in its very course.*"[3] What becomes the primary point of interest for the occasion of this chapter is the radical assertion of gender's refusal *as* one's (non)gender and precisely that as necessary to adopt on the road to revolution, radicality, and thoroughgoing abolition.

We know that there is a cost to deeming something true about oneself. That cost—wherein cost can be sutured to price, and the ontological gravity comes into view due to this, as if Foucault and James Baldwin spoke in a kind of Black and queer communion—depletes the capacity to emerge through and as oneself not tethered to the coercive demand to maintain legibility on the grounds of current metrics.[4] These metrics, at base, are violent. Violent because they precede a subject's ability to name itself or to remain unnamed; they precede a subject's ability to appear as a subject, which is to say that such metrics curtail one's subjectivity and disallow one to say "I" in different ways or not at all. The point I am trying to illustrate is one of how we come to express who we are and on what grounds we *get to* and *have to* express that which we are. And, in a bit of a paradoxical, contradictory commentary on the previous sentence: What happens to those who attempt to assert their me-ness by way of a vitiation of and refusal to adhere to that which qualifies one for the status of "me"?

In clarification, my aim in this chapter, then, will be the following: What happens when one's body belies what they wish it to be? For those of us who are *read* as cis, have not undergone the alterations potent with gendered signification, and are not trans(gender) in a sense that registers with how such an identity is made tentatively legible, what claim do we have to a gendered subjectivity that is in fact a nonconfession, a confessional refusal, a desire for *facelessness*? And how might (my) Blackness muddy the already muddy waters of gender alignment, that uneven epidermis indexical of an anoriginal lawlessness lacerative of the "cis" of cisgender, intimate with the "trans" of transgender—especially knowing that cisness itself is a racialized regulatory regime? In this chapter I have no straightforward argument, really, only a byzantine desire for a way of moving in the world and among others on grounds unstable, being and becoming a nobody, a faceless being not *without* gender per se—oh, how known it is that I *have* a gender, one everyone assumes and insists on and demands of me, ontologically—but with a subjectivity that vibrates away from perinatal circumscription toward [insert *nothing* here]. In a desire for facelessness and confessional refusal, I am intrigued by the contours of the engendered world when living unto a way of being that is not coerced to confess its gendered self, or confined to the normative registers of the body-made-legible.

I.

What is this obsession, religious and secular, with confession? It is a practice that rose to salience after the advent of Christianity, a religion that had as one of its fundamental traits the notion of the individual's requirement to find the truth of their self. That excavated truth, immutable and revelatory, decisively bore on one's salvation. And after this discovery, one needed to, by divine decree, manifest that truth in ways legible to all others. Or else one was not living truthfully.[5] The form such truthful manifestation took was, and is, the confession. It is a confessional that exceeds the practice of revealing one's sins to an ordained church official, though this excessive confessional, this pervasive imposed confessional sociality, as it were, is indexical of the religious practice. The modality expanded into all realms of one's personhood and acted as a way to live truthfully with others, yet a truthfulness that was given over as such to the precise extent to which it adhered to legible notions of the good, the natural, and the divine.

The confession or, alternatively, as Foucault calls it, the avowal, is disingenuous from the start. The being or beings who stand in judgment of the confession's veracity care little for persuading the confessor of the unimpeachability of that which is confessed. The aim, instead, is to extract the confession in a particular way and to have the truth expressed in a particular way. And this is a quotidian phenomenon, though Foucault may have undersold this aspect of the confession in his emphasis on it as a singularized act. Confession's constancy, its quotidian lilt, resounds from the juridical trial to the confessional booth, all the way to the implicit calls to tell the truth of your status in the world, your adherence to the world's grammars, your alignment with extant vectors of legibility. And this happens more than once, twice; this happens at every moment at the level of ontology, an ontology woven through constitutively with, among other vectors, gender. The confession must be "I am a man," "I am a woman," over and over, repeatedly to the sanctioned and institutionalized arbiters (doctors, judges, government documents) and again to others deputized as arbiters (growing children on the playground, peers, strangers, teachers, parents). And the perverse twist is that the demand for confession is presumed therapeutic, a necessary salve for that which ails the confessor; the twist, in short, is that normative violence is served up as the only thing that will propitiate the anguish one is feeling by virtue of that normative violence.

In a reading of the French psychiatrist Dr. Leuret, Foucault understands the avowal of madness as functioning for Leuret as a means by which the confessing patient "seal[ed] the certificate that imprisoned him [sic]." One must confirm their own madness, in this case, which can be extended as the demand to confirm one's perinatal assignation, what is mistakenly taken to be the observation and recording of birth sex. That is, not only is one diagnosed by an external authority but one must also confirm that determination for themselves, verify nonconsensually the accuracy of that determination. To affirm that which was bestowed, or more accurately imposed, onto one's person—*as* one's person—is to say, as Foucault concludes, "'I give you the right to lock me up; I am giving you the possibility of healing me.' This is the meaning of the avowal of madness [or one's purported gender]: avowal signs the asylum [or gender binaristic] contract."[6] This is then detrimental for those who may be subjectivating themselves through genderfluidity, gender queerness, nonbinariness, or transness inasmuch as these present a kind of gendered impurity. And if the very ability to tell the truth about one's gender, which is to say to adhere to legible nodes of where and how gender manifests to verifying hegemonic gazes, is predicated on a "tight connection" "between purity and truth-telling (only the pure can tell the truth . . .)," then to tell the truth of an impurity from an impure subject becomes an impossibility. To emerge as proximate to transness, to be and become trans, is indeed to become what Dean Spade calls an impossible person.[7]

As all of this pertains to the occasion of this chapter specifically, I submit here that gender is one of the chief forms of inhabiting the world as a subject, which implies the requisite to live one's *gender* truthfully, a truthfulness whose probity rests on an adherence to a normative understanding of binary gender. One is also evaluated on the grounds of how their body is rendered legible based on those binaristic, cis-normative assumptions, making even departures from these assumptions retroactively conform to a binary codified as legitimate through a normative evaluation of gender-potent corporeal sites. In other words, if one identifies as, say, a trans woman, even if the evaluator is supposedly "cool" with such a gender identification, you best believe that the trans woman better "*look like*" a woman—feminine, unadulterated, and deprived of any trace of "male" privilege. And that measurement, always relative to cis normativity, occurs again and again, and the same queries and standards abound. *When did you know you were a woman? Have you had the surgery? Do you feel trapped in the wrong body?* You must say from a very young age, you must say yes, and you must say absolutely. So, you must confess, on their terms, to their questions, always through, nevertheless, the narrowed scope of the gender binary.

This sentiment of wanting out of the scope of intelligibility is what I wish to expound upon via the confessional. Not only is one made to adhere to cis normativity, where deviations from perinatal assignation are deemed pathological; there is also a strain of coercion in spaces offering themselves as liberal or radical and justice-oriented too. One is, of course, forced to confess to the Starbucks barista their gender in ways immediately transparent so as to make the social and economic exchange seamless—sirs and ma'ams, respective Johns and Janes foundational for the flow of sociality. Indeed, such a social interaction is stalled and disallowed its continuance until gender is assigned and known, as the ability of the barista to uninterruptedly say "ma'am," for example, is necessary for the conversation, the social interaction, to proceed. Gender must be placed, sedimented, known, and untroubled *in order for* sociality to happen.[8] Also, one is made to confess even when organizing and movement-working with those who might deem themselves radical. Consider that when I show up to the meeting for social justice doers with the ways my body presents itself—being read almost exclusively as a cis man, and perhaps being impacted by latent assumptions of the hypermasculinity my Blackness may precipitate—despite my nonbinariness and refusal of gender normativity's hold over me, there is a discourse present that demands I not only reckon with but *accept* and *reiterate* male/masculine privilege as an ethical gesture. They say that someone who looks like I do must acknowledge the reality of how my body accrues benefits bestowed by patriarchy. And if I do not acknowledge this, I wrongly try to rebuke the privileges I undoubtedly, unceasingly, always and forever, have. I fail to *check* my privilege. I know, I think, what they mean, and I know the kinds of politics and discourses from which they draw. It seems too often, though, that the requisite to acknowledge and check is in fact a requisite to content myself with the existing order as if it is natural, as if nothing can—*or should*—be done about it (like, I don't know, nonbinariness and a commitment to a refusal of the behaviors of masculinity, of masculine privileges, of the logics that inhere in the acceptance of masculinity as my, or anyone's, province). It seems often that they want me to be a man. And how cruel is that, how violent, to me and others. In a sly undermining of the political valence and intention of nonbinariness (for example, to subvert, interrogate, and displace the assumption that a body means something a priori and that gender can be assumed by making recourse to the corporeal surface), I am called to deem and make myself, over and over, a legible man in a perverse commitment to gendered ethics.

At issue is something quite mutedly profound: "The problem is that of knowing how subjects are effectively tied within and by the forms of veridiction in which they engage," as Foucault writes.[9] One cannot give a "veridiction of self" (not veridiction of *the* self, as the self cannot be preconstituted and then verified; its selfness emerges as it is verified) in terms not permissible as constitutive of selfhood. This ongoing process that is never finished but always a quotidian practice of reassuring others of one's selfsameness, a selfsameness that is the same as the self, permissible by normative logics, verifies power. The one who must speak of themselves is the subjugated; to speak is to announce one's beholdenness to having to absolve the violence characteristic of that ontologizing beholding. To be beheld is to be subject to the ways one must appear in order to be answerable to the metrics by which bodies are beheld. And, indeed, these bodies do not preexist their beholding; to be beheld is to be fixed into the parameters by which bodies are said to exist as such, making the gaze a formative one rather than a transparent one, an act of making rather than an act of revealing. So we must begin not from the premise of there being truths out there we need only to uncover. There are no preexistent genders that we need only get people to see the "naturalness" of, no bodies out there that are simply *there* needing only to be respected. Hence when it comes to gendered subjectivity that escapes, to whatever extent, the regime of Gender, the aim is not to establish its unimpeachable locus on a given site of an already-complete corporeality. We cannot point to intrinsic unfalsifiable truths as if they fall outside the orbit of the contingent forms such desires, impulses, dispositions, or affects are permitted to take, for "Nothing in man [*sic*]—not even his [*sic*] body—is sufficiently stable to serve as the basis for self-recognition or for understanding."[10] It becomes then a question as to whether it is possible for there to be a body external to its construction, its traces of investments and politics and history and oversights, and constitutive outsides. Where this leads this meditation is toward a desire for interaction on different terms, terms not predicated on legibilizing scripts for the body. Terms that will surely stall the interaction with that Starbucks barista, making us receive our coffees a bit later than usual, but hopefully on much more loving, open grounds of exchange. And if one must be gendered in a fundamental, "truthful" way in order to be a body that is interactive—if one must be disciplined from the jump, corralled by gender into a body on terms not, and never, its own—then where we land here, indeed where I think I want to land, is proximate to a non- or dislocation Paul Preciado has expressed so succinctly: "I do not want the female gender that has been assigned to me at birth. Neither do I want the male gender that transsexual medicine can furnish and that the state will award me if I behave in the right way. I don't want any of it."[11]

I want to reckon with and amplify the claim that gender is fundamentally disciplinary. I mean genders *as such*—even genders that one may purportedly self-determine, genders that might supervene along the byzantine discursive framework of trans, genders that might be bent or blended—are disciplinary. So if genders are disciplinary vehicles, and if discipline is a nonconsensual, coercive web of both entrapment and production, then gender is a nonconsensual and coercive subjugating and producing modality. It is here that I tentatively submit the necessity for gender abolition, which might be characterized through facelessness. To emerge into "gendered" sociality via Preciado's "I don't want any of it." Gender as a regime of subjectivation necessitates that one fit somewhere, that one settle. And this is precisely the fold in which I want to insert a disruption. Consider here the possibility of a gendered dormancy in how coercion, discipline, and station operate. To have a gender is to be given a gender, to be given a station and a place, to be placed. And that is more than description; that is coercion, discipline. Gender

> ha[s] its own system of coercion, which seemed to be the code, but which in fact was discipline. There had to be a place, a location, a compulsory insertion: "One sleeps at home, said the judge, because in fact, for him, everything must have a home, some dwelling, however magnificent or mean; his task is not to provide one, but to force every individual to live in one." Moreover, one must have a station in life, a recognizable identity, an individuality fixed once and for all: "What is your station? This question is the simplest expression of the established order in society; such vagabondage is repugnant to it, disturbs it; one must have a stable, continuous longterm station, thoughts of the future, of a secure future, in

order to reassure it against all attacks." In short, one should have a master, be caught up and situated within a hierarchy; one exists only when fixed in definite relations of domination: "Who do you work with? That is to say, since you are not a master, you must be a servant, whatever your station; it is not a question of your satisfactoriness as an individual; it is a question of order to be maintained." Confronted with discipline on the face of the law, there is illegality, which puts itself forward as a right; it is indiscipline, rather than the criminal offence, that causes the rupture. An indiscipline of language: incorrect grammar.[12]

It seems that we are simply following, voluntarily or naturally, an innocent code that we can opt out of if we wish. But that code is disciplinary. We must occupy a gendered place; we must be able to be slotted in, known untroublingly and immediately, compulsorily. We must have, as it were, a gendered home, and there are only condos or colonial-style homes, only two kinds of homes you can have, no bungalows or ranch-styles or split-levels or apartments. And if you call your home split-level, they will tell you, no, that is not a home but the perversion of your god-given home. You are and will always be living in a colonial. Our gendered identities must be recognizable, a recognition that has investments and agendas and biases and is subject to verification by the powers that not only be but demand how we be too. To ask "What is your station?" is to ask, in one context, "What is your gender, M or F?" One cannot and should not float free, a gender vagrant, for one must always have papers of verification—where is your birth certificate verifying this so-called gender? Where is your ID, your passport? In what way, in other words, are you specifically serving power's ends? We are forced to measure up. What I seek in facelessness, an evasion of biometric surveillance techniques that are always and already disciplinary techniques, is a living ungrammatical, an "anagrammaticality," an *incorrect grammar* as what is reached for when subverting gender's hold.[13] And the subversion of gender's hold, inasmuch as gender as such is the disciplinary, violent apparatus, is the abolition of gender.

II.

It feels like I'm always bringing up Blackness when I talk about gender because I am. That is because Blackness matters, and it matters in more ways than many others seem to think it matters—as, simply, an additional quality ascribed to those within the present relevant demographic (for example, trans people *who are Black*). I bring up Blackness in large part as a reckoning. That is, Blackness as a modality of tinkering, as it were, and as what Che Gossett via a blackening of Judith Butler has called Blackness's gender trouble, works on the regime of gender in service of its dissolution. Of peak interest is the nature of that dissolution; of peak interest, one might say, is the nature of that denaturing.

My concern is where we locate the zones of constitutive bodiness. Because *the* body is not a passive entity whose boundaries are limned in advance and is not a transparent, readily legible thing we merely assess on its own terms, it is imperative to note the incredible impurity of discourses concerning what the body is. The body—which should perhaps always be in skeptical scare quotes—is forced to announce its contours within the limits of an ontology that dictates what can rightly be claimed as a proper body. In other words, the body does not mean on its own, we know; thus, I wish to think about the assertion of something like nonbinariness even or especially when one's body (take, for instance, mine) does not adhere to the contours of what a nonbinary body must look like *as an assault on the logics that constitute bodiness*. Where nonbinary signifies or is presumed to necessitate androgyny or the perfect harmony of equal parts masculine and feminine, there is a departure from such thinking here in favor of nonbinariness not as a uniform, if you will, of a gendered middle ground but as a vitiation of the perceived body as saying anything, from the start, truthful about its gender. Which means truthful about itself, inasmuch as gender is constitutive of bodiness. It is an avenue into thinking the very question of the body, an avenue among others. And via that thinking, how might the assumption of a body and all its attending categorical constituents—themselves hegemonic and normative bestowals—be withered away with the goal of abolition? What Foucault's facelessness aspires toward in my meditation is the vitiation of the body.

But what is so wrong with the body? Well, I follow Dionne Brand's thinking on this front. She writes in Verso 16.3 of *The Blue Clerk*, her compilation of essay poems philosophizing about writing and the world, "I do know that the bodies that we inhabit now are corpses of the humanist narrative. Awful corpses. And, when we appear on the street, that is what we are appearing as. So, I can only give you this view of it. We inhabit these bags of muscle and fat and bones that are utilized in humanist narrative to demonstrate the incremental ethical development of a certain subject whom is not we."[14] What we call our bodies are the scabs of an insufficient, violent humanist narrative that has constructed certain bodies as more valuable and, indeed, human than others. To double down on the unimpeachability of the body is to also double down on that humanist narrative. And this results in a doubling down on the violence of that narrative. I do not want that narrative and thus do not want the body or the racializations or the genders that are constitutive and compulsory under the narrative. Blackness and nonbinariness, then, are political projects, and subjective projects too, that aim to forsake the joints of that narrative. Because when we appear, we appear as this humanist narrative, a narrative of violence and white supremacist cis normativity. I desire facelessness—and express that facelessness, however unreceived it is, as a certain iteration of Blackness and nonbinariness—and that facelessness means I do not appear under the rubrics of the aforementioned narrative. It is a facelessness that does not possess that fixture of consolidated personhood, attending to which would be a name, a history, an identity. Facelessness exceeds the definitional insofar as definitions need a subject, a skeleton, a structure to drape over, whereas facelessness is precisely beingness outside the grammars on which beingness rests. What often happens is a forcing into the narrative, a forced confession along the melodies and notes of that narrative. But that subject "is not we," as Brand says, so what is being sought via Blackness and nonbinariness is a stalwart movement toward a certain subjectivity of not we-ness.

I am focusing on the convergence of Blackness and nonbinariness not to asseverate a specificity that no other demographic assemblage (though I would not say this is a "demographic") can highlight; rather, the focus here is in service of uncovering how the two serve as analytics toward dissolving gender's hold. Blackness and nonbinariness work in tandem for gender abolition, their Heideggerian toward-whichness that of doing things to gender such that gender no longer is, which is, in turn, where the subject emerges differently.

As encapsulative of this, I offer Eva Hayward's second round of starfish lessons. Hayward writes of changeability in "More Lessons from a Starfish: Prefixial Flesh and Transspeciated Selves." Specifically, I am drawn to the following sentence: "Our bodies are scarred, marked, and reworked into a livable gender trouble, sex trouble, or uneven epidermis."[15] Here, Hayward is speaking of the corporeal flesh of the transsexual. And while there is a generative conversation to be had between transsexuality and its racialized discourse, my interest in this passage is the sentence's latter desirous concatenation of *livable gender trouble, sex trouble, or uneven epidermis.* This is a site of futurity, what we might become. Its thrust is that of how to live the unlivable, as it were. Inasmuch as normative ontology marks nonnormative genders as unlivable, and inasmuch as Blackness is cast in part as proximal to a death-boundedness, I find deeply rich the possibility of *living* in the gender and sex trouble, the unevenness of the epidermis.

Certain modes of subjective expression are deemed unlivable and unworthy of life. This is not new. But what intrigues me is what the ripple effects of living in unlivable subjectivities would not only look like but necessitate. That is, if we in fact live nonnormative genders—genders that are not, properly, genders—what will need to shift? What will we be unable to maintain if we live these genders that are not genders, considering the myriad ways our societal, existential, institutional, and historical doxa are predicated on, are enabled fundamentally by, a cis-normative worldly orchestration? It becomes imperative to live the trouble that arises when one's nonnormativity is pressed to adhere to, to make itself legible via, to *confess*, binary gender. Doing such would advance the radical abolitionist ethics so many purport but do not leap to actualize. To have no face would throw askew the very coherency of a body, or even personhood. To have no face here would be to refuse confession; to have no face would dovetail with living the troubling of sex and gender—as if, we have known since at least the publication of that famous 1990 text from Routledge, the two are intelligible without one another, discrete and transparent characteristics—and to have no face is to live the troubling of the epidermis: the process of racialization imposed on us and deemed necessary for social viability. Abolition of these categorical coercions is movement toward a world that refuses the violences of the world we have been given. Insofar as nonbinariness is a *refusal* of the processes of normative gender, and insofar as Blackness names an antecategorical lawlessness in excess of the epidermis, moving unto facelessness is a Black and nonbinary endeavor in service of a radical change—the abolition of gender, sex, and race, these hegemonic bestowals and coercive perinatal assignations.[16] Where coerced subjective confession serves to buttress the evaluative criteria already extant, which have long served to proliferate the violences in our midst, to end these violences one must not confess, and on the grounds of that nonconfession find others who are refusing confession. This refusal is how we find others who wish to assume a radical comportment relative to power. To refuse the confession is a testament to an allegiance to other realms, other ways to be.

III.

It was a questing for noncoercive communion.

—ASHON T. CRAWLEY, *THE LONELY LETTERS*

A Twitter user I followed when I still had a Twitter account, who at the time of this writing went by the name bitcher (@Lurdia), tweeted an encounter. "[M]e: I'm non-binary," the user wrote, followed by a response: "cis ppl: wow, you go girl! live in your truth you strong, independent, woman! using they is totally valid, chica!"[17] Such an encounter, one I've experienced myself though slightly differently, befalls this meditation's desire for a way to move throughout the world. That is, at issue here is not only the misgendering that "cis ppl" do in moments like this, which to be sure is no small matter as it attests to the violence that can happen even in purportedly justice-oriented spaces; the issue too is the opening declaration. But what is not being asserted is that bitcher (@Lurdia) should not tell others of their nonbinary identification. What is being asserted is a yearning for interrogating the grounds on which one is called to profess a presumed status whose implication is one of stability. To have to say that one "is" nonbinary is part of a social field that demands that one make themselves known from the jump, uncomplicatedly, and thus carry with them a legible archive of proper ways they should be interacted with. My aim in this critique is to offer not the declaration of oneself as nonbinary but a subjective emergence through nonbinariness, a distinction that moves from possession of an identity (I am nonbinary) to modalities of emergence and engendering (what effects will relationality and the world undergo were "I" to emerge and relate on grounds that assumed the subversion of the binary). That is what I want. The history of gender's imposition has touched us—or more closely, slapped us, punched us—in so many places and in so many ways, and to announce one's nonbinariness is not another addition to how gendered history might touch us better but the enunciation, the *re*nunciation, of being touched. How might we move toward nonbinariness as more than a declaration—as an interrogation, identification-as-interrogation? I suppose what this chapter has amounted to is facelessness as the beginning of what gender might be without a body, an instantiation of the impossibility of being touched. To yearn to be without a face is an analytic gesture toward the deprivation of the corporeal instantiations of constitutive personhood; thus to be without a face is to be without footholds for given ontologies to latch onto. And this necessitates the obliteration of the Human promulgated in Black studies and a vitiation of the gender binary promulgated in trans and non-binary studies. Facelessness via the Blackness and nonbinariness established throughout these pages is a movement toward Denise Ferreira da Silva's call to be "nobodies against the state," a state that functions fundamentally by the subjugation and eradication of "the black, sexual, trans body"; and, relatedly, a movement toward Tourmaline's call to become "undercover nobodies."[18] This Black and trans no-body has no face, because the Black and trans, the Black and nonbinary, reference those whose breadth cannot abide the consolidating subjective congealment of faces.

One's movement toward facelessness precipitates a tremulous kind of relation to oneself and, surely, to others. The kind of nonbinary that does not shroud or define me but allows me to emerge differently, flittingly, a nonbinary I do not feel I can claim at times—for even in the trans sociality I find so inviting and capacious, there is at times an implicit, even rarer an explicit, demand for untroubled linear shuttling between an identifiable "man" or "woman" that bears no traces of the other. This essay is an attempt to live toward facelessness; in facelessness is the beginning of what we might call, truthfully, life.

NOTES

1 Foucault, *The Archaeology of Knowledge*, 17.
2 See Foucault, *Wrong-Doing, Truth-Telling*.
3 Gonzalez, "Communization and the Abolition of Gender" (emphasis in original).
4 I'm referencing Foucault's "How Much Does It Cost to Tell the Truth?" in which he asks, "How much does it cost the subject to be able to tell the truth about itself?" as well as James Baldwin's notion of the "price of the ticket," where there is a price paid to, effectively, become white or become in proximity to whiteness through assimilation. Cost and price resound generatively and converge to create a way of looking at confession as that always linked to coercion, normativity, and a kind of conditioning torture, to draw on Denise Riley's epigraph.
5 See Foucault, *Wrong-Doing, Truth-Telling*, 91–92. He writes, first, that the need to avow the truth about oneself, to confess, "hardly existed" before the onset of Christianity as a pervasive structuring force. Further, he notes that in Christianity "there is an obligation to search for the truth of oneself. There is an obligation to interpret this truth through all obstacles in order to take a decisive move or step toward one's salvation. And finally, third, there is an obligation not only to discover the truth, but to manifest it" (92).
6 Foucault, *Wrong-Doing, Truth-Telling*, 13.

7 See Spade, *Normal Life*. Spade writes, "Trans people are told by the law, state agencies, private discriminators, and our families that we are impossible people who cannot exist, cannot be seen, cannot be classified, and cannot fit anywhere" (19).

8 I'm thinking here of the encounter Judith Butler conveys, in which Butler was staying in a hotel room in London to which a custodian needed brief access to check the minibar (see "Judith Butler—The Difference of Philosophy," March 6, 2015, https://www.youtube.com/watch?v=WecaTBx64p0). As Butler recounts it, upon opening the door, the custodian said, "Excuse me Mr. . . . madam . . . Mr. . . . madam . . ." to which Butler responded, "Is it really important to determine my gender in order to check the minibar?" The interaction *could not occur* until gender was placed, definitively and untroublingly. Indeed, think too not only about Butler's own nonnormative gender expression and general butchiness but also about the ways the custodian was curtailed. The delimited class interaction compelled this custodian to mark deference via the vector of class by circumscribing gendered possibility. Which is also to say, perhaps that custodian yearned for different, more open gendered language but was pummeled into the gender binary via class expectations. What if the custodian didn't have to confess class-cum-gender? What if the custodian was allowed to be faceless?

9 Foucault, *Wrong-Doing, Truth-Telling*, 20.

10 Foucault, *Language, Counter-memory, Practice*, 153. See also Butler, "Foucault and the Paradox of Bodily Inscriptions."

11 Preciado, *Testo Junkie*, 138.

12 Foucault, *Discipline and Punish*, 291.

13 See Sharpe, *In the Wake*. Sharpe thinks about what she calls anagrammatical Blackness, which denotes the anagrammatical as indexical of potentiality and violability, as an opening rift that expresses Blackness through an anewness, putting pressure on meaning.

14 Brand, *Blue Clerk*, 91.

15 Hayward, "More Lessons from a Starfish," 74.

16 I allude here to Moten, in *The Universal Machine*. Of Blackness, Moten writes, "There is an imposition onto the figure of the black that would signify the confluence of racial identity and racial inferiority, there is also, in a way that is prior to the regulative force of that imposition and calls it into question, a resource working through the epidermalization of afantasmatic inferiority as the anti-epidermalization of the radical alternative" (185).

17 See their post here: https://twitter.com/Lurdia/status/1160210641552138241.

18 In "Poethical Readings/Intuiting the Political," Denise Ferreira da Silva says in full, "If the state is ready to kill to defend itself from the black, sexual, trans body brought before it, do we want to be somebody before the state, or no-body against it?" See also Stanley, "Anti-trans Optics." In turn, Tourmaline says (see Gossett, "Commencement Address"), "If the state, capitalism, and surveillance want us to be visible somebodies, it might be a good time to be undercover nobodies."

Brand, Dionne. *The Blue Clerk: Ars Poetica in 59 Versos*. Durham, NC: Duke University Press, 2018.

Butler, Judith. "Foucault and the Paradox of Bodily Inscriptions." *Journal of Philosophy* 86, no. 11 (1989): 601–7.

Crawley, Ashon T. *The Lonely Letters*. Durham, NC: Duke University Press, 2020.

da Silva, Denise Ferreira. "Poethical Readings/Intuiting the Political." Tramway, Glasgow, April 18, 2015. https://arika.org.uk/intuiting-politica/.

Foucault, Michel. *The Archaeology of Knowledge*. New York: Pantheon, 1982.

Foucault, Michel. *Discipline and Punish: The Birth of the Prison*. Translated by Alan Sheridan. New York: Vintage, 1995.

Foucault, Michel. *Language, Counter-memory, Practice: Selected Essays and Interviews*. Edited by Donald F. Bouchard and Sherry Simon. Ithaca, NY: Cornell University Press, 1980.

Foucault, Michel. *Wrong-Doing, Truth-Telling: The Function of Avowal in Justice*. Edited by Fabienne Brion and Bernard E. Harcourt. Chicago: University of Chicago Press, 2014.

Gonzalez, Maya Andrea. "Communization and the Abolition of Gender." *Anarchist Library*, 2011. https://theanarchistlibrary.org/library/maya-andrea-gonzalez -communization-and-the-abolition-of-gender.

Gossett, Reina. "Commencement Address at Hampshire College." May 17, 2016. http://www.reinagossett.com/commencement-address-hampshire-college/.

Hayward, Eva. "More Lessons from a Starfish: Prefixial Flesh and Transspeciated Selves." *Women's Studies Quarterly* 36, nos. 3–4 (2008): 64–85.

Moten, Fred. *The Universal Machine*. Durham, NC: Duke University Press, 2018.

Preciado, Paul B. *Testo Junkie: Sex, Drugs, and Biopolitics in the Pharmacopornographic Era*. Translated by Bruce Benderson. New York: Feminist Press, 2013.

Riley, Denise. *The Words of Selves: Identification, Solidarity, Irony*. Stanford, CA: Stanford University Press, 2000.

Sharpe, Christina. *In the Wake: On Blackness and Being*. Durham, NC: Duke University Press, 2016.

Spade, Dean. *Normal Life: Administrative Violence, Critical Trans Politics, and the Limits of Law*. Durham, NC: Duke University Press, 2015.

Stanley, Eric A. "Anti-trans Optics: Recognition, Opacity, and the Image of Force." *South Atlantic Quarterly* 116, no. 3 (2017): 612–20.

PART IV
ANTI-TRANS
POLITICS

JOANNA WUEST

ASSUAGING THE
ANXIOUS MATRIARCH

7

Social Conservatives, Radical Feminists,
and Dark Money against Trans Rights

> How wrong does something have to be for a Christian
> pro-family organization and a radical feminist organization
> to oppose it together? Privacy and safety matter.
> —AUTUMN LEVA, FAMILY POLICY ALLIANCE, "UNLIKELY
> ALLIES FOR PRIVACY AND SAFETY"

In a video advertisement opposing the Barack Obama administration's 2016 trans-inclusive Title IX reforms, the policy director of the Family Policy Alliance (FPA), Autumn Leva, posed the question outlined in this chapter's epigraph. Emboldened by the impending inauguration of Donald Trump, Leva announced an unlikely coalition of Christian conservatives and trans-exclusionary radical feminists (TERFs)—who have since come to style themselves as "gender-critical" feminists—united against the rapid expansion of transgender legal rights.[1] In the following years, this coalition and its allies in the Trump administration attempted to roll back nascent reforms in the courts, the federal bureaucracy, state legislatures, city councils, and local school districts. Their goal was and is to restrict the meaning of "sex" in antidiscrimination law to the category of "biological sex," a designation that constructs sex in the dyadic form, the feminine half of the gender binary.[2] It has since become common to see radical feminists such as the members of the TERF group Women's Liberation Front (WoLF) appear on Fox News talk shows and in the campaign materials of much larger conservative Christian foundations and political action committees denouncing trans rights.[3]

In some ways, there is little novel about this alliance. The present-day conservative-TERF partnership looks far less anomalous when situated in the longer history of women's rights and social conservative collaborations. Throughout the 1970s and 1980s, activists of varying ideological stripes pushed for victims' rights legislation that resulted in increased sentences for violent offenders and restrictions on the production and distribution of pornography.[4] In each of these instances, radical feminists teamed up with the newly formed Religious Right and conservative law enforcement advocates under the banner of protecting women and locking up male predators. Though some rightly caution against ignoring historical alliances among trans and feminist activists, these collaborations typify a persistent strain of anti-trans politics that is packaged as "pro-women."[5] Accordingly, these forces have advanced their joint projects with the rhetoric of women's rights, safety, privacy, and dignity.

Much like their forebearers, this new alliance pits cis women against the figure of a violent, masculine male perpetrator. In their messaging against bathroom access policies, opponents portray the threat to women as stemming from either trans women themselves or the specter of the male predator, the latter of which is portrayed as constantly lurking behind the doors of public restrooms to which trans advocates have handed him the keys.[6] In construing the enemy as phallic in nature, both TERFs and Christian conservatives reify the category of cis woman through both biology and the language of victimization, all the while eliding the reality of trans women's disproportionate vulnerability to the very violence they are accused of enacting. Some social conservatives have even adopted principles from feminist theory and activism as wide-ranging as women's agency and autonomy to antiracism. The Christian traditionalist group Alliance Defending Freedom (ADF), for instance, has invoked an explicitly antiracist feminist message—one construed in the form of an *antagonistic intersectionality* that pits Black cis women against trans women—in a recent federal case against inclusive school district policies.

This uncanny alliance is made possible in part by the congruencies between the two groups' philosophies of sex and gender that—while conflicting
at the level of ontology over whether "woman" is a purely natural kind or one
that draws from biology but has been rationalized to justify a social subordination to men—overlap in politically significant ways. For instance, both
conservatives and TERFs assert sex's biological reality at the level of reproductive organs and sex chromosomes; in doing so, they argue for an approach to
antidiscrimination law that matches this purported reality.[7] These disparate
groups also share a deep commitment to sex-panic tropes—the rapacious and
looming child predator, the libidinally driven transgender menace, the cis
woman and child as defenseless victims—that portray trans rights reforms as
an impossibility, a mere invitation to sexual marauding and social instability.[8]

These historical parallels and overlapping theories of sex's essence,
however, are not enough to explain the peculiar emergence of this cross-
ideological coalition. It is not clear at first why a massively well-funded array
of organizations like the FPA, the ADF, and the Heritage Foundation (together, their annual operating budgets total well over $100 million) would
bother working alongside small activist sects like WoLF, which as of 2018
functioned with under $50,000 annually, at least $15,000 of which came from
an ADF grant.[9] A deeper look reveals that *all* of these groups receive significant funding from billionaire-funded, right-wing, dark-money networks,
which seek to exploit fears of eroding gender norms to garner support for
various deregulatory political projects.[10] Since the 1970s, libertarian industri-
alists like Richard Scaife and Charles Koch have funded this brand of blue-
collar social conservatism. Organizations like the Concerned Women for
America and the Heritage Foundation were funded by right-wing donors
who sought to camouflage their class program with the visage of social tra-
ditionalism.[11] Today those same donors are financing the attack on trans
rights while simultaneously undermining everything from public education
to social services to the Affordable Care Act.[12]

This chapter explores how social conservative organizations have provided
the political muscle and money for campaigns against trans rights while
spokespersons for gender-critical or TERF ideologies have functioned as an
important piece of political theater. The argument begins by delineating the
construction of this coalition, its allies in government, and its "counterattack"
against what it perceives to be an attack on the very nature of sex and gender.
The chapter turns from there to the courts, where groups like the ADF have
attempted to remake antidiscrimination law to exclude gender identity from

statutory, bureaucratic, and constitutional protections. It examines, too, how the ADF selected a person of color (POC) cis woman called Alexis Lightcap as the face of its anti-trans campaign in the courts. In concluding, the chapter asks what a political economic analysis of this gendered reactionary politics might expose about these strange shifts in language and allies.

COALITION, CAMPAIGN, LEGAL TERRAIN: TRANS RIGHTS REFORM AND ITS OPPONENTS

From the moment he took office in 2017, Donald Trump created a fertile ground for anti-trans politics. His administration incessantly promoted the idea that, in order to protect (cis) women, the trans-inclusive bureaucratic policies, executive orders, and judicial opinions of the Obama era needed to be repealed, overturned, and replaced. Secretary of Education Betsy DeVos and Attorney General Jeff Sessions immediately began this work by revoking their departments' 2016 directives, which had encouraged states and school districts to implement restroom access policies for trans students and workers, reversing them by early 2017. The following year, the Department of Education began to reject complaints made to its civil rights office by trans students who had been barred from accessing the restroom or locker room that best matched their gender identity.[13] In May 2020, the Department of Education went on the offensive when it issued a letter threatening to withhold Title IX funding from states that allow trans women to compete in women's high school athletics.[14]

On the healthcare front, a leaked memo from the Department of Health and Human Services (HHS) in 2018 revealed the Trump administration's plans to impose a strict biological definition of sex to exclude trans people, and in the subsequent year the administration proposed stripping gender-identity language from the Affordable Care Act's antidiscrimination provisions.[15] A version of the 2018 HHS rule was adopted in June 2020. At the state level, a new crop of anti-trans healthcare laws aimed at banning gender-affirming care for minors has sprouted in state legislatures and governorships. As of July 2023, twenty-one states have imposed such bans.[16]

Admittedly, social conservatives have not always been effective in their anti-trans agenda even when the conditions for victory appear favorable. This is evinced most strikingly in Trump-appointee Justice Neil Gorsuch's central role in the Supreme Court case *Bostock v. Clayton County* (2020), in which the majority ruled in favor of a trans plaintiff alleging that the provision against sex discrimination in Title VII protected her from workplace discrimination.[17] Though trans advocates claimed a decisive victory in that case, the Trump administration and its allies doubled down on opposition by promoting a Department of Housing and Urban Development (HUD) rule change that would restrict access to women's homeless shelters on the basis of biological sex.[18]

This institutional backdrop provides some context for how and why emergent coalitions and campaigns of interest groups and social movement forces opposed to trans rights have come to cloak themselves in the rhetoric of women's equality, safety, and dignity. Take, for example, the Hands across the Aisle Coalition (HATAC), an organization that styles itself as a bipartisan, ideologically ecumenical group of women united in defense of traditional conceptions of sex and gender.[19] As its website explains, its members include "women from across the political spectrum [who] have come together to challenge the notion that gender is the same as sex." Working against internal divisions for the common goal of curbing trans rights expansions, the group of "radical feminists, lesbians, Christians and conservatives" has vowed to defend its "hard-won civil rights" against sex discrimination from "erasure." Its leadership includes those of wide-ranging perspectives, from lesbian rights advocate Miriam Ben-Shalom, who fought against the federal government's exclusionary military practices in the 1980s and 1990s, to members of the Women's Liberation Front and the FPA. Ben-Shalom's participation in this coalition is less an indication of a late-life rightward turn than it is exemplary of just how contingent the relationships between trans-inclusive gender-equality campaigns and more traditional women's and LGB-equality projects truly are.

What brings these disparate activists and nonprofit leaders together is a shared project of, according to the HATAC website, "reclaim[ing] the definition of sex as a binary concept that refers to one's biological status as male or female" and a rejection of an ideology that "reduces women to nothing more than body parts." The group holds a common belief that there is some essence to womanhood that allows for the construction of a coherent biological category. In another section of its website titled "Gender Identity Harms Women," HATAC spells out this theory that the category of woman is distinct (and untraversable) from its male opposite. For the radical feminists in its ranks, this means perceiving the gender/sex distinction as one that has overlain a socially constructed notion of gender as applied to those persons with certain reproductive capacities.[20] For the Christians, *man* and *woman* are rendered distinct entities according to natural law and the biblical tradition.

As HATAC explains, "Psychology (feelings) cannot change your ontology (being)."[21] Though they begin from disparate premises and philosophical commitments, these logics converge at the notion of a true female essence, one that is most readily discernible at the level of an immutable biology.

As one of its founding acts against the culture of "gender identity ideology," HATAC penned a letter to HUD Secretary Benjamin Carson to protest another Obama administration–era act of gender reform. In 2016, HUD directed beneficiaries of federal funding such as women's homelessness and domestic violence shelters to serve trans women. As a matter of protecting victims' safety and privacy from "the risks of violence faced by women housed with transgender-identified males" (that is, trans women), HATAC members called for Carson to repeal this directive. In a demonstration of its deep bench of coalition partners, HATAC had its memo signed by representatives of Concerned Women of America, over a dozen FPA and Family Council state chapters, the Texas Eagle Forum, and the American College of Pediatricians (a small conservative medical community whose name erroneously implies a connection with the larger and much more prestigious American Academy of Pediatrics). Beyond the HUD letter, groups like the Heritage Foundation, a titan of modern conservativism, have also hosted panels with HATAC members.

In an era of feminist backlash to Trump's misogyny and new energy to resist sexual assault stemming from the #MeToo phenomenon in which slogans like "Believe All Women" have become ubiquitous, social conservatives and TERFs have branded their own project as one that exalts women's voices and agency. Founded in 2016 during the North Carolina HB2 bathroom bill saga, the FPA's "Ask Me First" campaign encouraged women to voice their discontent with policies that "allow men to enter women's spaces," reforms that the FPA characterized as fundamentally "anti-women." Unlike HATAC, Ask Me First's opposition rested not only in a theory of essence but also in a normative appeal to the democratic voice of women and their representation in legislatures and executives. Ask Me First questioned, for instance, the democratic commitment to trans rights proponents in public office whom they accuse of not being "interested in talking with us—the women who will be most impacted by these rules—to learn how we feel about [them]." Though liberal feminist commentators have worked to denounce these and other attempts to keep the "believe women" trope from expanding beyond its own preferred ideological interpretation, the social conservative message has proliferated in these and related operations.[22] The latter has now joined a constellation of similar sex-panic concerns on the right, ranging from Senator Josh Hawley's war against sex trafficking and the porn industry to the QAnon conspiracy-driven crusade against an imagined globalist child-sex ring.[23]

In a series of Ask Me First video advertisements, the FPA told the stories of cis female student athletes, radical feminists, and victims of male-perpetrated violence, all of whom protested not having been "asked first" about the presence of trans girls and women in spaces that they felt that cis girls and women ought to have exclusive right to occupy. In one segment, an Alaskan student athlete spoke on the unfairness of being forced to compete against "biological males" without having a say in the matter.[24] Since this early debate over sex and sports in Alaska, the fight over what constitutes fair competition has spread across conservative states and even to the US House of Representatives. In March 2020, Idaho became the first state to pass one of these laws, titled the Fairness in Women's Sports Act, which resembles those in other states with titles such as Save Women's Sports (the original title of the Idaho legislation). This law was promoted by legislators and a governor who expressed concern with "athletes who were identified as boys on their birth certificates but now identify as female and wish to compete as such."[25]

Additionally, the Ask Me First campaign incorporated perspectives from WoLF. In a feature titled "Unlikely Allies for Privacy and Safety," WoLF's board chair and former American Civil Liberties Union (ACLU) attorney Kara Dansky explained that "on certain issues like gender identity, pornography, and prostitution, WoLF finds that the left has pretty much sold out women."[26] In her own Ask Me First interview, she described the "bathroom agenda" as going beyond restroom politics and would spell the end of sex-segregated facilities in general. Dansky explained that her organization had turned to alliances with Christian conservatives because traditional liberal women's rights organizations and trans rights proponents in government had ceased to represent women's interests. As a whole, these video ads laid the victim narrative on thick with dramatically dour mood-setting music and heartfelt testimonials, all of which served to shore up fear and resentment against alleged instances of male trespassing on women's turf.

The FPA's Ask Me First project and others like it have provided the battle cries for opponents of trans rights expansions. They used these videos and messages in legislative and ballot referenda campaigns in fights to roll back antidiscrimination policies in cities and states across the United States. In one early attempt, the FPA's Alaskan state chapter instigated a ballot referendum in 2018 to repeal an Anchorage antidiscrimination ordinance passed three

years before. Alaska Family Action's "Protect Our Privacy" project emphasized the safety, privacy, and dignity of women and children who were framed
as both survivors and future victims of predatory violence. Most strikingly,
the organization released an advertisement featuring a POC trans woman
making the case against the trans rights ordinance. In her statement, she im-
plored that policy makers heed the concerns and "boundaries" of cis women.[27]
Ironically—tragically—the boundary erected here was one between cis and
trans women, the former defined as real and the latter as an open invitation to
the potential of male violence (whether that violence be attributed to creep-
ing male predators or trans women themselves).

Upon losing the ballot referenda in Alaska, a larger coalition, including
the ADF, Focus on the Family, and the Family Research Council, attempted
the first statewide repeal of an antidiscrimination ordinance in Massachusetts. "Keep MA Safe," as its proponents styled their joint efforts, ran a repeal
campaign that highlighted the same slew of issues that defined the Alaska
one. Though conversations about TERF ideology in the United States generally point to the United Kingdom when making transnational linkages
and comparisons, the Keep MA Safe campaign promoted the work of a geo-
graphically closer set of allies in Canada. In a link to a "Violence Database"
curated by the group WOMAN Means Something, the Keep MA Safe website
showcased a comparative take on the notion that the category "woman" indicates some essential and stable content, which cannot be traversed through
the logic of gender identity. Despite the much larger coalition assembled for
the MA fight, the ballot referenda campaign here failed as well, prompting
statements from the various organizations about the necessity of pursuing
future work to protect the privacy and dignity of women.[28]

Undeterred by these early losses, the social conservative-TERF alliance has
marched on to new legislative terrains. In the winter of 2019 and spring of
2020, these groups spurred GOP lawmakers to introduce bans on physicians
from providing gender-affirmative medical treatment to minors.[29] In at least
seventeen states during this period, legislators considered bills promoted by
WoLF, the ADF, and other social conservative organizations. At the site of
one of these first legislative showdowns in South Dakota, WoLF representatives argued that it was incumbent on state governments to help children
"survive girlhood" and to resist the "new misogyny" latent in gender-identity
ideology.[30] At a Heritage Foundation event, spokespersons from these
organizations declared that such medical interventions invited "unwanted
sexualization" by introducing children en masse to concepts like sexual ori-

entation and gender dysphoria in education curricula. From 2021 onward, these bills have become increasingly widespread. In 2022, an astounding 238 bills that either banned trans girls from sports or refused healthcare to trans youth were filed in state legislatures.[31] By the summer of 2023, such laws had become so common that three in ten trans or gender-expansive minors were legally prohibited from seeking gender-affirming medical care.[32]

REMAKING FEMINIST JURISPRUDENCE
AND ANTIDISCRIMINATION LAW

Over the past decade, Christian conservative legal organizations have begun to retool right-to-privacy legal arguments against bathroom access policies, laws, and judicial rulings.[33] Though privacy has been celebrated by some liberal feminists and largely condemned by social conservatives since the days of *Roe v. Wade* (1973), a number of organizations, including the ADF, the Family Research Council, the Liberty Counsel, and the Heritage Foundation, have seized on the notion that privacy might roll back recent trans rights victories. In an early example of one of these cases, the Pacific Justice Institute filed suit in 2013 against a trans-inclusive Colorado public school district for allegedly "elevating the rights of one self-proclaimed transgender student while minimizing the privacy rights of all the biologically female students."[34] Since then, numerous other conservative groups have adopted this litigation strategy in attempts to invert the privacy ideal in everything from feminist constitutional jurisprudence to civil rights statutory law.

The turn to the courts and privacy claims represents two concurrent trends that characterize the social conservative legal agenda in both its more short-term tactical maneuvering as well as its long-term vision for the law. First, the pivot to the courts has sometimes occurred after incurring a loss before a legislature or in a ballot referenda campaign; taking a page out of the minority rights legal advocacy book, these litigants have learned that if you cannot win democratically, you might claim victory via judicial decree. Upon losing both an Anchorage, Alaska, city council vote against a gender identity–themed antidiscrimination ordinance and then again in the statewide attempt to repeal such laws, the ADF turned to the courts to beat back the reform on a new front.[35] In that case, the ADF represented Downtown Hope Center, a faith-based nonprofit women's shelter run by Christian conservatives that had barred trans women from attaining their services against the orders of the Anchorage Equal Rights Commission. The ADF invoked the

Alaskan state constitution's right-to-privacy provision as a means of protecting women from being forced "to change, sleep alongside, and interact with men in intimate settings," again propping their argument on the claim that trans women are men. Though the ADF has failed repeatedly to convince a judge of this position, it did secure an initial victory for Downtown Hope Center in 2021 based on the Supreme Court's anti-LGBTQ+ ruling in *Fulton v. City of Philadelphia* (2021).[36]

Second, these right-to-privacy legal challenges are constitutive of the right-wing's decades-long scheme to install conservative ideologues in the judiciary.[37] After 2017, the Trump administration and GOP Senate Majority Leader Mitch McConnell accelerated this appointment strategy; they were successful in placing a sizable new cohort of young conservatives eager to remake the law in their own image.[38] Emboldened by this influx of ideological allies, social conservative litigators and firms have leveraged the principle of privacy in attempts to shape both the interpretation of statutory civil rights law and constitutional law. For an instance of the former, the ADF and others have argued that Title IX's guarantee of gender equity requires sex-segregated bathroom and locker-room facilities to protect each cis student's "partially clothed body" from the gaze of trans students. Additionally, in positing that there is some fundamental liberty claim to privacy inherent in the Constitution, the ADF and others have now begun to argue that the nation's highest governing principles might allow for—or perhaps even *require*—such discrimination on the basis of gender identity.

The ADF has taken the lead in the most high-profile cases that involve this broader attempt to reshape case law. The most prominent of these cases began in 2016 with Boyertown Area School District's adoption of a trans-inclusive bathroom access policy. The policy, which was implemented in accordance with the US Departments of Education and Justice Title IX guidance issued earlier that year, was quickly challenged by the ADF. Assembling a group of four cis male and female students in a case that made its way up to the US Supreme Court's long list of cases to consider for its 2019 term, the ADF claimed that the new policy violated each plaintiff's "constitutionally protected privacy interest in his or her partially clothed body."

In the *Boyertown* case, the ADF claimed that—contrary to the Obama administration's interpretation—Title IX and the US Constitution required a traditional sex-segregation scheme and that the rights of trans students needed to be balanced with the privacy rights of their cis classmates; for instance, in the event that a trans student did feel comfortable using a restroom or locker room that matched their assigned-at-birth sex, a single-stall room would be made available to them. Citing from Justice Ruth Bader Ginsburg's opinion in the 1996 landmark sex-discrimination case *United States v. Virginia*, the ADF seized yet another staple of feminist doctrine for anti-trans ends. In drawing from this case, which dealt with systemic sex discrimination in Virginia's military academy admission policies, ADF attorneys asserted that "privacy needs driven by the real physiological, reproductively grounded differences between males and females have been recognized and protected by myriad courts, including the United States Supreme Court."[39] Thus, while the ADF conceded that *some* accommodations might be made for trans students, their wholesale integration into sex-segregated spaces was deemed anathema to law. Together, this statutory right, combined with claims about a constitutional right to bodily privacy, allowed the ADF to frame its project as one that balances competing rights claims—cis women's privacy versus trans rights—rather than one of outright animus against a gender minority population.[40]

WoLF made a similar series of legal arguments in support of the ADF's case. In one brief, WoLF attorneys argued that the Obama administration's interpretation of "sex" signaled "a truly fundamental shift in American law and policy that strips women of their Constitutional right to privacy, threatens their physical safety, undercuts the means by which women can achieve educational equality, and ultimately works to erase women and girls under the law." WoLF too condemned the opposition's arguments as laden with an "old-fashioned sexism," which reifies what it means to be truly a man or woman, cis or trans. In support of this claim, WoLF pointed to arguments made by those like the American Civil Liberties Union, the National Center for Lesbian Rights, and other trans advocates who couched their claims for rights expansion in studies showing that trans children are "born that way" in that they possess some neuroanatomical or other physiological difference that renders them the "opposite" biological sex. The radical feminists here denounced such definitions of sex as reinforcing ideas about the innately nurturing and maternal qualities of biological women.[41] These and a host of other arguments demonstrate WoLF's attempt to position itself as the true proponent of gender equality against those trans advocates who were so quick to cast aside the rights of all others—women particularly—in their demands for accommodation.

The ADF has also reformulated the principle of antiracism in its plaintiff selection and parallel media strategy. Alexis Lightcap, an African American cis female student, became the face of the ADF's privacy litigation against Boyertown School District. Though Lightcap was only one of several other plaintiffs, she became the face of the litigation by writing opinion pieces in national and regional newspapers and by making speeches on the steps of federal courthouses. Across all these venues, Lightcap framed her opposition to her high school's bathroom policy in terms of her own experience with racial discrimination and the hardships she endured as a woman of color. In a November 2018 editorial for *USA Today*, Lightcap wrote, "As a black girl who grew up in a predominantly white neighborhood, I know what it's like to be treated unfairly, picked on, and made fun of by insensitive people. I won't accept anyone being bullied or discriminated against—and that absolutely includes my classmates experiencing gender dysphoria. They deserve our love and support. Even so, my privacy shouldn't depend on what others believe about their own gender. . . . My reason for suing was to restore the bodily privacy we used to enjoy in locker rooms and restrooms on campus."[42] In this statement and in subsequent interviews, Lightcap deployed the logic of positionality as a shield against charges of discrimination. How could Lightcap be accused, after all, of not understanding prejudice considering her own experiences? Though the litigation itself was funded and directed by a movement generally lambasted for its white racial character and its male-skewed perspective, the ADF's choice of plaintiff made the *Boyertown* case about balancing the rights of many different and diverse students; in this mode, the case could be framed as one about just accommodations rather than outright discrimination or unconstitutional animus. The ADF's racially conscious social conservativism thus took on an antagonistic intersectional form, one that leveraged the racial and gender experiences of a cis woman to cast the categories and interests of trans women and women of color as discrete and divergent.

Despite its pretentions to pluralism, Lightcap's portrayal of her own experience of privacy violation is undergirded by a logic that undermines trans women's claim to their gender identity. In a video produced by ADF to accompany its litigation, Lightcap recounted seeing a man in her high school bathroom. Narrating this moment of alleged trauma, she described that upon seeing "a reflection of a man [in the mirror] . . . my whole body went into immediate shock.[43] There is an ambiguity in this testimony about whom exactly Lightcap saw in that restroom. Though she often refers to the clinical diagnosis of gender dysphoria when referring to trans classmates, it is impossible to discern whether this story recalls a meeting with an opportunistic male student exploiting the reform policy or if it demonstrates Lightcap's perception that trans women are men suffering from a psychological malady, which affords them some form of accommodation but does not allow them access to the women's restroom. Whereas the former meaning displaces trans women entirely by invoking the looming threat of would-be male predators, the latter denies the possibility that trans women are "real" at least in a biological respect (and, by extension, a civil rights distinction).

There is a parallel here between Lightcap's portrayal of her trans classmates and the media and trial depictions of Latasha King, a trans feminine POC who was murdered by a fellow student in Oxnard, California, in 2008. As retold in an account of the trial of King's killer, Gayle Salamon illustrates how a young Black trans person's identity was depicted as inherently suspect and dangerous. Salamon shows, for instance, how behaviors as innocuous as King's gait were construed as sexualized provocations. Whereas gender identity is anything but certain or stable in this telling, what is clear is that King's gendered expressions represented a threat, an act of aggression, in the eyes of many students and teachers.[44]

Perhaps the ambiguity in Lightcap's narrative is intentional as such uncertainty and anxiety about gender is central to the panic around bathroom access reforms. Lightcap's recognition of the medical classification of gender dysphoria then might not be taken so much as a recognition of *identity* per se, but instead as a prefatory clause—a cover—that abstracts away the conundrum of trans personhood while instantiating the imagined threat of the predacious male figure as the more concrete specified referent. Trans identity in this mode is most "real" in its threat; it is at once impossible to register and to define (is it an affliction? a diseased state of being but a subjectivity in need of some accommodation nonetheless?) while also constituting a very real and material menace. Whatever Lightcap and the ADF presume trans people to *be*, what is clear is that they construe trans rights as an undue abrogation of cis students' privacy rights.

Though the Supreme Court denied an appeal in the *Boyertown* case in the spring of 2019, the ADF and its allies have continued their fight to imbue privacy with anti-trans sentiment. That following October, Lightcap spoke in favor of the ADF's Title VII employment-discrimination case—now known as *Bostock v. Clayton County*—in support of the funeral home that fired a transgender employee. Making the case against a broad interpretation of sex-based civil rights law, Lightcap condemned those protesting her efforts to "speak up for women" and her prayers that "the laws will continue to protect and respect women."[45]

Others joined Lightcap in subsequent months, demanding that the Trump administration step in if the courts would not. Trump's 2017 repeal of the Obama Title IX directive was not enough for those like Doreen Day, the senior director of government relations for Concerned Women for America, who called for stronger efforts to rein in school districts like Boyertown. In a piece for the *Daily Signal*, Day proclaimed that "it's time for the Trump administration to step up and do its job enforcing Title IX. Girls will either be protected as female," she cautioned, "or continue to face greater risk and discrimination."[46] Whether the call has come from religious litigators, social conservative lobbyists, or radical feminists, the message has been the same: cis women deserve their privacy, dignity, and safety from those very reforms that might secure those same rights for trans women.

THE POLITICAL ECONOMY OF GENDER REACTION

What is to be done in an era of increasing appropriation and obfuscation of feminist principles and antidiscrimination legal doctrine in the service of constricting trans rights? One could, of course, deride the conservative, cis-centric agenda as a cynical co-optation and assert instead that one or another trans-inclusive feminist ideologies represents the true or at least *truer* nature of these categories and commitments. One too might draw a throughline between these and earlier moments in American history when terms like *privacy* and *safety* were invoked with chivalrous overtones to keep women restricted to the domestic sphere.[47] The parallels are indeed striking. Restrictions on the rights of trans women and others who live outside the gender binary lead such nonconformists out of public life, relegated to either the closet or the confines of their homes (and, in the case of those turned away from women's shelters, the streets).

These arguments and allusions may well be part of an effective progressive strategy for reclaiming such language. But on their own, they fail to offer—and may even foreclose—reflections on how we have arrived at this moment of unlikely alliances and rallying cries.[48] We might instead adopt a political economic outlook to see what these strange bedfellows and shared slogans reveal about the broader scene of feminist politics.

In the twenty-first century, gender ideology plays a peculiar role—though in many ways a still utterly constitutive one—in culture, law, and the labor market.[49] Feminist political projects have benefited women in an upper class–skewed segment of the population, while gendered modes of work and inequality persist in low-paid care and service industries that are populated with working-class, poor, and migrant labor. Transgender rights have also proven assimilable into this class politics as evinced by Fortune 500 corporate boycotts over discriminatory state legislation. Nonprofits like Freedom for All Americans now organize corporations in fights that aim to unite people of faith to business leaders to conservatives to women's safety advocates in the pursuit of trans rights. Notably, this advocacy also rearticulates the category of womanhood, swallowing up trans personhood into a relatively undifferentiated and declassed whole; when it does identify intra-category inequalities, it does not tend to interrogate how its base material commitments—that is, generating profits or garnering high-dollar campaign donations—might foreclose the possibility of ever ameliorating them.[50]

The 2020–2023 state legislative cycles have illuminated the utter weakness of business-backed advocacy and the broader instability of existing trans rights victories.[51] In fomenting an emboldened reaction to progressive gender norms, social conservatives and their dark-money donors persist in taking the form of the anxious matriarch, purportedly protecting mothers and children all in the service of their own class agenda. Thus, the performance of a gendered pluralism defines today's embittered, protracted conflicts. At present, almost no one is "against" women's autonomy, agency, or diversity. Rather, we are all "women's rights" advocates now.

To break the cycle of unstable liberal progress and conservative reaction, we might better attend to the political economic source of these campaigns against transgender rights. Egalitarians neglect the foundations of right-wing backlash at their own peril, given that present incursions on civil rights have accompanied an all-out war against the ideals of democracy and equality. The ongoing assault on trans life may be only the beginning of what terrible reaction might fester in the ruins of democratic life.

NOTES

1   Taylor, Lewis, and Haider-Markel, *Remarkable Rise of Transgender Rights.*
2   Wuest, *Born This Way.*
3   Burns, "Rise of Anti-trans 'Radical' Feminists, Explained."
4   Gottschalk, *Prison and the Gallows*; Wypijewski, *What We Don't Talk About.*
5   Heaney, "Women-Identified Women."
6   Schilt and Westbrook, "Bathroom Battlegrounds and Penis Panics."

7   Karkazis, "Misuses of Biological Sex," 1898.

8   Lancaster, *Sex Panic and the Punitive State*.

9   Baker, "Fake 'Radical Feminist' Group Actually Paid Political Front."

10 Wuest, "Dead End of Corporate Activism."

11 Phillips-Fein, *Invisible Hands*; Mayer; *Dark Money*.

12 Center for Media and Democracy, "Contributions of the Bradley Foundation"; Kotch, "ALEC Leaders Boast about Anti-abortion, Anti-trans Bills."

13 Balingit, "Education Department No Longer Investigating."

14 Eaton-Robb, "Transgender Sports Inclusion Violates Others' Rights."

15 Green, Benner, and Pear, "'Transgender' Could Be Defined Out of Existence; Keith, "HHS Proposes to Strip Gender Identity."

16 Freedom for All Americans, "Legislative Tracker."

17 *Bostock v. Clayton County*, 590 U.S. ___; US Department of Health and Human Services, "HHS Finalizes Rule on Section 1557."

18 Cunningham, "HUD to Change Transgender Rules."

19 Barthélemy, "Christian Right Tips to Fight Transgender Rights."

20 Jeffreys, *Gender Hurts*.

21 Though Ben-Shalom has cited her own Jewish faith as a constitutive element of her political activism, there is no reference to a perspective on gender and sex extending from any religious tradition besides Christianity.

22 Faludi, "'Believe All Women' Is a Right-Wing Trap."

23 I owe this insight to Briana Last, who has kept a close eye on the connections between those like *New York Times* columnist Nicholas Kristof's own misguided attempts to rein in sex trafficking and Hawley's cynical deployment of related tropes.

24 Family Policy Alliance, "Ask Me First about Fairness."

25 Minsberg, "'Boys Are Boys and Girls Are Girls.'" See also Save Women's Sports, accessed June 8, 2020, https://savewomenssports.com/state-legislation.

26 Ask Me First, "Ask Me First."

27 Alliance Defending Freedom, "Unintended Victims of Bathroom Bills."

28 Salsberg, "Massachusetts Voters Uphold Transgender Rights Law."

29 Bosman and Smith, "Doctors Could Face Criminal Charges."

30 Schmidt, "Conservatives Find Unlikely Ally."

31 Lavietes and Ramos, "Nearly 240 Anti-LGBTQ Bills Filed in 2022."

32 Human Rights Campaign, "Map: Attacks on Gender Affirming Care by State."

33 Adler, *Gay Priori*, 93. For a more complete legal history of right-to-privacy and gender-equality claims, see Wuest, "Conservative Right to Privacy."

34 Ford, "Anti-LGBT Group Admits It Invented Story."

35 Kelly, "Discrimination Complaint against Downtown Anchorage Women's Shelter Opens Up Political Front."

36 Alliance Defending Freedom, "Court Ruling Protects Anchorage Faith-Based Women's Shelter."

37 Hollis-Brusky, *Ideas with Consequences*.

38 Montgomery, "Conquers of the Courts."
39 Wardlow, "Re: Student Privacy in Locker Rooms."
40 According to *Romer v. Evans*, 517 US 620 (1996), a reform based in outright animus toward such a minority group would likely be deemed unconstitutional.
41 Fine, *Delusions of Gender*; Jordan-Young, *Brain Storm*; Richardson, *Sex Itself*.
42 Lightcap, "My High School's Transgender Bathroom Policies."
43 Alliance Defending Freedom, "Doe v. Boyertown Area School District."
44 Salamon, *Life and Death of Latasha King*, 30.
45 Lightcap, "Protestors Won't Silence Me."
46 Day, "Only Trump Has the Power."
47 Allen and Mack, "How Privacy Got Its Gender."
48 Schreiber, *Righting Feminism*.
49 Brenner and Ramas, "Rethinking Women's Oppression"; Watkins, "Which Feminisms?"
50 Wuest, "Sanders Campaign Goes beyond Intersectionality."
51 Wuest, "State, Economy, and LGBTQ+ Civil Rights."

BIBLIOGRAPHY

Adler, Libby. *Gay Priori: A Queer Critical Legal Studies Approach to Law Reform*. Durham, NC: Duke University Press, 2018.
Allen, Anita L., and Erin Mack. "How Privacy Got Its Gender." *Northern Illinois University Law Review* 10 (1991): 441–78.
Alliance Defending Freedom. "Court Ruling Protects Anchorage Faith-Based Women's Shelter." December 21, 2021. https://adflegal.org/press-release/court -ruling-protects-anchorage-faith-based-womens-shelter.
Alliance Defending Freedom. "Doe v. Boyertown Area School District." Accessed June 8, 2020. http://www.adfmedia.org/News/PRDetail/10239.
Alliance Defending Freedom. "Downtown Hope Center v. Municipality of An- chorage, et al." *ADF Legal*. Accessed June 8, 2020. https://adflegal.blob.core .windows.net/mainsite-new/docs/default-source/documents/resources/media -resources/cases/the-downtown-soup-kitchen-d-b-a-downtown-hope-center-v. -municipality-of-anchorage/hope-center-v-anchorage—one-page-summary.pdf ?sfvrsn=fa9b07be_6.
Alliance Defending Freedom. "Physical Privacy Policy." Accessed May 28, 2020. https://adflegal.blob.core.windows.net/web-content-dev/docs/default-source /documents/resources/campaign-resources/marriage/safe-bathrooms/local -student-physical-privacy-policy.pdf?sfvrsn=2/.
Alliance Defending Freedom. "The Unintended Victims of Bathroom Bills and Locker Room Policies." Accessed June 3, 2020. https://yesprop1.com/videos/.
Alliance Defending Freedom. "US Supreme Court Won't Weigh In on Whether Schools Can Allow Violation of Students' Bodily Privacy." Accessed June 8, 2020. http://www.adfmedia.org/News/PRDetail/?CID=101258.

Ask Me First. "Ask Me First." Accessed June 1, 2020. http://www.askmefirstplease.com
/?fbclid=IwAR2fA_kJEdcGC15etSLwgHOAsi8PvjgPHZoHVHecNxi2Qb69F
EdBhnjS6oU#home.

Baker, Rani. "Fake 'Radical Feminist' Group Actually Paid Political Front for Anti-
LGBT James Dobson Organization." *Trans Advocate*, April 10, 2017. https://
www.transadvocate.com/fake-radical-feminist-group-actually-paid-political
-front-for-anti-lgbt-james-dobson-organization_n_20207.htm.

Balingit, Moriah. "Education Department No Longer Investigating Transgender
Bathroom Complaints." *Washington Post*, February 12, 2018. https://www.
washingtonpost.com/news/education/wp/2018/02/12/education-department
-will-no-longer-investigate-transgender-bathroom-complaints/.

Barthélemy, Hélène. "Christian Right Tips to Fight Transgender Rights: Separate
the T from the LGB." *Southern Poverty Law Center*, October 23, 2017. https://
www.splcenter.org/hatewatch/2017/10/23/christian-right-tips-fight-transgender
-rights-separate-t-lgb.

Ben-Shalmon, Miriam. "Audio." Library of Congress, October 26, 2011. https://
memory.loc.gov/diglib/vhp-stories/loc.natlib.afc2001001.43276/.

Bosman, Julia, and Mitch Smith. "Doctors Could Face Criminal Charges
for Treating Transgender Teens." *New York Times*, January 27, 2020.
https://www.nytimes.com/2020/01/27/us/south-dakota transgender
.html?fbclid=IwARoNtwBpHXFbp9gkM6cuf-hnT_1WfNsFDmHxkS
-Z6JjfgaegBxRA5kjgVhE.

Brenner, Johanna, and Maria Ramas. "Rethinking Women's Oppression." *New Left
Review* 144 (1984): 33–71.

Burns, Katelyn. "The Rise of Anti-trans 'Radical' Feminists, Explained." *Vox*, September 5, 2019. https://www.vox.com/identities/2019/9/5/20840101/terfs-radical
-feminists-gender-critical.

California Family Council. "AB 2943." Accessed May 28, 2020. https://californiafamily
.org/oppose-ca-ab-2943-ab-1779-and-ab-2119-reference-materials/.

Center for Media and Democracy. "Contributions of the Bradley Foundation."
Accessed May 11, 2022. https://www.sourcewatch.org/index.php/Contributions
_of_the_Bradley_Foundation.

Complaint for Attorneys for Plaintiff. *Downtown Soup Kitchen d/b/a Downtown Hope
Center v. Municipality of Anchorage, Anchorage Equal Rights Commission, and
Pamela Basler* (No. 3:18-cv-00190-SLG). 406 F. Supp. 3d 776 (D. Alaska 2019).

Cunningham, Paige Winfield. "HUD to Change Transgender Rules for Single-
Sex Homeless Shelters." *Washington Post*, June 14, 2020. https://www
.washingtonpost.com/politics/hud-to-change-transgender-rules-for-single-sex
-homeless-shelters/2020/06/12/d47a5744-ad03-11ea-9063-e69bd6520940
_story.html.

Day, Doreen. "Only Trump Has the Power to Keep Men Out of Girls' Restrooms."
Daily Signal, July 5, 2019. https://dailycaller.com/2019/07/05/denny-trump
-restrooms/.

Eaton-Robb, Pat. "Transgender Sports Inclusion Violates Others' Rights." Associated Press, May 28, 2020. https://apnews.com/5c1d9682fb92ed9c277c7e139bdab9ed.

Faludi, Susan. "'Believe All Women' Is a Right-Wing Trap." *New York Times*, May 18, 2020. https://www.nytimes.com/2020/05/18/opinion/tara-reade-believe-all -women.html.

Family Policy Alliance. "Ask Me First about Fairness: Tanner." August 2, 2017. https:// www.youtube.com/watch?v=Jk_CKFkm8sI.

Family Policy Alliance. "Unlikely Allies for Privacy and Safety." July 9, 2017. https:// www.youtube.com/watch?v=84zEJS_8KD4.

Fine, Cordelia. *Delusions of Gender: How Our Minds, Society, and Neurosexism Create Difference*. New York: W. W. Norton, 2010.

Ford, Zach. "Anti-LGBT Group Admits It Invented Story about Transgender Student Harassing Classmates." *Think Progress*, October 17, 2013. https://thinkprogress .org/anti-lgbt-group-admits-it-invented-story-about-transgender-student -harassing-classmates-updated-d66f40c01517/.

Freedom for All Americans. "Legislative Tracker." Accessed June 1, 2020. https://www. freedomforallamericans.org/2020-legislative-tracker/2020-student-athletics/.

G. G. v. Gloucester County School Board, No. 15-2056 (4th Cir. 2016).

Gloucester County School Board v. G. G., No. 16-273 (vacated and remanded 4th Cir. 2017).

Gottschalk, Marie. *The Prison and the Gallows: The Politics of Mass Incarceration in America*. Cambridge: Cambridge University Press, 2004.

Green, Erica, Katie Benner, and Robert Pear. "'Transgender' Could Be Defined Out of Existence under Trump Administration." *New York Times*, October 21, 2018. https://www.nytimes.com/2018/10/21/us/politics/transgender-trump -administration-sex-definition.html.

Hands across the Aisle Coalition. "Gender Ideology Harms Women." Accessed June 8, 2020. https://handsacrosstheaislewomen.com/gender-ideology-harms -women/.

Hands across the Aisle Coalition. "Home." Accessed June 8, 2020. https:// handsacrosstheaislewomen.com/home/.

Hands across the Aisle Coalition. "Our Letter to HUD." Accessed June 8, 2020. https://handsacrosstheaislewomen.com/our-letter-to-hud/.

Heaney, Emma. "Women-Identified Women: Trans Women in 1970s Lesbian Feminist Organizing." *TSQ* 3 (2016): 137–45.

Heritage Foundation. "Biology Isn't Bigotry: Why Sex Matters in the Age of Gender Identity." February 16, 2017. https://www.heritage.org/marriage-and-family /event/biology-isnt-bigotry-why-sex-matters-the-age-gender-identity.

Heritage Foundation. "Summit on Protecting Children from Sexualization." October 9, 2019. https://www.heritage.org/marriage-and-family/event/biology-isnt -bigotry-why-sex-matters-the-age-gender-identity.

Hollis-Brusky, Amanda. *Ideas with Consequences: The Federalist Society and the Conservative Counterrevolution*. Oxford: Oxford University Press, 2015.

Human Rights Campaign. "Map: Attacks on Gender Affirming Care by State." July 25, 2023. https://www.hrc.org/resources/attacks-on-gender-affirming-care-by-state-map.

Jeffreys, Sheila. *Gender Hurts*. New York: Routledge, 2014.

Joel Doe et al. v. Boyertown Area School District, No. 17-3113 (US 2018, *cert denied*).

Jordan-Young, Rebecca. *Brain Storm: The Flaws in the Science of Sex Differences*. Cambridge, MA: Harvard University Press, 2011.

Karkazis, Katrina. "The Misuses of Biological Sex." *Lancet* 394 (2019): 1898–99.

Keep MA Safe. "Home." Accessed June 3, 2020. https://www.keepmasafe.org/.

Keith, Katie. "HHS Proposes to Strip Gender Identity, Language Access Protections from ACA Anti-discrimination Rule." *Health Affairs*, May 25, 2019. http://www.healthaffairs.org/do/10.1377/hblog20190525.831858/full/.

Kelly, Devin. "Anchorage Assembly Passes LGBT Rights Law." *Anchorage Daily News*, September 29, 2015. https://www.adn.com/anchorage/article/anchorage-assembly-debates-lgbt-rights-law/2015/09/30/.

Kelly, Devin. "Discrimination Complaint against Downtown Anchorage Women's Shelter Opens Up Political Front." *Anchorage Daily News*, March 14, 2018. https://www.adn.com/alaska-news/anchorage/2018/03/14/discrimination-complaint-against-downtown-anchorage-womens-shelter-opens-up-political-front//.

Kotch, Alex. "ALEC Leaders Boast about Anti-abortion, Anti-trans Bills." *Exposed by CMD*, October 4, 2021. https://www.exposedbycmd.org/2021/10/04/alec-leaders-boast-about-anti-abortion-anti-trans-bills/?eType=EmailBlastContent&eId=cf745228-ac07-4f00-8373-b43277121667.

Lancaster, Roger N. *Sex Panic and the Punitive State*. Berkeley: University of California Press, 2011.

Lancaster, Roger N. *The Trouble with Nature: Sex in Science and Popular Culture*. Berkeley: University of California Press, 2003.

Lavietes, Matt, and Elliott Ramos. "Nearly 240 Anti-LGBTQ Bills Filed in 2022 So Far, Most of Them Targeting Trans People." *NBC News*, March 20, 2022. https://www.nbcnews.com/nbc-out/out-politics-and-policy/nearly-240-anti-lgbtq-bills-filed-2022-far-targeting-trans-people-rcna20418.

Lightcap, Alexis. "My High School's Transgender Bathroom Policies Violate the Privacy of the Rest of Us." *USA Today*, November 29, 2018. https://www.usatoday.com/story/opinion/voices/2018/11/29/transgender-bathroom-debate-privacy-school-lawsuit-column/2123946002/.

Lightcap, Alexis. "Protestors Won't Silence Me on Transgender Issues." *Morning Call*, November 20, 2019. https://www.mcall.com/opinion/mc-opi-rights-to-privacy-dignity-20191120-egspgivuhzd2fogqgy27wz4qgq-story.html.

Mayer, Jane. *Dark Money: The Hidden History of the Billionaires behind the Rise of the Radical Right*. New York: Anchor, 2017.

Minsberg, Tayla. "'Boys Are Boys and Girls Are Girls': Idaho Is First State to Bar Some Transgender Athletes." *New York Times*, April 1, 2020. https://www.nytimes.com/2020/04/01/sports/transgender-idaho-ban-sports.html.

Montgomery, David. "Conquerors of the Courts." *Washington Post*, January 2, 2019. https://www.washingtonpost.com/news/magazine/wp/2019/01/02/feature /conquerors-of-the-courts/?noredirect=on&utm_term=.309ed171b7b4.

Pacific Justice Institute. "Update: Colo. School Story Sparks Backlash by LGBT Activists." October 17, 2013. https://www.pacificjustice.org/press-releases/update-colo -school-story-sparks-backlash-by-lgbt-activists.

Parker v. Hurley, No. 07-1528 (1st Circ., January 28, 2008).

Petitioners' Application to Extend Time to File Petition for *Writ of Certiorari. Joel Doe et al. v. Boyertown Area School District et al. and Pennsylvania Youth Congress Foundation* (No. 18-568) (submitted to Justice Samuel Alito, US Supreme Court).

Phillips-Fein, Kim. *Invisible Hands: The Businessmen's Crusade against the New Deal*. New York: W. W. Norton, 2010.

Protect Our Privacy. "Yes on Prop 1: Protect Our Privacy." Accessed June 3, 2020. https://yesprop1.com/.

Richardson, Sarah S. *Sex Itself: The Search for Male and Female in the Human Genome*. Chicago: University of Chicago Press, 2013.

Roe v. Wade, 410 US 113 (1973).

Salamon, Gayle. *The Life and Death of Latasha King: A Critical Phenomenology of Transphobia*. New York: New York University Press, 2018.

Salsberg, Bob. "Massachusetts Voters Uphold Transgender Rights Law." *Boston .com*, November 6, 2018. https://www.boston.com/news/politics/2018/11/06 /massachusetts-voters-uphold-transgender-rights-law.

Schilt, Kirstein, and Laurel Westbrook. "Bathroom Battlegrounds and Penis Panics." *Contexts*, August 20, 2015. https://contexts.org/articles/bathroom-battlegrounds -and-penis-panics/.

Schmidt, Samantha. "Conservatives Find Unlikely Ally in Fight against Transgender Rights: Radical Feminists." *Washington Post*, February 7, 2020. https://www. washingtonpost.com/dc-md-va/2020/02/07/radical-feminists-conservatives -transgender-rights/.

Schreiber, Ronnee. *Righting Feminism: Conservative Women and American Politics*. Oxford: Oxford University Press, 2008.

Southern Poverty Law Center. "American College of Pediatricians." Accessed June 8, 2020. https://www.splcenter.org/fighting-hate/extremist-files/group/american -college-pediatricians.

Taylor, Jami K., Daniel Clay Lewis, and Donald P. Haider-Markel. *The Remarkable Rise of Transgender Rights*. Ann Arbor: University of Michigan Press, 2018.

United States v. Virginia, 518 US 515 (1996).

US Department of Education. Memo, June 6, 2017. Accessed June 8, 2020. https:// assets.documentcloud.org/documents/3866816/OCR-Instructions-to-the-Field -Re-Transgender.pdf.

US Department of Health and Human Services. "HHS Finalizes Rule on Section 1557 Protecting Civil Rights in Healthcare, Restoring the Rule of Law, and Relieving

Americans of Billions in Excessive Costs." June 12, 2020. https://www.hhs.gov
/about/news/2020/06/12/hhs-finalizes-rule-section-1557-protecting-civil-rights
-healthcare.html.

US Departments of Justice and Education. "Dear Colleague Letter." February 22, 2017.
https://www2.ed.gov/about/offices/list/ocr/letters/colleague-201702-title-ix
.pdf/.

Wardlow, Douglas G., to Anoka-Hennepin School Board. "Re: Student Privacy in
Locker Rooms, Restrooms, and Overnight Accommodations." Southern Poverty
Law Center. Accessed March 15, 2017. https://www.splcenter.org/sites/default
/files/adf-ltr-anoka-hennepin-school-board.pdf.

Watkins, Susan. "Which Feminisms?" *New Left Review* 109 (2018): 5–76.

Welch v. Brown, 834 F.3d 1041 (9th Cir. 2016).

WOMAN Means Something. "Violence Database." Accessed June 4, 2020. http://
womanmeanssomething.com/violencedatabase/.

Women's Liberation Front. "Brief of *Amicus Curiae* Women's Liberation Front
in Support of Petitioners. No. 18-658, 18 December 2018." Accessed June 8,
2020. https://www.supremecourt.gov/DocketPDF/18/18-658/76683
/20181218150007157_37309%20pdf%20Chavez.pdf/.

Wuest, Joanna. *Born This Way: Science, Citizenship, and Inequality in the American
LGBTQ+ Movement*. Chicago: University of Chicago Press, 2023.

Wuest, Joanna. "A Conservative Right to Privacy: Legal, Ideological, and Coalitional
Transformations in U.S. Social Conservatism." *Law and Social Inquiry* 46, no. 4
(2021): 964–92.

Wuest, Joanna. "The Dead End of Corporate Activism." *Boston Review*, May 18, 2022.
https://bostonreview.net/articles/the-dead-end-of-corporate-activism/.

Wuest, Joanna. "The Sanders Campaign Goes beyond Intersectionality." *Nation*,
February 24, 2020. https://www.thenation.com/article/politics/sanders
-intersectionality-working-class/.

Wuest, Joanna. "State, Economy, and LGBTQ+ Civil Rights." Law and Political Economy Project blog, February 22, 2022. https://lpeproject.org/blog/state-economy
-lgbtq-civil-rights/.

Wypijewski, JoAnn. *What We Don't Talk About: Sex and the Mess of Life*. London:
Verso, 2021.

JULES GILL-PETERSON

CARING FOR TRANS KIDS, 8
TRANSNATIONALLY,
OR, AGAINST "GENDER-
CRITICAL" MOMS

In 2020, the legislative attacks began in South Dakota. Almost like clock-work, the US presidential primary cycle began to hoard national attention away from a concurrent state legislative cycle, a diversion vital to authoritarian political movements because their diffuse machinations are cloaked by the former's spectacle, giving them their teeth. In January the South Dakota House of Representatives entertained Bill 1057, which proposed criminalizing the delivery of healthcare to trans children under the age of sixteen by prose-cuting doctors for providing such care. Why South Dakota? And hadn't this already happened, say, *four years ago*? As an article in the *Nation* that many trans advocates shared online detailed, South Dakota was indeed a legislative laboratory for opening new fronts in the American right's anti-trans crusade, owing to its smallness and, consequently, its sensitivity to targeted invest-ments of outside money.[1]

Several years later, after more than twenty other states have succeeded where South Dakota failed, it might seem quaint, but it's worth revisiting the reaction at the time. The bill languished procedurally, which led the media to declare its ostensible "death," or that it had been "effectively killed." A grim but hardly incidental choice of words, given how central the image of dead children has been to responses to anti-trans political violence. Four years prior, when American Civil Liberties Union lawyer and trans activist Chase Strangio helped organize against a nearly identical bill, he declared, "If I were a kid in South Dakota today, I probably wouldn't survive into adulthood."[2] In the manic rush to press against the rapid proliferation of similar state bills that followed in the first few months of 2020, the specter of death was regularly invoked. *Trans children will die* as a result of such legislative efforts to ban "lifesaving healthcare"—that is, puberty blockers, hormone replacement therapy, and surgeries endorsed by every relevant major medical association.[3] This is the terrain in which trans people are asked to relate to state power and the crisis of liberalism's version of democracy. A siege mentality in which the stakes are permanently as high as life or death, whatever else our lives, or deaths, might actually consist of. This cyclicality brandishes in me a virulent cynicism that burns into the ashes of pessimism. The threatened foreclosure of trans futurity occurs at increasingly regular intervals, as the presidential election cycles of 2016 to 2020 and their attendant anti-trans bills in South Dakota show. At the time of this writing, perhaps the intervals have collapsed; the threat is now constant. And as this writing ages, there will surely be many more such moments. The state of constant threats could become banal, crises ordinary, losing something of their affective punch. I also sincerely worry about the growing endorsements of state-sponsored exposure to premature death, both in the sense of exposing trans people to greater vulnerability by prohibiting any of the weak and biopolitical hopes offered by medicine, and in the sense of intensifying the material conditions that precipitate—and provoke people to relish in the desire for—suicide. To lock people into a cycle of legislation that produces suicidality and resistance that pushes back by evoking that suicidality, in turn, is nothing short of a description of horror.

Such horror can produce a mode of knowing: it reveals a fetish of state power and, especially, of electoral politics in liberal democracy. That is, the massive amount of time spent debating trans people's existence on the narrowest possible grounds of citizenship—protection from formal discrimination in public accommodation, employment, and housing as well as access to private healthcare—wastes incalculable energy that could be expended organizing in coalition around many economic and racialized issues that actually affect most trans people, but also masses of non-trans people. A list of such urgent priorities includes the criminalization of sex work, overpolicing and mass incarceration, housing unaffordability, public healthcare, access to immigration, income inequality, and welfare.[4] While the battle over banning pediatric trans healthcare is not hypothetical in impact, it still affects only the *smallest* sliver of trans children who currently have, or had, access to gender-affirmative care, largely thanks to white, middle-class resources and parental advocacy that survives legislative ban. Even though bans harm those children, they nevertheless make no obvious material difference in the lives of the vast majority of trans children, who do not enjoy the fear of having healthcare withdrawn from their lives.[5] Nevertheless, I find it impossible to haughtily dismiss the efforts to resist these legislative measures, as if they are not the means through which the state inflicts political violence that certainly will kill some trans people and wear many more down. Yet, if one of the primary values of intersectional thought is avoiding zero-sum games, then there is something in this horrifying and pessimistic terrain worth not just investigating for its effects but mobilizing.

When one news outlet reported on the "death" of the South Dakota bill, it quoted a local seventeen-year-old trans activist, Quinncy, who had spent considerable time fighting it and who gave a haunting rendition of the outcome: "It's gone. . . . I don't have to worry about it until next year."[6] As a trans adult, I worry about youth like Quinncy. To be sure, my accumulated worries about trans children and adults are so numerous that to catalog them alone would overtake the word limit of the present writing. Still, I worry what the impact of fighting such legislation over and over, both when it passes and is defeated, will be for someone like Quinncy. What kind of childhood is that? The Trans Day of Remembrance, an important project of mourning and militancy for Black and brown trans women, has become enshrined by and for mainstream consumption in recent years, intensifying the trans necropolitics so aptly described by C. Riley Snorton and Jin Haritaworn by converting death into a spectacle.[7] As with those trans women of color, youth like Quinncy are being locked into a pattern of survival predicated on endless exposure to death that the public demands to consume in order to care about them.

This is a worry that has to do, equally, with my status as a trans adult and something about Strangio's hypothetical South Dakotan childhood. I wonder, in this moment of resurgence for anti-trans feminists, and the hypervisibility engulfing trans women, especially those who are Black, or brown, if the question isn't so perverse as the very viability of something like "trans women and children"? That is to say, conversely, that I worry that the anti-trans tidal wave, drawing on immense preexisting reserves of white supremacy and misogyny, flirts first and foremost with the perverse proposition that trans women and children ought not to exist.[8] This view explains the aggregate effect of efforts to make trans life impossible by, for instance, eliminating medical care or investigating the families of trans children as presumptive child abusers.[9] While horrifying to observe, there is a lesson in taking up this situation beyond its life-or-death rhetoric. Young trans life is not solely contingent on legislation, and trans women of color's lives are not solely contingent on being saved from spectacular violence like murder. This is true *in addition to the fact* that trans children like Quinncy are endangered by legislation and Black and brown trans women are being killed in unprecedented numbers. Trans women and children should not have to die, or be threatened with endless danger and death, to establish that their lives *might* be worth valuing.

I have written elsewhere of the riddle of being myself a trans woman of color who wrote a book about trans children, but for whom the writing of that book did little to nothing to clarify how I can actually care for such children outside of my writing.[10] And so with the acknowledgment that I'm here, once again, *writing*, I'd like to dig deeper into my sense of figurative (but, as we shall see, this means material) entanglement with trans children, for we are two kinds of trans people with especially big targets on our backs. Yet we have also been prohibited from entering into relation by successful efforts to *force* a barrier between adults and children through legislation— and the far-right talking point, aided and abetted by anti-trans feminists, that trans women are per se "groomers" of children, or sexualized aggressors in general.[11] To begin to scratch at this prohibition and what it covers up is to ask a question that moves past the figurative framing of saving vulnerable lives because trans women of color and trans children are equally in need of saving. Tallying the psychic and physical cost of political struggle, of sustaining the ability to care about, and react to, the state's hysteria around trans life, leads somewhere else.

The coalition of anti-trans political forces flourishing today has realized that driving a wedge between trans adults and children is highly effective, since children are very easy targets for political violence to begin with, but doubly so when that compounds with our culture's arrogant assumption that children cannot really know themselves (and so it goes, their gender). I find myself stuck with the problem of how to find a different maternal relation between myself, as a trans woman of color, and trans children. "Different" not merely because my socially reproductive labor as a trans woman is cast as inferior, or an affront to literal reproduction, but because, as we shall see, it is in fact certain *mothers*, claiming to act in protection of "their" children, who are the most respectable face of anti-trans efforts in the United States and the United Kingdom.

I have some choice words for them, and so I write.

The remainder of this chapter serves two ends that, I hope, may prove not to be wholly incommensurate. First, it will indict the transnational network of anti-trans political alliances across the United States and United Kingdom that explicitly targets children for harassment, bullying, and legislative and administrative violence, with the outcome of exposing them to forms of premature death, social and literal. The mode of indictment will be to insist on placing such efforts in the context of a global resurgence of ethnonationalism—in the United States and United Kingdom, in particular, of white supremacy and its authoritarian appeals to state power to protect variously aggrieved white citizens.[12] To make a certain point about ostensibly unlikely bedfellows, the object on which I will focus is the most respectable one possible: the so-called gender-critical moms who extensively use the sentimental and feminist resources long accorded to white women in both countries to pursue the eradication of trans children as a mode of maternal protection. Second, I will reflect on the problem of how to find a different maternal relation between trans women and children, for it is obvious that the gender-critical model leaves little salvageable in the normative role of "mommy" for those of us who desire both livable presents and futures for all trans people, women and children included. The broader problem, as I see it, is one of trans life and death as entangled objects of nationalism and biopolitics.

The flourishing of anti-trans sentiment, and its specific utility to cultural and political movements, spans the right and the left in both the United States and the United Kingdom. Trans children in particular find themselves in the crosshairs of a series of battles, in addition to the aforementioned state legislative efforts in the United States: bans on trans children's participation in education and organized sports; the saturation of corporate media outlets with moral panic stories about children influenced into transition; the legitimizing circulation of pseudoscientific concepts like "Rapid Onset Gender Dysphoria"; the figural beating of children in the ostensibly justified concern of high-profile feminists and their aggrieved figureheads, such as J. K. Rowling; and the invocation of trans children as an index of moral degeneracy by movements with reactionary and authoritarian goals. This loose and formally unaffiliated field joins the Make America Great Again (MAGA) movement and pro-Brexit partisans, as well as Evangelical and anti-immigrant movements, with academic feminists, trans-exclusionary gays and lesbians, and anti-vaxxer skeptics of biomedicine. The cultural, political, and policy outcomes of these movements are equally wide-ranging and diffuse. They are unexpectedly collective, yet simultaneously not.[13] In the United States, of course, efforts to make trans healthcare illegal or prohibited from insurance coverage are joined by coordinated efforts to reclassify trans people out of recognition by the federal administrative state, as well as the overturning of an array of civil rights, including the right to abortion.[14] In all of this, trans people as figures have become lightning rods around which to organize culture wars and attempt to mobilize voting or ideological blocs.

In the United Kingdom, the contest for the leadership of the Labour Party in 2020 became embroiled for some time in a battle between the trans-affirmative and anti-trans Left, followed two years later by escalating anti-trans promises in the Conservative Party leadership race.[15] Perhaps just as noteworthy, the extreme and unrelenting onslaught of moral panic articles about trans people, especially children, in major media outlets seems to correlate to the imperiling of otherwise rather mundane (but vital) reforms to the Gender Recognition Act in England.[16] This spectacular set of libelous claims about trans people in the media has likewise succeeded in preempting broad public recognition of the brutal wait times, archaic gatekeeping, and general impossibility of accessing trans healthcare through the National Health Service.[17] As any casual perusal of the subreddit r/TransDIY will demonstrate, trans people of all ages in the United States and United Kingdom face a similar problem of inaccessibility to the means of transition, despite the massive differences between a nationalized healthcare system and privatized healthcare networks.

In this larger social context has emerged the seemingly bizarre camp of "gender-critical" feminists, a mix of academics, activists, and people who present themselves publicly as lesbians, mothers, and other concerned centrists. Bizarre, in part, because it remains unclear how one might ever explain a dogmatically deterministic point of view of biology and social roles as "critical" of gender, particularly in comparison to other feminist theories of the same. Nevertheless, this phraseology has caught on as an alternative to the stigmatized term born of the 1970s, another decade in which feminists pursued this cause so vociferously: trans-exclusionary radical feminist (TERF).[18] In a brilliant essay detailing the ways in which the gender criticals have, in the broader authoritarian and ethnonationalist resurgence of the twenty-first century, configured trans people's existence as a problem of free speech, Grace Lavery points out the aggrieved and surreal terrain on which the whole gambit rests. "The startling rapidity with which controversies surrounding trans people regenerate and supplant each other, along with the perpetual sense that trans discourse exists precisely *as* discourse to stifle and suppress speech," she observes, "sustains a sense of crisis around trans issues while making individual outrages difficult to contest."[19]

In other words, the aggrieved white subject of contemporary US and UK identity politics entertains her *public* humiliation at the hands of an imagined trans aggressor—so often, unsurprisingly, a phallic trans woman—which serves the dual ends of dismissing the widespread violence, poverty, and marginalization that trans people structurally endure by transforming them into predators and simultaneously justifying any number of nearly hysterical responses and hypothetical substitutions that can direct real outcomes without saying as much.[20] These dynamics of substitution and disavowal are intensified and often directly rely on the conflation of gender and sexual deviance in the form of naked racism, especially anti-Blackness.[21] In this way, the outrageous accusations that children are being led into clinics and convinced, en masse, to jump on hormones or get surgeries can function despite being easily falsifiable.

The work of sustaining this claim in the public sphere relies on the respectability of its speakers, for their aggrieved identity must be worn on their sleeves to solicit sympathy. The identity of "mom" fits that need perfectly. The fear of gender-critical moms that "biological males" will invade girls' sport and dominate their daughters, for instance, folds back onto a feminized vulnerability for which they, as mothers, can uniquely demand retribution because they have felt it too—even though they have not. The issue becomes a matter of sentiment, of feeling one's way through the political, and disqualifying trans people's feelings from entering the equation.[22] For what is at stake is not a contest over the truth of sex and gender, but rather "an argumentative trope that began as a claim about the proper governance of the public sphere," as Lavery puts it, one that then "mutates by degrees into an ambient cruelty, felt in every domain but precisely never spoken."[23] In this way, Lavery helps us understand, the participation of these liberal feminists in authoritarian and ethnonationalist strategies "is not merely an abstract echo of Trumpian rhetoric *but evidence of a preference for Trumpist political tactics.*"[24] She would know, for that last line is written in reference to a campaign by gender-critical feminists to inundate Lavery with threats, dox her colleagues at the University of California, Berkeley, and circulate harassing materials about her and her husband online. (I would know too, as I regularly receive graphic messages promising violence, sexual assault, and death in my inboxes and social media replies.)

Perhaps the most respectable iteration of gender-critical feminists comes not from PhD-holding scholars at well-known universities (though the contest here would be close, I admit), but in the form of what I will call, for full rhetorical effect, their "mommy groups."[25] Many of these were formed not around the politicization of free speech, but rather an ostensible critique of contemporary biomedicine and xennial gender taxonomies, particularly the online uptake of an entirely made-up concept, "Rapid Onset Gender Dysphoria" (ROGD), in 2018. There are already several fantastic and granular critiques from Julia Serano, Florence Ashley, Lisa Farley and R. M. Kennedy, and Victoria Pitts-Taylor of how ROGD passed itself off as based in legitimate research when it was in reality a rather basic, fabricated social contagion theory dressed up in the clothes of an acronym: the proposition that children who otherwise had never expressed any gender inclinations different from what was assigned at birth would suddenly come out as trans, experience severe dysphoria, and wish to immediately transition, all because of peer influence. Tellingly, the ROGD study's data were the perspectives of parents that the author found on an anti-trans website.[26]

Taking Lavery's point seriously that the aggrieved form of such rhetoric secures its absurdity, I will pass on the opportunity to prosecute ROGD's innumerable illogics and unrealities after those who work in the social sciences already have. While it would be rather easy to adversarially and rationally dissect the discourse in which gender-critical moms traffic, such a critical endeavor is misguided to the extent that it imagines critique capable of deactivating the political strategy in question. In short, I see no compelling evidence for that capability in trans studies or in critical scholarship more broadly—it is frankly not what we are typically called to do in our work. Perhaps critics must confront more honestly the libidinal desire to engage in critique in the first place if its purpose is to inflate its effects. It may be that the pleasure of critique is the only thing we critics feel entitled to, especially in trans studies, because we implicitly know the scalar ineffectiveness of our work from the very beginning.[27] More to the point, as a historian of sex, gender, and medical science, I would add that binary sex and gender are themselves, *normatively and through the functioning of their systematicity*, wildly inconsistent, incoherent, and illogical categories. That is not their deficiency: it is their greatest strength. As I argued in *Histories of the Transgender Child*, the thesis of sex and gender's inherent plasticity allowed for indeterminacy and outright illogic to regenerate and salvage the governmentality built into those categories over the course of the twentieth century. To put it plainly: ideology based on the binary gender is largely impervious to rational critique.

A better question, to me, would be: *How* have informal but highly successful transnational political movements in two countries enabled gender-critical moms to publicly prosecute trans children and respectably amplify their vulnerability to premature death? Here we might briefly examine the aggrieved fantasy of white women's citizenship that authorizes their agenda. As a selection of their online presence through Transgender Trend, Gender-criticalresources.com, and 4thWaveNow makes clear, the political position of the imperiled white mom produces some of the most powerful alibis available to authoritarian projects because it marries them to liberal democracy and state power.[28] (I should add that the whiteness of these moms is generally unmarked by them, and I expect they would react to the charge of whiteness as an anchor of identity politics with resentment—which I should think would ratify the assertion.) Many of these groups actively supported a more extreme position in 2020 than that of Republican state legislators at the time, arguing that trans healthcare should not be available to anyone under eighteen.[29] Transgender Trend, perhaps the most directly antagonistic in its name, is typical of these organizations that pitch themselves as educational resources for worried mothers who feel overwhelmed by trans cultural visibility and unsure what information to trust. Much of the website's content critiques the scientific and medical discourses that inform not just pediatric trans medicine, but normative definitions of sex, gender, and sexual orientation in general. Not categorically anti-science, Transgender Trend instead promotes its own reading of scientific data on detransition, behavioral psychology, and adolescent brain development, posturing them as renegade or brave for their lack of credentialed support.[30] Their website is largely a clearinghouse of links to social media (especially YouTube videos) and other online forums that host long-running harassment of trans-affirmative organizations, particular those in the United Kingdom, like Mermaids, that have received charity status and funding for work on access to healthcare.

There is so much one could say and analyze here to fully appreciate what is at stake, but I am most interested in the actual fantasized child being protected by these white moms through their assault on trans kids. Though the figure of the trans woman is otherwise wildly oversaturated in anti-trans rhetoric, and most of these gender-critical mom groups are careful to mention both trans feminine and trans masculine people in their materials, an unmistakable impression forms that the actual object of concern is quite specific: white children, assigned female at birth, whose identities as trans masculine or nonbinary would represent, in this fantasy, an unconscionable dilution of white womanhood.[31] As one "resource guide" for nervous parents of teenagers puts it explicitly, "In recent years, there has been an unprecedented and unexplained rise in the number of natal females presenting as transgender. There is concern that identifying as transgender and transitioning by binding, taking hormones, or undergoing 'top surgery' may be the newest culturally mediated way that female adolescents are giving expression to and coping with the intense discomfort that most young women feel with their bodies."[32]

At first glance, this is a novel historical development, given how misogynistic and pornofied the character and scope of *all* trans discourses have been since the turn of the twentieth century.[33] The ostensible feminism at hand may make this focus on "the intense discomfort that most young women feel with their bodies" unsurprising, but it places their project in a much longer history of white women's feminism as oriented toward hegemonic state power. As Kyla Schuller has pointed out, white womanhood played a historically decisive role in the nineteenth century in securing whiteness both as a regime of political domination *and* as a motif for liberal citizenship. Schuller underlines that there is no false consciousness afflicting white women, despite many protestations to the contrary over their support of Donald Trump and Republicans in the United States, or of the Conservative Party in the United Kingdom. Rather, "there is a deeper, more structural reason why white women vote for misogynist, white supremacist candidates despite a century and a half of feminist organizing," writes Schuller. "Simply put: sex difference is itself a racial structure."[34] Given that "sex difference helped qualify individuals for life" in monumentally significant ways in the nineteenth century, as Schuller's book *The Biopolitics of Feeling* details, it comes to be today that "white Republican women who vote for sexual assaulters are not identifying with their whiteness over gender," as many pundits have presumed. "Rather, they are enacting their womanhood itself: both absorbing and smoothing over the flow of sensation and feeling that makes up the public sphere."[35] To transpose this insight to gender-critical moms: they are likewise mobilizing in defense of white womanhood to maintain durable regimes of political domination and citizenship in the public sphere, which they sense to be especially threatened by the fantasy that a generation of children might elect to give up their "white female" social position assigned at birth and its civilizational mandates. Or, more pointedly, they substitute the domestic threat of a trans masculine child for the broader political strategy underway that seeks to remove trans people entirely from the public sphere and, therefore, from citizenship.

Part of what I mean to suggest in this reading, then, is that trans-affirmative politics, particularly around children, are caught in the snare of a biopolitical game about the interminable crisis of the liberal public sphere. While right-wing political movements work to enshrine exposure to premature death through legislation or administrative fiat, the affirmative defense of trans life is undercut from both sides by being restricted to a narrow conversation over normalizing healthcare models *and* the gender-critical mom's crusade to preserve white womanhood's (social *and* biological) reproductive vitality over trans life. In other words, while the prevailing indifference to trans life is one problem, the white maternal claim to be saving or protecting the child's life from a fatal transness is equally deadly. Trans politics has been put in the service of nationalism in both the United States and the United Kingdom so that white women, historically central emblems of such racializing configurations of nation-as-family, fantasize the ruin that would arise if their children assigned female at birth should live otherwise. (This is why the rhetorical claim to be anti-trans *in defense of* lesbians, or gay children, falls flat.) Inside the terms of this battle there is precious little space to react, other than the very understandable and polemic invocation of trans children's inevitable deaths.

The problem, though, is that the shared political fantasy of cis-normative citizenship here is actually *bio* political, and so it indulges openly and shamelessly in the rationalization of "letting die" as a form of social hygiene for the nation. This is, likewise, what subtends the transnational mode of mutual reinforcement at hand, so that local forms of ethnonationalism in the United States and United Kingdom, or Canada and Quebec, or Hungary and Russia, or in Latin America and even more specific national contexts like Brazil, can mobilize a vaguely racialized and cisgender fantasy of imperiled citizenship despite immense differences of culture, language, religion, and nationalist political cultures. The biopolitical foundation of this mode of gendered and racial citizenship makes anti-transness a transnational phenomenon. In light of that, I find it unconvincing to counter these anti-trans forces with the claim that they are exposing trans children to premature death, as if that will move them (or the imagined liberal center of the non-trans public) to recant. The letting-die of trans children is precisely the desired outcome that such groups never have to disclose because it is taken as a given in a biopolitical domain invested in sex and gender as legitimately administrable axes of biological and political life. The protection that gender-critical moms envision is meant to be deadly to some; otherwise it cannot secure the futurity of white womanhood and, with it, the nation. (One proof for this that I lack the space to unwind, though its evidence abounds these days: much of the putative parental concern over puberty suppression and adolescent hormone therapy is the loss of an entirely hypothetical, future reproductive potential. There is a longer genealogy to investigate concerning the alliance between anti-abortion and anti-trans activists.)[36]

If the maternal relation of protection is so thoroughly shot through by this biopolitics of white womanhood, where does that leave the second task I gave this essay? Is there a possibility of a different maternal relation between myself, as a trans woman of color, and the trans children for whom I sincerely worry? In truth, I remain ambivalent, for all the reasons enumerated here and more. What I do think, however, is that an antiracist and trans feminist political movement that understood its antagonists to be operating in an ethnonationalist *and* biopolitical mode might operate from the assumption that *the affirmative defense of trans life cannot side with medicine, human rights, or the state against them, and that it also cannot oppose attempts to increase vulnerability to premature death by opposing trans life to death.*[37]

Affirmatively, such a politic might also make something unexpected out of one of the other discarded relics of bygone feminism. I'm speaking of the phrase "women and children," which I suggested at the outset might be reinvigorated otherwise as an intersectional, coalitional politic prioritizing "*trans* women and children *of color*," specifically.[38] It might look something like a strategic "nothing for us without us" approach, one indebted to Black feminist analyses like the Combahee River Collective of differential systems of oppression that make coalition essential to transformative change, rather than a flat identity politics that revolves around state recognition.[39] I will leave the elaboration of this politic to other writing, for I think the critique outlined above takes priority. What's more, the critique has yet to be recognized in a widespread way by trans-inclusive feminists, by trans studies, and by the larger public sphere in which trans life and death are still narrated as opposite phenomena. Yet since my motive in this writing was the urgent problem of how to care for trans children outside of the normative maternal relation and outside of the scene of writing, I will end with a speculative coda of sorts about one domain in my life where I have experienced nonprotective care for, and solidarity with, youth: teaching.[40] Think of what follows as a love letter to the possibility of intergenerational trans kinship in a nonreproductive sense. No one is raising anyone else in this situation and, so, importantly, no one is reproducing themself in anyone else. This mode of care and cohabitation across difference glimpses solidarity outside of the reproduction of preexisting and toxic forms of social and biological kinship. It remains improvisational because of its institutional context: the university is an unlikely place for genuine care to take root. Allergic to the extreme idealization of trans women of color in the academy, I also refuse to metaphorize the kind of maternal relationship I am chasing as if it were like the kinship tradition of the Black and brown ballroom world, where there are real mothers and children whose livelihoods have none of the institutional affordances of the university. What I am after is a mode of intergenerational care that does not imitate being a white mom, whom I simply cannot become.

I can't help but think of this as a teacher. I returned to campus one fall after a year away on fellowship during which I had also begun my transition. I was, I thought, in the childhood of my womanhood. I didn't know how I would handle that and be a professor. At times, I nearly didn't. Mercifully, the semester saw me teaching a course of my own design on contemporary trans literature. To my immense delight I found my students to be overwhelmingly, and by their own enthusiastic declarations on the first day of the semester, trans and nonbinary. But that delight was accompanied by an immediate and immense weight of responsibility that wore heavy on my adult-trans-child-self. Many of my students, especially those in their first semester of college, had lived publicly trans lives longer than I, including during high school. I experienced them as consequently older than me, something that I registered as a deep need for care during a semester where I was struggling to reexperience long-dormant, dissociated trauma that transition had reignited in part because I had not had their childhoods. Such feelings infantilized me.

And yet I also sense that my students, besieged by the anti-trans present in which we all lived, but one that they perhaps absorbed more anxiously than I, also desperately needed me as a grown trans woman. That I needed to incarnate for them a basic, living possibility for futurity in femme and brown form by showing up every week to teach, to be "gay as hell" (as they put it), and to confer on them the hope of collective persistence, of love. And so, I had to "grow up" right before their eyes each week, even as I tried to tell them it was safe, in my classroom, to feel our shared weakness of being young and trans in this world. The pain and honor of our four months together was something about how our classroom forced us out of bed, into a room with potential kin, and kept time for us by making space. How awful it felt, at the end of term, to say goodbye. I felt the naked fear of not being able to see them twice a week and thereby know, if only superficially, that they were alive, that they were breathing, that they were thinking and laughing and recognizing in one another a personhood so rarely acknowledged outside of our classroom. Encrypted inside that fear and the temptation for me to play a protective role, a second feeling: the sorrow that I would be without them. That I would have to live and try to live well enough, on my own, without their demand for my presence to tether me, for they were not my children after all. For weeks after the end of the semester, I would wake up in the middle of the night from a nightmare, worried about one or another student. Eventually, those dreams started to fade. And a year later, when I stepped back into the classroom to teach that course again, I felt the tender sweetness of seeing that we had found each other yet again. That we would get to do it all again. That what can't last forever, or guarantee life, also offers the relief of ending and then starting again.

NOTES

1   Gordon-Loebl, "How Did South Dakota Become a Factory for Anti-trans Legislation?" In the years since this bill failed to pass, the landscape has worsened considerably. The years 2021 and 2022 witnessed record waves of anti-trans legislation in the vast majority of state legislatures, soaring to over two hundred at the time of this writing. Levin, "Mapping Anti-trans Laws." While an array of anti-trans legislation has passed in a variety of states, including bills targeting children through sports, the banning, criminalization, or destruction of access to gender-affirming care have taken considerably more effort. In April 2021, Arkansas became the first state to ban pediatric gender-affirming care, overriding the veto of its conservative governor. Hutchinson, "Why I Vetoed My Party's Bill." In 2022, Alabama became the first state to successfully enforce a ban on gender-affirming care for anyone under the age of nineteen, quickly adapting to the overturning of abortion rights by the US Supreme Court to serve the state's argument in a federal court challenge to the law. Gonzales, "Alabama Cites Roe Decision." Meanwhile, administrative violence has become an additional tactic for politicians hoping to avoid the legislative process altogether. Florida invented its own standards of care to forcibly pull trans people at any age off gender-affirming care under Medicaid, which also opens the door to private insurers to withdraw coverage. In eight states,

trans people are already barred from Medicaid coverage for their gender-affirming care. Migdon, "Florida Publishes Rule Barring Medicaid Coverage."

2 Margolin, "Anti-trans Bill."

3 For representative examples of this invocation, see Wax-Thibodeaux and Schmidt, "South Dakota House Passes Bill"; Burns, "Bills Targeting Trans Kids"; and Dowshen, "Dangers of Criminalizing Medical Care for Trans Youth."

4 I elaborated this argument in "Anti-trans Laws Aren't Symbolic."

5 As sociologist Ann Travers has shown, very few trans youth actually have access to this kind of healthcare. See Travers, *Trans Generation*.

6 Fitzsimmons, "South Dakota's Trans Health Bill."

7 Snorton and Haritaworn, "Trans Necropolitics."

8 See also Hayward, "Don't Exist."

9 Gill-Peterson, "Anti-trans Laws Aren't Symbolic."

10 Gill-Peterson, "On Wanting Trans Women and Children (for Better or for Worse)."

11 Block, "Accusations of 'Grooming.'"

12 Although this chapter focuses on the United States and United Kingdom, I want to underscore that this phenomenon is not restricted to those two countries but is one with global reach and many flows. On the many links between European anti-trans campaigns and those across Latin America, see Correa, Patternotte, and Kuhar, "Globalisation of Anti-gender Campaigns." Importantly, as these authors observe, anti-trans political movements span the political spectrum, from conservative Catholics and right-wing populists to secular politicians and Marxists. See also Bassi and LaFleur, "Trans-Exclusionary Feminisms."

13 I am elaborating here on a longer conversation I had with Marquis Bey and Grace Lavery about the TERF industrial complex at the Clayman Institute for Gender Research at Stanford University on August 26, 2020. That conversation is available in podcast form in the September 9, 2020, episode of TFP *Clayman Conversations*, "The TERF Industrial Complex."

14 Wamsley, "Trans People."

15 Jacques, "Transphobia Is Everywhere in Britain"; Akmen, "Rishi Sunak."

16 Jacques, "Transphobia Is Everywhere in Britain."

17 Jacques, "Transphobia Is Everywhere in Britain."

18 Of course, the story told of the trans-exclusionary 1970s is very much a *story*, a narrative that serves the conflicts of the historical present more than it is an accurate account of the past, which makes it worth reevaluating. See Enke, "Collective Memory and the Transfeminist 1970s." Kind of a petty thing, but I published a very similar essay in the same publication two years earlier and Enke doesn't even cite me.

19 Lavery, "King's Two Anuses," 126.

20 I say "hysterical" with great irony, given its misogynist history—but one that I read as effectively ventriloquized to misogynist ends by white identity politics.

21 On this specific racial phenomenology of transphobia, see Salamon, *Life and Death of Latisha King*.

22 I am drawing here on the sentimental tradition of white women's moralizing politics, well developed in both the United Kingdom and the United States since the nineteenth century. See, for example, Berlant, *Female Complaint*.

23 Lavery, "King's Two Anuses," 128.

24 Lavery, "King's Two Anuses," 147n2 (emphasis added).

25 Perhaps the most famous of these groups is Transgender Trend, which bills itself as "an organisation of parents, professionals, and academics based in the UK" (Transgender Trend, "Transgender Trend—Who Are We?") and is often quoted in the UK press as if it were of equal credibility to trans activist organizations or medical associations. Far less formal is Mumsnet, an online messaging board that has acquired a reputation for being the premier infrastructure for people claiming the identity of mothers in the anti-trans movement—about which I say more below.

26 Serano, "Everything You Need to Know about Rapid Onset Gender Dysphoria"; Farley and Kennedy, paper presented at Youngsters 2; Pitts-Taylor, "How to Wait"; and Ashley, "Critical Commentary."

27 See Gill-Peterson, "On Wanting Trans Women and Children (for Better or for Worse)."

28 Though I find empirical or demographic considerations largely unimportant to my argument (being something like the other side of the perverse discursive coin that charges "But trans people are only 0.1 percent of the population!"), given the evidently outsized impact gender-critical moms have discursively, the Gender Critical Support Board website posts statistics on its home page, suggesting, at the time of this writing, that it has about two thousand members. See Gender Critical Support Board, "Support."

29 The FAQ page for 4thWaveNow dramatizes this tension perfectly. Its answer to "Do you oppose providing medical transition even to individuals over the age of 18?" is followed, farther down on the page, with "Does 4thWaveNow partner with conservative organizations?," to which the response is unambiguously "No, we do not." See 4thWaveNow, "FAQ."

30 Transgender Trend, "Resources for Parents."

31 A point for which I am grateful to Pitts-Taylor, in "How to Wait," who has spent significant time immersed in this discourse to come to that conclusion.

32 Marchiano, "Guidance for Parents of Teens with Rapid Onset Gender Dysphoria."

33 On the generalized pornification of trans women, see Lavery, "An Interview with Susan Stryker."

34 Schuller, "Trouble with White Women."

35 Schuller, "Trouble with White Women." See Schuller, *Biopolitics of Feeling*.

36 See, for example, the especially hysterical alarm sounded by Madeleine Kearns in "The Tragedy of the 'Trans' Child," which warns of the "ideology" that counsels

that "parents should consider greenlighting the surgical removal of their child's reproductive organs." This article is part of a particularly disturbing and vicious campaign against a *single* trans child in Texas, whose custody battle between a trans-affirming mother and anti-trans father became a cause célèbre for right-wing politicians. Much like my worry for the young trans activist Quinncy, I worry about the impact of national political campaigns to intimidate, harass, and suppress individual trans children. What kind of childhood is that?

37 In this thinking I am immensely indebted to the trans political analyses of Spade, *Normal Life*; and Stanley, "Anti-trans Optics."

38 I'm riffing specifically on Oakley, "Women and Children First and Last," 13–32.

39 Combahee River Collective, "A Black Feminist Statement." This is, in many ways, an unfairly abbreviated point on my part. My hesitation in elaborating is that I think such an intersectional, trans feminist, and coalitional politics would need to navigate the many pitfalls and possibilities cataloged, for instance, by Nash in *Black Feminism Reimagined*, and that is not the central aim of this writing. I am taking up these political and genealogical questions for trans of color feminism in a forthcoming essay, "Trans of Color Liberation: An Unauthorized History of the Future."

40 On the complexities of trans care, see Malantino, "Future Fatigue."

BIBLIOGRAPHY

Akmen, Tolga. "Rishi Sunak Has Pledged to Wipe Out Woke Culture 'Nonsense.'" *Times*, July 30, 2022. https://www.thetimes.co.uk/article/rishi-sunak-has -pledged-to-wipe-out-woke-culture-nonsense-zl5n96pgn.

Ashley, Florence. "A Critical Commentary on 'Rapid-Onset Gender Dysphoria.'" *Sociological Review* 68, no. 4 (2020): 779–99.

Bassi, Serena, and Greta LaFleur. "Trans-Exclusionary Feminisms and the Global New Right." Special issue, *TSQ* 9, no. 3 (2022).

Berlant, Lauren. *The Female Complaint*. Durham, NC: Duke University Press, 2008.

Bey, Marquis, Grace Lavery, and Jules Gill-Peterson. "The TERF Industrial Complex." Clayman Institute for Gender Research at Stanford University, August 26, 2020.

Block, Melissa. "Accusations of 'Grooming' Are the Latest Political Attack—with Homophobic Origins." *NPR*, May 11, 2022. https://www.npr.org/2022/05/11 /1096623939/accusations-grooming-political-attack-homophobic-origins.

Burns, Katelyn. "Bills Targeting Trans Kids Are Getting Defeated in State Legislatures." *Vox*, February 11, 2020. https://www.vox.com/2020/2/11/21133117/south -dakota-bill-trans-kids-defeated.

Combahee River Collective. "A Black Feminist Statement." In *This Bridge Called My Back: Radical Writing by Women of Color*, 2nd ed., edited by Cherríe Moraga and Gloria E. Anzaldúa, 210–18. New York: Kitchen Table Press, 1983.

Correa, Sonia, David Patternotte, and Roman Kuhar. "The Globalisation of Anti-gender Campaigns." *International Politics and Society*, May 31, 2018. https://

www.ips-journal.eu/topics/human-rights/article/show/the-globalisation-of-anti
-gender-campaigns-2761/.

Dowshen, Nadia. "The Dangers of Criminalizing Medical Care for Trans Youth." *The Hill*, February 8, 2020. https://thehill.com/opinion/healthcare/482057-the -dangers-of-criminalizing-medical-care-for-trans-youth.

Enke, Finn. "Collective Memory and the Transfeminist 1970s: Towards a Less Plausi-ble History." *TSQ* 5, no. 1 (2018): 9–29.

Farley, Lisa, and R. M. Kennedy. Paper presented at Youngsters 2: On the Cultures of Children and Youth. Ryerson University, May 11, 2019.

Fitzsimmons, Tim. "South Dakota's Trans Health Bill Is Effectively Dead, Opponents Say." *NBC News*, February 10, 2020. https://www.nbcnews.com/feature/nbc-out /south-dakota-s-trans-health-bill-effectively-dead-opponents-say-n1134356.

4thWaveNow. "FAQ." Accessed March 13, 2020. https://4thwavenow.com/faqs/.

Gender Critical Support Board. "Support." Accessed March 13, 2020. https:// gendercriticalresources.com/Support/.

Gill-Peterson, Jules. "Anti-trans Laws Aren't Symbolic. They Seek to Erase Us from Public Life." *Them*, April 18, 2022. https://www.them.us/story/anti-trans-laws -public-erasure-dont-say-gay/.

Gill-Peterson, Jules. *Histories of the Transgender Child*. Minneapolis: University of Minnesota Press, 2018.

Gill-Peterson, Jules. "On Wanting Trans Women and Children (for Better or for Worse)." *Rambling*, November 26, 2019. https://the-rambling.com/2019/11/26 /issue6-gill-peterson/.

Gill-Peterson, Jules. "Trans of Color Liberation: An Unauthorized History of the Future." In *The Routledge Companion to Intersectionality*, edited by Jennifer Nash and Samantha Pinto, 325–34. New York: Routledge.

Gonzales, Oriana. "Alabama Cites Roe Decision in Urging Court to Let State Ban Trans Health Care." *Axios*, June 28, 2022. https://www.axios.com/2022/06/28 /alabama-roe-supreme-court-block-trans-health-care.

Gordon-Loebl, Naomi. "How Did South Dakota Become a Factory for Anti-trans Legislation?" *Nation*, June 27, 2019. https://www.thenation.com/article/archive /south-dakotan-anti-transgender-legislation/.

Hayward, Eva. "Don't Exist." *TSQ* 4, no. 2 (2017): 191–94.

Heaney, Emma. *The New Woman: Literary Modernism, Queer Theory, and the Trans Feminine Allegory*. Evanston, IL: Northwestern University Press, 2017.

Hutchinson, Asa. "Why I Vetoed My Party's Bill Restricting Health Care for Trans-gender Youth." *Washington Post*, April 8, 2021. https://www.washingtonpost .com/opinions/asa-hutchinson-veto-transgender-health-bill-youth/2021/04/08 /990c43f4-9892-11eb-962b-78c1d8228819_story.html.

Jacques, Juliet. "Transphobia Is Everywhere in Britain." *New York Times*, March 9, 2020. https://www.nytimes.com/2020/03/09/opinion/britain-transphobia -labour-party.html.

Kearns, Madeleine. "The Tragedy of the 'Trans' Child." *National Review*, November 21, 2019. https://www.nationalreview.com/magazine/2019/12/09/the-tragedy-of -the-trans-child/.

Lavery, Grace. "An Interview with Susan Stryker by Grace Lavery." *TSQ*Now*, July 29, 2020. https://www.tsqnow.online/post/an-interview-with-susan-stryker-by -grace-lavery.

Lavery, Grace. "The King's Two Anuses: Trans Feminism and Free Speech." *differences* 30, no. 3 (2019): 118–51.

Levin, Sam. "Mapping Anti-trans Laws Sweeping America: 'A War on 100 Fronts.'" *Guardian*, June 14, 2021. https://www.theguardian.com/society/2021/jun/14 /anti-trans-laws-us-map.

Malantino, Hil. "Future Fatigue: Trans Intimacies and Trans Presents (or How to Survive the Interregnum)." *TSQ* 6, no. 4 (2019): 635–58.

Marchiano, Lisa. "Guidance for Parents of Teens with Rapid Onset Gender Dyspho- ria." *Jung Soul*, October 27, 2016. http://thejungsoul.com/guidance-for-parents -of-teens-with-rapid-onset-gender-dysphoria/.

Margolin, Emma. "Anti-trans Bill Heads to Republican Governor's Desk." *MSNBC*, February 17, 2016. http://www.msnbc.com/msnbc/anti-trans-bill-heads -republican-governors-desk?cid=sm_fb_msnbc.

Migdon, Brook. "Florida Publishes Rule Barring Medicaid Coverage for Gender- Affirming Health Care." *The Hill*, August 13, 2022. https://thehill.com /changing-america/respect/equality/3598274-florida-publishes-rule-barring -medicaid-coverage-for-gender-affirming-health-care/.

Nash, Jennifer C. *Black Feminism Reimagined: After Intersectionality*. Durham, NC: Duke University Press, 2018.

Oakley, Ann. "Women and Children First and Last: Parallels and Differences between Children's and Women's Studies." In *Children's Childhoods*, edited by Berry Mayall, 13–32. Sussex, UK: Falmer Press, 1995.

Pitts-Taylor, Victoria. "How to Wait: Temporal Narratives of Gender Transition." Lecture given at the University of Pittsburgh, September 26, 2019.

Salamon, Gayle. *The Life and Death of Latisha King: A Critical Phenomenology of Transphobia*. New York: New York University Press, 2018.

Schuller, Kyla. *The Biopolitics of Feeling: Race, Sex, and Science in the Nineteenth Century*. Durham, NC: Duke University Press, 2017.

Schuller, Kyla. "The Trouble with White Women." Duke University Press blog, Jan- uary 11, 2018. https://dukeupress.wordpress.com/2018/01/11/the-trouble-with -white-women/.

Serano, Julia. "Everything You Need to Know about Rapid Onset Gender Dysphoria." *Medium*, August 22, 2018. https://medium.com/@juliaserano/everything-you -need-to-know-about-rapid-onset-gender-dysphoria-1940b8afdeba.

Snorton, C. Riley. *Black on Both Sides: A Racial History of Trans Identity*. Minneapo- lis: University of Minnesota Press, 2017.

Snorton, C. Riley, and Jin Haritaworn. "Trans Necropolitics: A Transnational Reflection on Violence, Death, and the Trans of Color Afterlife." In *Transgender Studies Reader 2*, edited by Susan Stryker and Aren Aizura, 66–76. New York: Routledge, 2013.

Spade, Dean. *Normal Life: Administrative Violence, Critical Trans Politics, and the Limits of Law*. Durham, NC: Duke University Press, 2015.

Stanley, Eric A. "Anti-trans Optics: Recognition, Opacity, and the Image of Force." *South Atlantic Quarterly* 116, no. 3 (2017): 612–20.

Transgender Trend. "Resources for Parents." Accessed March 13, 2020. https://www.transgendertrend.com/resources-for-parents/.

Transgender Trend. "Transgender Trend—Who Are We?" Accessed May 8, 2023. https://www.transgendertrend.com/about_us/.

Travers, Ann. *The Trans Generation: How Trans Kids (and Their Parents) Are Creating a Gender Revolution*. New York: New York University Press, 2018.

Wamsley, Laurel. "Trans People Say They #WontBeErased as Trump Administration Mulls Defining 'Sex.'" *NPR*, October 22, 2018. https://www.npr.org/2018/10/22/659553583/trans-people-say-they-wontbeerased-as-trump-administration-mulls-defining-sex.

Wax-Thibodeaux, Emily, and Samantha Schmidt. "South Dakota House Passes Bill Resisting Medical Treatments for Transgender Youth." *Washington Post*, January 29, 2020. https://www.washingtonpost.com/national/south-dakota-house-passes-bill-restricting-medical-treatments-for-transgender-youth/2020/01/29/8578b550-413d-11ea-b503-2b077c436617_story.html.

GENERIC DEDUCTIVENESS   9

Reasoning as Mood in the Stoner Neo-Noir

> Sexuality is the area where the homogeneity of
> the new world manifests itself most clearly.
> Significantly the hero's erotic instincts are themselves
> all but extinguished by his epistemological confusion.
> —LARRY GROSS, "FILM APRÈS NOIR"

> ORDELL ROBBIE: You know you smoke too much
> of that shit, that shit's gonna rob you of your ambition.
> MELANIE: Not if your ambition is to get high and watch TV.
> —*JACKIE BROWN*, DIR. QUENTIN TARANTINO

It feels like everyone I speak to these days seems to say that they're tired of talking about trans*ness*, and only want to notice trans people and bodies— lives as they are lived. The authors collected in the recent volume *Trap Door* all seem to echo a point made succinctly by Morgan Page: that trans visibility entrenches trans inequity, by drawing attention and prestige to a minority of trans celebrities, while directing state and public violence to the less presti- gious majority.[1] A central mechanism of biopolitical governance, "visibility" functions through a logic of racial selection. Jules Gill-Peterson argues that the historical construction of the cis body in the early twentieth century served to rationalize the eugenic science of racial plasticity.[2] Eva Hayward and Che Gossett have argued that the generalization of trans modes of analysis outside the remit of the transsexual has led to the catastrophic neglect of, especially, those subjects whose subjection by cisness is most violently enforced: Black trans women living with HIV/AIDS.[3] Insofar as there is a trans everywhere, it screams to stop the theorizing and attend instead to the mechanical reproduction of death by racial capitalism and the global transnational state.

As a result, there are not one but many cisnesses that we are up against. There is the cis-normative movement in social policy, which is not so much a designation as a project of social cleansing; there is that thinking, which attempts, for example, to make a firm distinction between "reversible" and "irreversible" spots of time; there is, perhaps most basically, the cisness of ontic legibility that names a body or mind "cis" if it is uncontaminated by the touch of conscious design, and "trans" the moment that a motive is traceable. There is the voice in a head, which endows each value system with a currency—which distinguishes between natural and synthetic hormones (or breasts, whose growth may be catalyzed but is never caused by hormones) or between the true and the false transsexual. To lay these resistances out for analysis, then, would be to reveal that "cis" and "trans" are hardly ontologized concepts—they are felt limits encountered at the edge of every project of self-knowing or world-building. "Leave us alone" is the cry of trans feminism against cisness: a mode of collective conjuration that demands its own closure to contradict the sequence of medico-political reopenings, rephrasings of old demands, re-enforcements of stale injunctions.

As if to produce a psychic equilibrium with this demand for nonvisibility, nonconceptualizability emerges as a coeval power of scrambled knowledge, a sequence of mythologemes flitting back and forth between minute and gigantic scales. Conspiratorial thinking runs through trans knowledge for much the same reason gossip does: they both feel fun, and the particular kind of fun they feel is an especially effective compensation against the otherwise depressive effects of nonconceptualizability—loneliness, confusion, feeling stupid. The meme would be an effective vehicle of compensation if it bypassed interpretation and landed on the mutually presencing nodes of feeling-togetherness, which otherwise may as well have been abolished along with the concept. A meme becomes, one hopes, a mood; a mood might freeze into a meme—which, if it does, it does by sloughing off every possible trace of historical specificity. Walter Benjamin writes that the dialectical image is that "wherein what has been comes together in a flash with the now to form a constellation."[4] A meme, by contrast, is that image wherein the conceptualizability of history as a dialectical particular recedes entirely, and the limitless negativity of space capacitates the co-being of a you and a me, *not* as positively related subjects in a historically determined configuration, but as objects thrown into the same slipstream of cosmic indifference.

Memes are, among other things, instruments of conspiratorial knowing. They evoke knowingness in the absence of knowledge, the negative imprint of a dialectical image. The art historian Michael Fried referred to this condition as "deductive structure": the minimalist notion that the content of an art object should derive, as literally as possible, from its form—that the dimensions of a canvas determine the marks one puts on it.[5] Memes refuse to stipulate whether there is one mood or many moods; instead, they repair the schizoid split between singular and plural, bypassing theory and conceptualization and returning knowledge to the presencing zone of affect. The process reverses what Stephen Colbert used to call "truthiness"—the self-satisfied structure of knowledge that vibes out on the purported credibility of a given ideologeme, rather returning us to the vacuity of knowledge claims in untheorizable space, the essential untruthiness of the mood. Yet there is a certain dogged optimism too: an effort to show one's working, to draw lines and scratch lines over them, to build architectural palimpsests from one's cognitive labor, to build a house from one's own delusion.

Although, again, *is* Charlie Day deluded? Is this space he has furnished propositional—does it make a claim?—or is it purely the negative architecture of nonpropositional, nonconceptual, nonabstract deductiveness? Would deductiveness shorn of proposition indeed be in any way distinct from delusion? This question approaches the condition of the cultist who awaits the apocalypse on a particular day and, when the day passes, decides that his calculations, but not his premises, were misguided. Interminable deduction—the work of the day (the working day) as the labor of fitting in the latest *drop* (for QAnon) or *root* (for queer Twitter) with the schematically absented nontheory toward which one is moving. The rationale, to adopt the form of R. D. Laing's formula in *Knots*, would be something like

· I know that I was gay when I was a child, because I am gay, and when I was a child I liked *Space Jam*, and *Space Jam* is gay.

- I know *Space Jam* is gay because I am gay, and I liked it when I was a child.
- When I was a child, I did not know *Space Jam* was gay, but I should have known *I* was gay, because I enjoyed *Space Jam*.[6]

And the conspirator reappears as the absented subject who knows only what she does not know (but should have known) and who suspects that the shared condition of "should have known"—of belated nonknowledge—is the negative condition of the mood. And if that subject appears narcissistic (which, of course, it does), it is a narcissism of the primary kind, rather than the secondary: developmentally dashed, the primary narcissist is the infantile type who simply has not had cause to differentiate between the negative space of mind and the negative space of world. Different than the pathological secondary narcissist, the mature subject self-replicates by investing objects with her own ego-libido and loves only the parts of herself she finds in the world.[7]

Deductiveness, on the other hand, was stoner logic—this much seemed obvious . . .

The work of psychoanalysis depends on the unsutured copresence of interpreter and witness. This is, as Paul Ricœur points out, one of the central problematics of Freud's work: it seems as though Freud is interested sometimes in meanings, sometimes in the mechanics of what happens. Yet what Ricœur names this "mixed discourse" he also calls the *"raison d'être* of psychoanalysis," as he attempts to think through the notion that Freud's mission was to make interpretation part of the act of witnessing, and witnessing part of the act of interpretation, without surrendering either to the other.[8] "How can the economic explanation be *involved* in an interpretation dealing with meanings; and conversely, how can interpretation be an *aspect* of the economic explanation? It is easier to fall back on a disjunction: either an explanation in terms of energy, or an understanding in terms of phenomenology. It must be recognized, however, that Freudianism exists only on the basis of its refusal of that disjunction."[9] Unpeeling the implications of that refusal leads Ricœur into *The Interpretation of Dreams*, the inaugural text of psychoanalytic method, and in particular to observing the coordination of the hermeneutic and the descriptive in the Freudian *Deutung*, or interpretation. Interpretation is the "mixed discourse" par excellence, because "to say that a dream is the fulfillment of a repressed wish is to put together two notions that belong to different orders: fulfillment (*Erfüllung*), which belongs to the discourse of meaning, and repression (*Verdrängung*), which belongs to the discourse of force."[10] For Ricœur, interpretation is not (just) a hermeneutics, but rather that "putting together" of hermeneutics with descriptive analysis, such that the subject of interpretation in *The Interpretation of Dreams* is not the dream—Freud's is not a dictionary of metaphysical symbols—but the mechanic of interpretation itself.

A "refusal" to disentangle mechanics from hermeneutics, however, is not only the destination of a science of interpretation, but the premise of an autoanalysis, in which not merely were the witness and interpreter identical, so too was the analytic subject, the dreamer himself. Psychoanalysis, infamously, started with a notoriously unsuccessful instance of self-exculpation: Freud's own dream of "Irma's Injection."[11] That dream, the subject of Freud's initial autoanalysis, revealed nothing more repressed by the dreamer-analyst than the latent thought, "I am not responsible for the persistence of Irma's pains," but, as Freud's friend Max Schur realized as early as 1966, nothing could have been further from the truth: Emma Eckstein, a patient of Freud's, had been subject to a serious surgical malpractice at the hands of Freud's confidant Wilhelm Fliess, who had left half a meter of medical gauze inside her nasal cavity, which had triggered the seepage of blood that Freud had diagnosed as hysterical, "occasioned by longing."[12] The episode illustrates with horrifying clarity the notion that, in the text of psychoanalysis, there is no mechanical description that is entirely devoid of hermeneutic overdetermination.[13]

Schur also realized that Eckstein played an important role in an equally formative moment in Freud's early career: the first stirrings of doubt in the so-called seduction theory of the origin of hysterical neurosis. That theory, which Freud elaborated in a paper entitled "The Aetiology of Hysteria" and delivered to the Vienna Psychiatric Society on April 21, 1896, held that the origins of hysterical symptoms in his patients (including Eckhardt's) were repressed memories of sexual abuse, usually carried out by their fathers; this view was treated skeptically by the society and dismissed as "a scientific fairy tale" by the sexologist Richard von Krafft-Ebing, who was in attendance.[14] That skepticism, in turn, led Freud to abandon the seduction theory altogether over the following year, explaining at last to Fliess in September 1897 that "it was hardly credible that perverted acts against children were so general."[15]

This narrative is well known outside the ranks of those who read Freud's letters because of two connected critiques leveled against Freud in the 1970s and 1980s: in an essay entitled "The Sexual Abuse of Children: A Feminist Point of View," delivered by the feminist activist Florence Rush at the April 1971 New York Radical Feminists Rape conference, and *The Assault on Truth:*

Freud's Suppression of the Seduction Theory, a systematic critique of psychoanalysis by Jeffrey Moussaieff Masson.[16] These two texts took Freud's malpractice in the Eckstein case, and his ambivalence about the reception of his 1896 paper, as evidence of a wider "cover-up" of child sexual assault, which in turn led psychoanalysis structurally to undervalue the testimony of patients reporting childhood sexual abuse.[17] Scholars tend to agree not only that Rush and Masson overstated the significance of Freud's abandonment of the seduction thesis—after all, he continued to believe that *some* of his patients had been sexually assaulted, and his later work was primarily concerned with posttraumatic symptoms—but that Rush in particular had mistaken the argument of Freud's 1896 paper based on the account of it he offered nearly forty years later in the *New Introductory Lectures on Psychoanalysis*.[18] Yet the accounts that Rush and Masson offered were persuasive enough to stimulate public interest in the notion of repressed memory of childhood sexual assault.

The subject of a "seduction theory," if one takes the argument as seriously as Rush and Masson urged, is radically at odds with the subject of psychoanalysis. As Ricœur showed, psychoanalysis operates by endlessly imbricating explanation and interpretation, orienting each process around the other, and binding the witness ever more firmly into the position of interpreter. But the position of someone whose memories themselves are repressed, whose project of cognitive reunification depends on the interpretation of memories whose mechanic is utterly absent to them but which nonetheless emerges into consciousness with the full force of literal truth, has sundered forever any dialectical mechanism. Rather, the work is simply to build truth via a process of permanent deductiveness, inferring lifeways from truths one inherits from a memory-function beyond even the minimally felt temporal continuity of consciousness. The subject of a seduction theory wakes up, receives narrative fragments whose ontology they are required to assume, and builds narrative in all directions toward and away from them. The affective texture of self-knowing is deductiveness; the medium is mood.

One might also hypothesize that the genre of such a project of deduction would be neo-noir, that genre of emerging Hollywood narrative coincident with Rush and Masson, two of whose early successes—Robert Altman's updated adaptation of *The Long Goodbye* (1973) and Roman Polanski's *Chinatown* (1974)—share more than their location in the dusty, semi-Western expanse of Los Angeles. Classic Hollywood noir movies, especially the works of Alfred Hitchcock, have long been associated with classically Freudian psychoanalytic accounts of subjectivity.[19] In D. A. Miller's essay "Anal *Rope*," for example, the heterosexual gaze of Hitchcock's camera associates the shadowy backsides of the gay male characters with the fear of castration that characterizes Oedipal maturity. Thus the visual and technical aspects of noir filmmaking reproduce—or perhaps have been cut to reproduce—the psychic conditions of Oedipalization, the developmental framework with which Freud supplanted the seduction thesis.

Neo-noir, on the other hand, is characterized by a certain aesthetic scrappiness, a multiplicity of visual and textual elements whose clutteredness signifies not merely the overdetermination of clues or data, but more crucially their inassimilability, the overabundance of knowable things. This aspect of neo-noir is highlighted in Larry Gross's 1976 essay on the "sociological" rather than "psychological" aspect of neo-noir, "Film après Noir: Alienation in a Dark Alley." While the traditional dick's greatest skill is his sense of timing, the neo-dick bumbles through a set of plots that happen *to* him: though both Altman's and Polanski's heroes are detectives, neither is exactly trying to solve a crime, and until *The Long Goodbye*'s Philip Marlowe (Elliot Gould) kills Terry Lennox (Jim Bouton) after speaking the last line of the film, neither escapes for even a second the complete control that other characters—Lennox, and *Chinatown*'s Noah Cross (John Huston)—have over them. Gross refers to these movies' understanding of protagonism as "a purely figural abstracted conception of a hero" and elaborates that subtle phrase, "purely figural," with an observation about Elliot Gould's dick: "[Marlowe's] nicotine addiction, his clothing, his catch-all line 'It's all right with me,' are foregrounded signs of a purely figural existence rooted in Hollywood's past."[20] His personhood has been vaporous, diffuse. Through a curious device of sound editing, Elliot Gould's mouth is, for most of the movie, kept out of shot, so his mumbling monologue, which is more or less uninterrupted for the whole two hours, feels like one line in the ambient soundscape, another instrument in the slow jazz variations on John Williams's title tune, as though Marlowe's interiority were itself an ambient effect, absorbed rather than emitted by the actor.

Is there a historical claim to be made? Neo-noir emerges as a response to the public collapse of faith in the psychoanalytic settlement of this question and the attempt to reopen the question of repressed memory? I wasn't sure . . .

Emma Heaney asked me to write something autotheoretical—"is that what you would say you do? I know not everyone likes the term . . ."—about the unusual position I've played in the "terf wars" of the last couple of years.

"An object of other people's paranoia" was her phrase. Damn straight. Earlier today I received a bizarre email from an anonymous account—bizarre, except I get messages like this every day. It describes a scene in which I interrupt some regular working-class men going about their business, desperate for them to make me feel like a woman. When one of the men starts to undress, my heart leaps. Turns out he's asking me to iron his shirt. If that's a joke, this whole damn system is a joke.

In thrall to a sexual masochism she can name but hardly control, this "flustered" and evening-gowned gull "zeroed in" on these polite ("heck") but strip-happy joes, only to realize that patriarchy's disinterest in satisfying even *masochistic* desire when it is articulated from a place of conspicuous femininity subs out the sauce and reapplies the beefcake. Male body as threat of nonsexual sadism—exhilarating, my Aunt Fanny. Femininity is the spectacle of wanting to get fucked and getting *fucked* instead.

How does it feel to be the object of someone else's paranoia? Hell, it feels great. Len Gutkin suggests that the traditional dick's anomie might have been constructed, by Raymond Chandler at least, through an ambivalent negotiation with the Wildean epigram—itself evidence of a more fundamental ambivalence about the figure of what Chandler called "the homosexualist."[21] Obviously, I'm getting high on it. Yesterday, a man named Adam Hibbert—and what a name for a white-bread chump—ran a Twitter thread asking "why is Grace Lavery an icon and Rachel Dolezal is a pariah?"[22] The missile was precision-tipped to produce the compensatory affect of stupefied but asymptotic assent: *good question, mmm, yes, this is the question, once you've framed the question this way, the absurdity of this whole situation is revealed.* What fascinates str8 ppl about transsexuals is the same as what fascinates everyone else: the superfluity of embodiment—always "figural," but never "purely" so. But the value they extract from us is of another kind entirely: it is the promise that politics might be conflictual again, that competing interests (even on the left) might be enumerated and split. A political scientist colleague of mine, who insisted on pronouncing the word "trans" to rhyme with "barns," once explained to me during a meeting that debates over trans women's access to public restrooms would have the salutary effect of ending the détente between anti-sex feminism (which, he said, was rooted in American puritanism) and the sexually licentious liberalism of the boomer flower children.

"As a British Marxist, I'm thrilled," he added.

"Oh yeah?" I asked.

"The left has been complacent, papering over disagreements, unable to explain its positions, and that's why we've been unable to build a mass movement."

"Whatever you say, man."

"You don't agree?"

"I try not to discuss toilet architecture in the workplace . . ."

"—it's NOT just architecture—"

". . . but I do think that any unity forged in a bonfire of trans feminine vanity doesn't sound like a whole lotta fun to me . . ."

"But don't you see, it's not supposed to be *fun*—"

"Whatever you say, Doc. Whatever you say."

So it's not just paranoia. But it is paranoia too. I realize that, when I was talking about conspiratorial thinking earlier, I referred to a conspiracy theorist as a "conspirator." My lover, who read this, said, "But they're not conspirators, they're conspiracy *theorists*." I replied to indicate that, in my view, potatoes were very much like po-*tah*-toes, and that to theorize a conspiracy is to become a conspirator. That's the nonnegotiable reflex action to believing in a conspiracy. "Sure," said my lover, "but they'd never admit it."

I could have been clearer. But that's the problem: I don't remember what side I'm on, theorist or conspirator. That's another aspect of the neo-noir to add to the list of decathexes: the institutions that might have allowed one to know by whom one is claimed have blurred into one, and there are no sides, just ambience.

Around the house, I refer to the suspects by their last names. I don't pin those names to the corkboard, but I might as well: Stock, Linehan, "Posey Parker" (it's a nickname, so I use both), Jones. . . . Sometimes this group of brainiacs fills the whole page, and I see nothing more than a totality. Damn right, I'm paranoid. My ex told me I was a member of the Illuminati now. Maybe she was right.

I forget if they're brave warriors after truth, or deliberate misinformation peddlers. *The Invisibles* taught me that all conspiracy theories are true—aliens are among us; the Queen was complicit in the human sacrifice of the personification of the hunter goddess Diana—and that felt true, felt energizing.[23] Power protects power, so maybe the epistemic immiseration of the disempowered could produce the knowledge specific to the revolutionary class? "Queer theory" is increasingly named as the psychic blitzkrieg of the ruling class—it is on these grounds, and because I supposedly preach it, that dozens of people call me a pedophile online. QAnon, but starring queer academics.[24] Three days ago, in his essay explaining why I am "grooming" students by teaching texts by Foucault and Hocquengham, Graham Linehan twice uses the phrase "no wonder Lavery didn't want parents listening in."[25] Today he's speaking to the House of Lords.

Sure, Emma. Autotheory. That's what I do.

The neo-noir has always had an affinity with marijuana. And it's close kin with the stoner caper: the first Cheech and Chong movie, *Up in Smoke*, shares with *The Long Goodbye* a plot concerning smuggling people into Tijuana, and like Gould's Marlowe, the central pair are equally pestered by cops and organized criminals. Likewise, the animated stoner movie *Fritz the Cat* (1972) shares with *The Long Goodbye* a mumbly urban soundscape in which the speaking mouths are never seen—in the opening sequence, three working joes are speaking an apparently documentary dialogue, and the animation jump-cuts to reveal that these are cartoon animals, sitting on a girder.[26] The visual field has been crafted to the specifications of the audio track, not just in the sense that the cartoon characters are moving their mouths along to prerecorded audio, but in a more capacious sense: in order to illustrate the sense of quotidian Manhattan hubbub that the apparently found audio footage conveys, one of these animals is struggling to squeeze his sandwich, ballooning over with meat and lettuce, into his expanding mouth. The object and his body concertina in scale in wobbly dance: it's a stoned association, suspending the laws of physics and replacing them with mere scuzzy, fungible congruence. Later on, hippie animals smoke weed and play with each other's bodies in a bath: a bunny (after the Playboy Club waitresses, presumably) moans "I'm there, I'm there!" and could mean either that she is stoned or that she is coming; the two merge.

The motif of stoned, hippie sexual community recurs in *The Long Goodbye*, with the girls getting high with their boobs out on the balcony opposite Marlowe's apartment. "A melon party. Melon party!" he mumbles, rounding the corner. What makes this scene especially striking is the lack of visual interest that the camera extracts from the nymphets in blue jeans: their circle is closed, and Altman seems (typically, perhaps) happy to observe, rather than to penetrate, the social connections he depicts. The shot spreads open the landscape of Hollywood Heights—the apartment building scenes were shot at 2178 High Tower Drive—as if displacing from the bodies onto the landscape the possibility of exploration, incursion, escalation. Gross argues that

9.1. Still from *Fritz the Cat* (dir. Ralph Bakshi, 1972).

the erotic energies of the neo-noir hero are "all but extinguished," but it would be premature to conclude that the universes of these movies are themselves anerotic. Rather, the frazzled libido in neo-noir is no longer focalized through characters, but displaced onto closed communities of blissed-out stoner girls, nature chicks whose oneness with the landscape is a sexual, and not merely aspirational, fact.

If the ecological embrace of the landscape insures Altman's dick against the potentially castrating closure of the group of girls, the embrace of Mother Earth uses the particular landscape of Los Angeles, terra-cotta roofs smeared over canyons and hills.[27] At stake in this embrace is the scalability of pastoral: an urban site depicted as the oversaturation of space by the pleasures of space, greenery, and the "colonial style." Gould's shuffling but unfazed Marlowe acts as gofer for the girls—his first action is to head to the supermarket, and he agrees to pick them up some brownie mix, to ferry goods between the green world and that of shoddy commercialism. (Gould's Marlowe is above all a mule: he conveys brownie mix to the girls, Terry Lennox to Tijuana, and Roger Wade back to his cheating wife.) Weed, the part of the green world that the girls take into their bodies, cannot be obtained at the supermarket. *Chinatown*'s green worlds are entirely hypothetical, the film's title naming the Los Angeles that negates that green world altogether, and the patches of green in which Evelyn Mulwray (Faye Dunaway) fantasizes her safety are themselves evidence of the villainy of her father, Noah Cross. At an individual scale, because the saltwater from the Mulwray lawn proves that Cross killed Hollis Mulwray, but globally, because his plan to irrigate (and therefore greenify) and then incorporate the San Gabriel Valley is the motive behind his murderous and megalomaniacal plot.

9.2. Still from
The Long Goodbye
(dir. Robert
Altman, 1973).

Although neo-noir always possessed this affinity with marijuana, with its attendant oscillations between natural/synthetic, urban modern/rural pastoral, paranoia/imaginativeness, and torpor/spontaneity, it was not until the late 1990s revival of the genre that it moved, seemingly, to incorporate the ethos of stonerdom altogether, in Quentin Tarantino's *Jackie Brown* (1997); Guy Ritchie's *Lock, Stock, and Two Smoking Barrels* (1998); the Coen Brothers' *The Big Lebowski* (1998); and then later in David Gordon Green's *Pineapple Express* (2008); Thomas Pynchon's 2009 novel *Inherent Vice*, which Paul Thomas Anderson adapted into a movie released in 2014; and David Robert Mitchell's *Under the Silver Lake* (2018).[28] *L.A. Confidential* (1997), a pastiche of noir movies of the Otto Preminger type, rather than a neo-noir, had turned marijuana into an important element of the plot, but the movie itself didn't feel stoned, and its method of reasoning was essentially distinct: it is his unexpected retreat to traditional shoe-leather detection that gets Jack Vincennes (Kevin Spacey) to the truth, and killed; Ed Exley (Guy Pearce) gets there through archival work, and due to the villain's saying a shibboleth— "Rollo Tomasi"—that revealed he was Jack's killer. The movie contains none of the verbal or visual signs of deductiveness: the liquid-furrowed forehead melting, druggily, over the brow of crossed eyes; the stuttering dick's comically inarticulate attempt to persuade one of the str8s that he's on top of the facts.[29]

These signs are all exhibited in *The Big Lebowski*, which has generated enough scholarly attention to fill a volume jovially entitled *The Year's Work in Lebowski Studies*, which compiles essays exploring the resonances of the Coen Brothers' movie with high-cultural touchstones as far apart as the Fluxus movement, the Grail quest, and the New Left.[30] The film's appeal as a switch-point for various genres and apparently diverse lines of cultural influence has obscured, however, the degree to which *The Big Lebowski* so perfectly encapsulates the genre in which it does its own work: the stoner neo-noir. To stipulate three of the more emphatically realized of these effects:

1 **Circular bathos:** In the scene at his midcentury mansion, the pornographer Jackie Treehorn (Ben Gazzara) takes a call (on an anachronistic phone), writes something invisible to the camera on a pad of paper, rips off the top leaf, and then walks out of the frame. Our hero, the Dude (Jeff Bridges), perhaps remembering Cary Grant in *North by Northwest*, heads over to the pad and rubs a pencil over the palimpsest, to reveal what perhaps might be a secret message but in fact turns out to be a doodle of a male figure masturbating an enormous phallus. The joke is a little more complicated than it might appear: what the Dude realizes, when he sees the doodle, is that the cinematic genre whose conventions he was mimicking was, after all, no more capable of disclosing plot or assigning meaning than he could juice from his own posture of speculative, stoned immobility. It is like learning that the grown-up genres smoke weed too, and that the taste not merely for the sexual, but for the *dumbly* sexual, is a vector of continuity between the stoner counterculture and the rich str8 folks in the hills. The moment thus recapitulates visually the logic of the Dude's *conscious*, but equally failed, attempt at bathos a minute earlier:

> JACKIE TREEHORN: The new technology permits us to do exciting things with interactive erotic software. Wave of the future, Dude. One hundred percent electronic.
>
> THE DUDE: Uh-huh. Well, I still jerk off manually.
>
> JACKIE TREEHORN: Of course you do. I can see you're anxious to get to the point.

It is clear that the Dude's attempt to knock Treehorn off his future surfboard has failed, but it is less clear precisely what Treehorn's withering response is supposed to indicate: that the Dude is an analogue masturbator in a digital world (which, then, might position Treehorn's doodle as something of a defeat)? Or, with a more sadistic bent, that while he did not expect the Dude to have any opinion on "interactive erotic software" worth hearing, he is nonetheless disappointed by the sheer witlessness of his failure to play along (which might then exempt the character from the exposure of generic vacuity with the doodle)?

2 **Stickiness:** The language of *The Big Lebowski* is like that sticky icky—dank and difficult to dislodge. The stoner mind absorbs phrases from the str8

world and disgorges them back into it elsewhere. First, the Dude hears George Bush on the television telling Saddam Hussein "this aggression into Kuwait will not stand," and then later he spits it back at the titular Lebowski: "This will not stand, man. If your wife owes money . . ." Or, when the hifalutin Maude Lebowski (Julianne Moore), herself mimicking speech she considers beneath her, says that her father's wife "has been banging Jackie Treehorn, to use the parlance of our times," the phatic phrase reappears, once more in the face of the big Lebowski (David Huddleston), when the Dude refers to a "young trophy wife, I mean, in the parlance of our times." Yet here, Jeff Bridges's enunciation reveals that the character hasn't fully understood Maude's usage and seems to think the phrase means something like "nowadays, when things are so precarious."

3 **"New shit"**: The spectacle of stoned deductiveness requires the exhibition of conspicuous thought, of the exertive application of effort. The stoner hero is not a dick, exactly, since the dick (like Da Fino, a "brother shamus") is a schmo, and the stoner is nobody's fool but fortune's. So the labor of the nondick stoner is to produce not a solution to the case, but the *appearance* of working on the case, without forgetting that everything is, in reality, out of his control. His performance of reasoning is not persuasive ("new shit has come to light and—shit, man! she kidnapped herself!"), but nor exactly is it intended to persuade, since it would be just as useful from the Dude's perspective that the big Lebowski think him an earnest idiot as that he think him a credible detective.

There are more, obviously.

I don't know what I think about autotheory. It seems like one way out of the relevance-and-hype market of academic prose, which has been in rapid and unmanageable inflation for a few decades and which shudders still further with each spasmodic contraction of the labor market. I don't want to be relevant—I don't want (trans) to be theorized!—except if it be by happy accident, by being in the right place at the right time and letting history suffuse me. But I don't know the provenance of this wish. I'm skeptical of it. "Sometimes there's a man, and I'm not saying a hero, cuz what's a hero, but sometimes there's a man—and I'm talkin' about the Dude here—sometimes there's a man who, well, he's the man for his time and place" (*The Big Lebowski*).

The guiltless classicism of boomer historiography discloses itself each time history simply engulfs a passive dude, filling him with history in return for his injection of meaning: Forrest Gump showing his ass to LBJ.[31]

Look at history happening to me: Forrest Gump, Jeffrey "the Dude" Lebowski, Paul Preciado. Masculine men, each of them, but each also penetrated, oddly passive in the face of their own discourse, flirtatious and indirect. Preciado writes,

> I'm not interested in my emotions insomuch as their being mine, belonging only, uniquely, to me. I'm not interested in their individual aspects, only in how they are traversed by what isn't mine. In what emanates from our planet's history, the evolution of living species, the flux of economics, remnants of technological innovations, preparation for wars, the trafficking of organic slaves and commodities, the creation of hierarchies, institutions of punishment and repression, networks of communication and surveillance, the random overlapping of market research groups, the biochemical transformation of feeling, the production and distribution of pornographic images.[32]

Preciado (b. 1970) is supposedly a member of Generation X, rather than a baby boomer, but he has nonetheless absorbed the boomers' characteristic subordination of macrohistorical narrative into a series of private traversals: "you had to be there," but also, "if you can remember the sixties, you weren't really there." The passage smashes together two rhetorical figures: praeteritio and asyndeton. Praeteritio, the art of saying something under negation, works its scuzzy magic in that classic formulation of scholarly bad faith: "I'm not interested in ..." This isn't about *me*, this is about the world as it happens to me; it is a phenomenological inrush of historical matter that I hold in my emotional sensorium solely because there is nowhere else for me to hold it, but the body is as disposable a vessel as can be imagined. The hygienic discretion with which Preciado wipes away the traces of *auto* in his theory conspicuously draws attention to that which, in fact, it was never supposed to obscure: the phenomenologist's genial objectivity, his asserted capacity to withstand the battening of historical and chemical force with his disinterest manfully intact. Autotheory earns its bones behind the body of the autotheorist, inters him in a shallow grave of macrohistorical runoff. That runoff, meanwhile, splashes through the page as asyndeton, unsubordinated and polyvalent: as with Flaubert in Roland Barthes's description, "a generalized asyndeton seizes the entire utterance, so that this very readable discourse is *underhandedly* one of the craziest imaginable: all the logical small change is in the interstices."[33] Between the apparently disorganized phrases Preciado discloses an unspoken *auto*, which is to say an undisavowed *auto*.

What are the historical conditions of possibility for this image? History has taken Linehan (b. 1968) by surprise too, though he is a stunt autotheorist, who also believes that he can arrest the insanity of the present moment merely by exhibiting it, amplifying it in the emptiness of his own sensorium. It is a project of profound hostility to the *auto*, self-immolating in the service of a comic construction of history, as though Forrest Gump were *himself* trying to imagine the historical position of a Forrest Gump. The conspiracy, which is obvious to anyone inside this discourse and surreal to everyone else, is that the dating app Her, which claims to serve the lesbian community, in fact sells that community out by including men as sexual prospects.[34] Perhaps there are examples of this, but the only one that anyone will cite is now Linehan himself, goofily mugging from the isolation of his own self-exile. Does such a project of historical self-erasure possess a motivation, beyond the obvious desires inevitably caught in the undertow of such steamy negations? (Which is to say, the lesbian phallus.)[35] Perhaps this: that the trans woman Graham, who claims to be twenty-nine, has lied about her age and therefore performed a generational betrayal, and even (more fancifully) has traveled in time.

If the stoner non-dick (the Dude, Preciado) is the diagnostician of twentieth-century history, then what we learn is that diagnosis is betrayal, a treacherous renaming of the condition of historical being.

I wanted to write about my love affair with a lesbian named L—, and about the ways she has taught me to rename my body, as well as those parasomatic moods that govern my, for example, fidgetiness, or the psychosocial praxis that governs whether or not I am passable in a given frame. I wanted to write into my lover, to groove my words into her flesh, as I pump them out of her with my hand. This, I thought, would be an autotheory worth the name, would answer the stuntists and historical castrati, phallically would reconstruct the episteme of modernity from the lesbian pussy. I wanted to be born out of her into my own body, to birth her through my hole, and I wanted to mash my face into her clit until I gagged and choked, love and melody. Everything I care about is love; why does anyone write about anything else, ever?

I don't know, man. I don't know what I'm making, what I'm repairing. I feel stoned in love and I need a vocabulary. It's not autotheory, it's autocriticism, and it's only that because it isn't anything else.

To recap the argument. ("The story so far.") I have noticed that trans people seem weary of being the subject of endless theoretical speculations, of being positioned as either the apogetic example or the confounding case of queer theory. I have suggested that this weariness is felt through a curious epistemological condition that I have called "deductiveness," which proceeds by a series of enthymemes: inquiries in which neither conclusion nor premise is known. This mode of reasoning, I have argued, is rigorously depicted (or as rigorously as possible) in a genre of representation I have called stoner neo-noir, which has its roots in 1970s noir revivalism but also absorbs new, and generational, theories of historical causality ("boomer historiography"). I have also aligned this mode of reasoning with the 1970s challenge to psychoanalytic accounts of hysteria, and in particular with the attempt by Jeffrey Masson and Florence Rush to restore the so-called seduction thesis, which in turn enabled the so-called recovered memory therapy. Like the stoner neo-noir, recovered memory positions people as receivers of their memories, splitting the functions of witnessing and interpreting, prizing apart metapsychology and hermeneutics. We come to, with a new memory.

This literally just popped up on my computer. Coincidence? I wondered.

David Robert Mitchell's 2018 neo-noir *Under the Silver Lake* picks up a number of these themes.[36] The central character, Sam (Andrew Garfield), is a rapacious consumer and reproducer of conspiracy theories who has absorbed part of the paranoid relation to media that *The Invisibles* disseminated.[37] Since his life as a drifter in Los Angeles is suffused on all sides by media, from the smiling ophthalmology ad on a billboard saying "I can see clearly now" (a face half of which is eventually replaced by a clown) to the notices across the Silver Lake neighborhood saying "Watch out for the Dog Killer," he therefore develops a paranoid, 1990s method of reading his own existence out of the world. The film therefore affords an opportunity to distinguish between boomer (*The Big Lebowski*), Gen X (*Testo Junkie*), and millennial stoner neo-noir, and to thread through this genre a history of postmodern relation to genre. In *Under the Silver Lake*, the disintegrated subject of neo-noir moves into a phase of reenchantment and repair, where the melancholic effects of

9.3. Still from
*Under the Silver
Lake* (dir. David
Robert Mitchell,
2018).

split subjecthood have worn off, and we are left with a subject whose object-hood has been fully installed into the world of object-signs. Sam not only accepts his position as a powerless cipher of genre, but revels in it; unlike the Dude, then, he has cheerful, low-stakes sex with a handful of people—one of whom, his middle-aged, topless neighbor, seems to stand almost literally for the stoner girls in *The Long Goodbye*, in the same apartment (or same type of apartment), forty-four years later. (The later movie was shot at 3205 Los Feliz Boulevard, a fifteen-minute drive away on the other side of Griffith Park.)

The big Lebowski plots to embezzle funds from the Little Lebowski Urban Achievers charity and create the impression that either the Dude has stolen the briefcase or the kidnappers failed to make good on their ransom note. His scheme is the squalid and ordinary shittiness of a man who, for all his pretentions, is even worse with money than the Dude; when the Dude unveils what has happened, the Lebowskis are, perversely, each diminished by becoming equal with the other. The Dude requires no accommodation to the events of the plot ("let's go bowling") because he has ingested and normalized a difference: a doppelgänger initially troubling because of his difference from the little Lebowski, has been brought into the muck, much as the pig-cop in *Felix the Cat* is thwarted by being pulled into the bath orgy. *Under the Silver Lake* portrays the most paranoid conspiracies that deductiveness can produce (enthymemes without premises): the number of letters in each word in one song leads Sam to derive a code from the lyrics of another one, which produces the phrase "rub Dean's head and wait under Newton." Sam heads up to the Griffith Observatory, rubs the statue of James Dean, and crouches under the bust of Newton until he is visited by the "Homeless King" and taken to an underground system of tunnels—which eventually he learns are pyramid-style tombs build under the Hollywood Hills where wealthy Angelenos are buried alive with three "brides," so that, as the "Final Man" puts it, shortly before he himself is interred, "future men will understand that *we* were the modern kings. Rulers without statues or effigies." No renormalization for Sam, whose paranoia plot deprives of bathetic deflation, but the perverse normality of harmonization—a reunification of the sign deriving from the universalization of deductive reasoning.

It feels counterintuitive to align Freud, arch nominalizer of phenomena and traducer of fuzziness, with deductiveness—the feeling of thought deprived of premise or destination. Yet to return once more to the dream of "Irma's Injection," that dream by which (as we have seen) Freud deflected any regret he felt over Emma Eckstein and, plenty have argued, sublimated his feelings of unprofessional attachment toward Wilhelm Fliess, we can pay special attention to the moment when the dream violates both the natural physical order and, in its retelling, the syntactic organization of elements: "Not long before, when she was feeling unwell, my friend Otto had given her an injection of a preparation of propyl, propyls . . . propionic acid . . . trimethylamin (*and I saw before me the formula for this printed in heavy type*). . . . Injections of this sort ought not to be given so thoughtlessly. . . . And probably the syringe had not been clean."[38] In fact, Freud's list of chemicals slips into asyndeton, as the chemicals slip off the page and into Freud's line of imaginative vision, and he starts to slur his own words. The sequencing of elements emerges from phonic echoes—"propyls, propyls, propionic acid"— rather than from logical orientation. Freud is stupefied, for once. Fittingly, since the terrain into which he is passing here is a terrain in which the text of memory—the basis for what he thinks of as the "seduction theory"—is staring him right in the face.

NOTES

1 Tourmaline, Stanley, and Burton, *Trap Door.*
2 Gill-Peterson, *Histories of the Transgender Child.*
3 Gossett and Hayward, "Trans in a Time of HIV/AIDS."
4 Benjamin, "On the Theory of Knowledge, Theory of Progress," 462.
5 Fried, "Three American Painters."
6 Laing, *Knots.*
7 Freud, "On Narcissism."
8 Ricœur, *Freud and Philosophy*, 65.
9 Ricœur, *Freud and Philosophy*, 66.
10 Ricœur, *Freud and Philosophy*, 92.

11 Freud, *Interpretation of Dreams*, 96–121.

12 Gay, *Freud*, 84–87; Welsh, *Freud's Wishful Dream Book*, 23.

13 This is the subject of much scholarly analysis. For example, see Hunter, *Seduction and Theory*.

14 Masson, *Complete Letters of Sigmund Freud*, 184.

15 Masson, *Complete Letters of Sigmund Freud*, 264. See also Eissler, *Freud and the Seduction Theory*.

16 Masson, *Freud: The Assault on Truth*. Masson addressed connections between his work and Rush's in his essay "A Personal Perspective."

17 See Rush, *Best Kept Secret*.

18 Schimek, "Fact and Fantasy in the Seduction Theory"; Israëls and Schatzman, "Seduction Theory."

19 Though neither is at all an orthodox Freudian, Žižek and Miller both explore Freudian classicism in their books on Hitchcock. A version of this argument is also outlined in Larry Gross's 1976 essay "Film après Noir: Alienation in a Dark Alley," which first outlines the new noir of *The Long Goodbye* and *Chinatown* (as well as Jean-Luc Godard's *Alphaville*, John Boorman's *Point Blank*, and Nicholas Roeg's *Performance*). See Žižek, *Everything You Always Wanted to Know about Lacan*; Miller, *Hidden Hitchcock*; and Gross, "Film après Noir."

20 Gross, "Film après Noir," 45, 47.

21 Gutkin, "Dandified Dick."

22 Adam Hibbert (@adhib), Twitter, March 8, 2021, 5:19 a.m., https://twitter.com/adhib/status/1368868882971246597.

23 Morrison, *The Invisibles*.

24 Jane Clare Jones (@janeclarejones), Twitter, September 17, 2021, 9:32 a.m., https://twitter.com/janeclarejones/status/1438858335701327877; https://twitter.com/janeclarejones/status/1438858337467211776: "So, a request for someone to write something—shortish—for the next issue of TRN. Ideally an American, or someone living/has lived in the States. Am interested in exploring the whole 'post truth left and right' thing, specifically of course QAnon/Trans ideology, and would be particularly interested in an analysis that could link this to any notable aspects of American culture, history or politics . . . for example, religiosity, lack of material class politics, conspiracy theories etc."

25 Linehan, "Just So It's Absolutely Clear."

26 Bakshi, *Fritz the Cat*.

27 For an argument about neo-noir as revenge against midcentury modernist architecture, see the video essay by Andersen, *Los Angeles Plays Itself*.

28 All of these films, except for the British movie *Lock, Stock*, were set and filmed in Los Angeles too.

29 The release of *Inherent Vice* in 2014 prompted an essay by the film critic Chris Wade on "slacker noir," which defines the genre according to a protagonist's "wish to remove themselves from the action." Yet while this might apply to *Pineapple Express*, and more tendentiously to *The Big Lebowski* (tendentious because the

Dude does accept commissions from both Maude Lebowski and Jackie Treehorn to retrieve the missing briefcase), it can hardly apply to *Inherent Vice*, whose protagonist is a professional private investigator, albeit a stoned one; and even less to *Under the Silver Lake*, whose protagonist is an obsessive collator of clues and conspiracy theories. See Wade, *"Inherent Vice."*

30 Jaffe and Comentale, *Year's Work in Lebowski Studies.*

31 Zemeckis, *Forrest Gump.*

32 Preciado, *Testo Junkie*, 11–12.

33 Barthes, *Pleasure of the Text*, 9.

34 Ironically, or not, I was kicked off Her in 2017 for looking too masculine. To get back on the app, I would have needed to supply them with a passport or state ID illustrating the change in my gender markers. I didn't have such ID obviously; I just wanted to date people.

35 Butler, "The Lesbian Phallus and the Morphological Imaginary," in *Bodies That Matter*, 28–57.

36 Mitchell, *Under the Silver Lake.*

37 "I mean, I've just been thinking, why do we assume that all of this infrastructure and entertainment and open information beaming all over the place into every home on the planet is exactly what people tell us it is. Maybe there are people more important, more powerful or wealthier than us that communicate things or see things in the world that are meant for them and not for us. I think it's fucking ridiculous to assume that media only has one purpose . . . right?" (*Under the Silver Lake*).

38 Freud, *Interpretation of Dreams*, 107 (emphasis added).

BIBLIOGRAPHY

Andersen, Thom, dir. *Los Angeles Plays Itself*. Cinema Guild, 2014.

Anderson, Paul Thomas, dir. *Inherent Vice*. Warner Bros., 2014.

Bakshi, Ralph, dir. *Fritz the Cat*. Cinemation Industries, 1972.

Barthes, Roland. *The Pleasure of the Text*. Translated by Richard Miller. New York: Hill and Wang, 1975.

Benjamin, Walter. *The Arcades Project*. Translated by Howard Eiland and Kevin McLaughlin. Cambridge, MA: Harvard University Press, 1999.

Butler, Judith. *Bodies That Matter: On the Discursive Limits of "Sex."* London: Routledge, 1993.

Coen, Joel, and Ethan Coen, dirs. *The Big Lebowski*. Gramercy Pictures, 1998.

Eissler, K. R. *Freud and the Seduction Theory: A Brief Love Affair*. Madison, CT: International Universities Press, 2001.

Freud, Sigmund. *The Interpretation of Dreams*. Vol. 4 of *The Standard Edition of the Complete Psychological Works of Sigmund Freud*, edited by James Strachey, Anna Freud, Alix Strachey, and Alan Tyson. London: Hogarth, 1953.

Freud, Sigmund. "On Narcissism." 1914. In *The Standard Edition of the Complete Psychological Works of Sigmund Freud*, vol. 14, edited by James Strachey, Alix Strachey, and Alan Tyson, 67–102. London: Hogarth, 1957.

Fried, Michael. "Three American Painters: Kenneth Noland, Jules Olitski, Frank Stella." In *Art and Objecthood: Essays and Reviews*, 213–68. Chicago: University of Chicago Press, 1998.

Gay, Peter. *Freud: A Life for Our Time*. New York: W. W. Norton, 2006.

Gill-Peterson, Jules. *Histories of the Transgender Child*. Minneapolis: University of Minnesota Press, 2018.

Gossett, Che, and Eva Hayward. "Trans in a Time of HIV/AIDS." *TSQ* 7, no. 4 (2020): 527–53.

Green, David Gordon, dir. *Pineapple Express*. Sony Pictures Releasing, 2008.

Gross, Larry. "Film après Noir: Alienation in a Dark Alley." *Film Comment* 12, no. 4 (1976): 44–49.

Gutkin, Len. "The Dandified Dick: Hardboiled Noir and the Wildean Epigram." *ELH* 81, no. 4 (2014): 1299–326.

Hunter, Dianne, ed. *Seduction and Theory: Readings of Gender, Representation, and Rhetoric*. Urbana: University of Illinois Press, 1989.

Israëls, Han, and Morton Schatzman. "The Seduction Theory." *History of Psychiatry* 4, no. 13 (1993): 23–59.

Jaffe, Aaron, and Edward P. Comentale, eds. *The Year's Work in Lebowski Studies*. Bloomington: Indiana University Press, 2009.

Laing, R. D. *Knots*. Harmondsworth, UK: Penguin, 1970.

Linehan, Graham. "Just So It's Absolutely Clear." *Glinner Update*, March 6, 2021. https://grahamlinehan.substack.com/p/just-so-its-absolutely-clear.

Masson, J. Moussaieff, ed. *The Complete Letters of Sigmund Freud to Wilhelm Fliess, 1887–1904*. Cambridge, MA: Harvard University Press.

Masson, J. Moussaieff. *Freud: The Assault on Truth; Freud's Suppression of the Seduction Theory*. London: Faber and Faber, 1984.

Masson, J. Moussaieff. "A Personal Perspective: The Response to Child Abuse Then and Now." *Journal of Trauma and Dissociation* 18, no. 3 (2017): 476–82.

Miller, D. A. *Hidden Hitchcock*. Chicago: University of Chicago Press, 2017.

Mitchell, David Robert, dir. *Under the Silver Lake*. A24, 2018.

Morrison, Grant. *The Invisibles*. 3 vols. New York: DC Comics, 1996–2000.

Preciado, Paul B. *Testo Junkie: Sex, Drugs, and Biopolitics in the Pharmacopornographic Era*. New York: Feminist Press, 2013.

Ricœur, Paul. *Freud and Philosophy: An Essay on Interpretation*. Translated by Denis Savage. New Haven, CT: Yale University Press, 1970.

Ritchie, Guy, dir. *Lock, Stock and Two Smoking Barrels*. Gramercy Pictures, 1998.

Rush, Florence. *The Best Kept Secret: Sexual Abuse of Children*. Englewood Cliffs, NJ: Prentice Hall, 1980.

Schimek, Jean G. "Fact and Fantasy in the Seduction Theory: A Historical Review." *Journal of the American Psychoanalytic Association* 35, no. 4 (1987): 937–65.

Tarantino, Quentin, dir. *Jackie Brown*. Miramax Films, 1997.

Tourmaline, Eric A. Stanley, and Johanna Burton, eds. *Trap Door: Trans Cultural Production and the Politics of Visibility*. Cambridge, MA: MIT Press, 2017.

Wade, Chris. "*Inherent Vice, The Big Lebowski*, and the Rise of 'Slacker Noir.'" *Slate*, January 9, 2015. https://slate.com/culture/2015/01/inherent-vice-the-big -lebowski-and-the-rise-of-slacker-noir-video.html.

Welsh, Alexander. *Freud's Wishful Dream Book*. Princeton, NJ: Princeton University Press, 1994.

Zemeckis, Robert, dir. *Forrest Gump*. Paramount Pictures, 1994.

Žižek, Slavoj, ed. *Everything You Always Wanted to Know about Lacan (but Were Afraid to Ask Hitchcock)*. London: Verso, 1992.

AFTERWORD

Toward a Feminism for the Living

To be against cisness is to orient oneself otherwise. It is a political and pedagogical stance, a process of learning to be disenchanted with the fictions that have established cis difference as the sacred destiny of settler dreams. In *Feminism against Cisness*, we learn of the methodological, material, and affective struggles of writing trans life in and against the currents of dominant cisgender narratives. The essays in this volume confront the inadequacy of history and theory to work against cisness through careful engagements with fragmented archives, transgressive storytelling, and conceptual meditations on cis difference as aesthetic and material imposition. As Emma Heaney powerfully suggests in the introduction, cisness is distinct from the analytical framework of sexual difference, a concept essential to feminist critiques of power. Cisness is the relentless invention and violent enforcement of biological certitude in science, law, education, policy, and economic life that delimits gender to the perceived sex of the body at birth and reinforces that assignment in social roles that follow. Cisness, the forced biologizing of sex as fact, obscures how sexual difference functions through complex ideologies of masculine domination over the feminine that live in and exceed gendered bodies. To be in opposition to cisness requires a hermeneutical approach that moves beyond critique toward a total reimagining of cis chronologies and the categorical impositions of cis difference that have fortified the framework of global white supremacy for centuries.

Abolishing cisness is an ongoing project that refuses the endless demands placed on trans people to be both the crisis and site of redemption for contemporary politics. Easier said than done perhaps. The contributions to this volume reveal the challenges of this project—the failed promises of historical presence in archives built to reinforce structures of gender difference, the nonconsensual demands of confession, the enduring misuse of political speech, and even the inadequacies of seemingly more transphilic genres of the revelatory memoir or autotheory. We confront a cruel reality: proof of the existence of trans people in the past and present is both essential and insufficient to dismantling cisgender economies that traffic in recognition, disclosure, and the perpetual diagnosis of trans people for easy consumption.

A key question animates this project: How do we write the lifeworlds of trans people who are denied basic access to life at every turn? Indeed, variations on *life* as living, livability, life-making appear again and again as a site of critique and aspiration across these contributions: Cameron Awkward-Rich's meditation on Sojourner Truth's "life" historically denied, Marquis Bey's "livable gender trouble," Kay Gabriel's "life worth living for everyone," Jules Gill-Peterson's pursuit of a "life outside of reproduction," Margaux Kristjannson and Emma Heaney's "life-making," Greta LaFleur's fleeting "affirmative articulation of trans lives," Beans Velocci's critique of new "structures that have occluded trans life," Joanna Wuest's critique of the alliances that build trans-exclusionary "public life," and Grace Lavery's weariness about the deductive reasoning of remembering trans life anew. The contributions explore hermeneutical approaches that defy cis norms, methods that further how we understand, envision, and write existence against the evidentiary, testimonial, and medicalized modes that this cis world demands.

Yet the seemingly endless incitement to discourse about *transness* dislocates trans existence from the nuances and complexities of life. Trans people are again and again rendered as abstractions, disembodied or disassembled objects subject to reform, correction, racialization, condemnation, criminalization, incarceration, and incessant social and political crises. The objectification of trans people takes another form as well, in political and academic theorizing that casts trans people as idealized subjects, the last *frontier* of good radical politics.[1] In this idealization, trans people of the past and present are exalted as the most ideal mode of revolutionary existence, a moral claim that distances the experiences and lifeworlds of trans people from the domain of political debate. Transness, as an abstract inquiry and object of biopolitical study, so often has little to do with the actual stuff of *living*: the everyday nature of hardship, conflict and rage, ambiguity, racial and economic subordination, violence, laughter, the material realities of poverty, deprivation, exploitation, familial love, and alienation.

LIFE VERSUS LIVING, OR, AGAINST THE CISNESS OF DEMOGRAPHY

Yet, I am left contemplating, what is the place of *feminism* in this project of being against cisness? Feminism has a complicated presence in this project. Across the volume, feminist thinkers are cited as key resources for this work against cisness, while exclusionary ideologies of women that claim the mantle of feminism are subjected to extended analysis. By undoing dangerous alliances built on cisness, these critiques reveal problems with exclusionary visions of feminism—from imperial white women's movements in the past and present that utilize Sojourner Truth as a strategic symbol to buttress white women's imperial citizenship, to trans-exclusionary radical feminist alliances with American conservatives that paradoxically promote violent bans to "protect" cis women, to contemporary "mom groups" who utilize the language of vulnerability to perpetuate trans-exclusionary policies that police children's bodies. These movements mobilize a rhetoric of racialized fear and white vulnerability and call it feminism, claiming the language of freedom and equality to enforce, institutionalize, and police cisness.

These histories of trans-exclusionary movements tell us of a past and present of authoritarian women who claim feminism *for* cisness. Yet, as Heaney suggests at the end of the introduction, feminist thought, in its commitment to critiquing the fundamentally unequal structures that organize sexual difference as an ideology of power, must be in opposition to cisness. Heaney argues that "the phrase feminism against cisness ought to be a redundancy" because feminism, in every sense, "should be *definitionally* against cisness" (emphasis added). For Heaney, myriad social movements, from women's marches to trans and third gender political protest, signify the ways people seek space against cisgender ideologies of masculinity.

I would suggest that the long-term project of imagining feminism cannot only insist that trans inclusion against cisness is feminist. To imagine a feminism against cisness, we must also critically assess how cisness has insidiously shaped even seemingly inclusive feminist frameworks and movements. We must critically reflect on just what definitional work is required for a feminism against cisness, as Heaney demands. Such a project against cisness requires comprehensive reevaluation of the material reality of feminist movements in the past and the many epistemological possibilities for feminist futures. It requires critique of trans-exclusionary white women and even progressive, inclusive feminisms in the United States and across the world that too often have had to rely on cis structures of knowledge to make an argument for women's rights in the twentieth and twenty-first centuries. In other words, the project of a feminism against cisness must critically interrogate the widespread feminist reliance on fields of knowledge that traffic in cis categories to prove women's political presence in social scientific disciplines of demography, population studies, and economic indices. These structures of knowledge reduce the political breadth of feminist ideas of women to simple descriptive biological fact.

The descriptive mode of cis demography—"women make up half of the world"—has served as the primary justification for feminist politics on the global stage in the past fifty years. In so doing, feminist movements around the world have had to rely on an unequal knowledge economy that utilizes demography to prove the value of women—especially the value of women's reproductive and informal labor—all while reinforcing cis categories as the only usable, measurable tools for policy change. No disciplines have had more impact on structures of knowledge that govern feminist movements and research around the world in the last fifty years than the interrelated fields of demography (technically, a social science) and population (technically based in statistics and applied mathematics). These knowledge economies have established a novel mode of understanding social life that M. Murphy has powerfully diagnosed as the "economization of life."[2] These forms of knowledge that populate everything from progressive feminist anthologies of the 1980s, to the abundant production of policy reports on women of the 1990s and 2000s, to legislative agendas and policy making at every level. These forms of knowledge have established cis difference as foundational to the study of women, using "vital data" as the foundation for all reports and studies on women. These fields of knowledge sustain the wildly unequal knowledge economy and policy machine on global women's and gender rights. These structures of knowledge extend far, in the United States and Europe, across US empire, and govern much of the world.

This knowledge economy of demographic data as social life dates back centuries, from the enumerative calculus of the Atlantic slave trade, Malthus's viral understanding of overpopulation, to the colonial census and settler colonial ethnology, all of which deployed and institutionalized biological sex difference as primary categories of social measure.[3] We might date the attachment of feminists to demography to a later iteration of population studies in the birth control movements of the early twentieth century of notables like Margaret Sanger who deployed the racialized language of population to argue for imperial women's rights and population control in the colonies.[4] But it is in the aftermath of the racist rhetoric of the "population bomb," during the inaugural United Nations International Women's Year in 1975, and subsequent Women's Decade between 1975 and 1985, that we see the formal entrenchment of the newly institutionalized postwar field of demography in global women's movements.[5] This moment from the 1970s onward built new and powerful knowledge infrastructures sustained through long-lasting frameworks for social scientific research on women that subsequently became the blueprint for sexual rights more broadly. These genres of the policy report and institutions of policy-oriented research were sustained by multiple international and national institutions, including the United Nations, independent nation-states, local and transnational feminist NGOs, and international foundations.[6]

This history is colored by structures of social scientific knowledge that have emerged alongside key political movements for justice in the last fifty years. Contemporary social movements for justice and rights are permanently transformed through Cold War technologies of governance, surveillance, and the management of populations; ongoing movements for decolonization; and the ongoing biopolitical calculus of dispensable life under perpetual war in the aftermath of 9/11. Even as radical, inclusive feminists around the world have sought to critique power and mobilize for substantive change, they have been largely limited by material circumstances that mandate the production of consumable knowledge by everyone from NGOs to modern nation-states and the United Nations. These structures of knowledge were strengthened through the rise of international foundations and development programs from the 1970s that deployed modern social science to prove the presence of women through demography and continue to thrive today.

To think forward for an ongoing global project of feminism against cisness, then, requires that feminists account for the history of cisness in its expansion in global infrastructures and knowledge economies from the 1970s onward that translated womanhood into a finite and measurable index, rather than a radically inclusive political category. As Murphy contends, to undo the power of these indices of population requires one to stand "#AgainstPopulation" itself.[7] Feminist research around the world is dependent on the global political economy of cisness through demography. Such a project might necessitate a return to the critical period of the 1970s and the massive explosion of feminist movements not only in the United States but across the world, not only to critique increasingly limiting visions of biological womanhood in "second-wave" feminisms of the First World but also to understand the origins of global feminist attachments to cis social science in efforts to put women "on the map." As we continue to pursue a feminism against cisness, we must account for knowledge infrastructures built in the past fifty years and how we are to contend with the inheritance of feminist reliance on cis knowledge forms in this ongoing abolitionist project.

Revisiting this history of policy making and knowledge production from the 1970s through the lens of being against cisness may offer us new avenues to critique powerful neoliberal institutions of human rights and development that continue to reductively mobilize feminist, third gender, queer, and trans issues around the world for material gains. Transnational institutions for sexual rights have proliferated while doing little to nothing to change the material realities of most of the women and sexual minorities in the world. Indeed, as feminist theorist Neferti Tadiar has powerfully argued, the development calculus of Third World human value in gendered reproductive and productive work has now paradoxically produced a "new political economy" where there is no longer "a distinction between life and labor" for people of the Third World. In the twenty-first century, demographic measures see life solely through people's economic productivity, while all other dimensions of most human lives are largely "expendable."[8]

A FEMINISM FOR THE LIVING

"There is not one but many cisnesses to be against," as Grace Lavery asserts in her contribution here. And, from the incredible breadth of this volume, it is clear there are many political possibilities available in building a feminism against cisness. To be against is to be in opposition, a negation, a form of resistance. Being against is also a form of protection, an expectation—*to shield against*. Feminism against cisness is perhaps best understood then as a project of negation and speculation, an abolitionist vision toward something new. This project is very different than the *demographic* calculus of speculative thinking that shapes so much of our world today in the form of economic futurity, market predictions, and the calculus of pandemic that measures life (and death) solely in terms of economic impact.

The rich history of radically inclusive feminist thought offers tools to think outside of the measurable calculus of life as vital statistic and to focus instead on the practice of living. It requires critical reflection on the inclusive possibilities of a trans feminism, as has happened over the past three decades, to critique feminist attachments to cis life and imagine a feminism that frees itself from the racialized colonial imaginaries that have established cisgender as the social, legal, and scientific norm around the world. Woman has functioned as a political category in excess of the biological since its inception, in the work of some of the earliest feminist thinkers across the world, from Sojourner Truth to He-Yin Zhen to Rokeya Sakhawat Hossain. We may need to return to these earlier political visions to undo the harm of biopolitical disciplines like demography that have so often co-opted and flattened liberatory social movements in the late twentieth century to the question of measure. From this volume, we learn that being against cisness is not solely about an antagonism to the institutional, social, legal, and medical imposition of cis norms. It is also an imagination of a future otherwise, a mode of dissent.

Feminism against cisness is an ongoing intellectual and practice-based project that aspires for new methods and disciplinary forms, even an entirely new lexicon to describe our social worlds with new ways of thinking and writing against the imposition of cis norms. Feminism against cisness must undo the cis basis of knowledge forms that have come to dominate so much of the work of feminists around the world. Feminisms offer a critique of the biopolitics of measurable life and death in disciplines wielded by the state to imagine a politics of sexual difference otherwise, outside of the measure of population, toward a critique of power.

To be against cisness requires that we reckon with feminism's attachment to cis gender categories and knowledge formations that may not be trans-exclusionary, that are certainly far more inclusive than the explicit modes of right-wing authoritarian movements that claim to be radically feminist but exist in contradiction to the fundamental tenets of global feminist thought. Most political movements based in feminist mobilization have found it challenging to translate the many political possibilities of the concept of woman into actionable language for policy change without submitting to disciplinary knowledge that transforms womanhood into the biopolitical category of demography. Our task then, is to imagine a vision of feminism toward the living, against the biopolitical economy of measurable life that has so fully overwhelmed policy today.

Building from the insights of this important volume, I see feminism against cisness as a project that moves away from the more policy-oriented structures that categorize women—away from vital statistics of demography and measurable understandings of lifespan in the form of sex ratios, birth rates, and death rates. I see in these amazing contributions a collective re-thinking of cis disciplinary knowledge used to describe, value, and act on behalf of trans people. In a time of pandemic, we have seen some of the most exaggerated versions of this calculus that prioritizes economic life over every aspect of living, that again and again reduces life to the question of labor value, that devalues the lives of so many in favor of "the economy" and getting "back" to "normal." Today we experience quite viscerally how the concept of life has been fully co-opted by the state as an economic measure of vital statistics, all while demonstrating the dispensability of life. In the face of such death, living may offer other ways to imagine the world, to meditate on what it means to be in and of social and political worlds.[9]

To pursue a feminism against cisness is to rethink feminist dependency on the biopolitics of life and commit to the collective work of building a feminism for the living.

NOTES

1 Thinking here with Jules Gill-Peterson's careful critique of the abstract idealiza-tion of trans women of color for contemporary politics away from the historical nuances of women's lives. See Gill-Peterson's lecture "Being Street."

2 Murphy, *Economization of Life*.

3 For brilliant analysis of this project of calculated enumeration and commodifica-tion in relation to structures of knowledge that shape the archives of slavery, see Morgan, *Reckoning with Slavery*. For more on the history of enumeration and the census in relation to categories of feminized sexuality in the colonial world, see Mitra, *Indian Sex Life*.

4 There is a rich global history on birth control movements. See, for example, Connolly, *Fatal Misconception*; Ahluwalia, *Reproductive Restraints*; Hodges, *Contraception, Colonialism and Commerce*; Bashford, *Global Population*; and Sreenivas, *Reproductive Politics*. On reproductive control and the new authoritar-ian visions of girl children as objects of protection, see Tambe, *Defining Girlhood in India*.

5 Erlich, *Population Bomb*.

6 I elaborate more on reckoning with the dominance of the genre of the social science report in feminist thought elsewhere, including Mitra, "The Report, or, Whatever Happened to Third World Feminist Theory?"

7 Murphy, "Against Population, towards Alterlife."
8 Tadiar, "New Global Political Economy."
9 By living, I also mean an understanding of mourning, the livingness of the dead that considers that the aftermath of a death for the living I am thinking here with the indispensable work of Asli Zengin on the struggles and lifeworlds of transgender communities and funerals in Turkey. See Zengin, "Afterlife of Gender."

BIBLIOGRAPHY

Ahluwalia, Sanjam. *Reproductive Restraints: Birth Control in India, 1877–1947*. Urbana: University of Illinois Press, 2010.
Bashford, Alison. *Global Population: History, Geopolitics, and Life on Earth*. New York: Columbia University Press, 2014.
Connolly, Matthew. *Fatal Misconception: The Struggle to Control World Population*. Cambridge, MA: Harvard University Press, 2010.
Erlich, Paul R. *The Population Bomb*. New York: Buccaneer Books, 1968.
Gill-Peterson, Jules. "Being Street: The Trans Woman of Color as Evidence, Imagining Trans Futures." Simpson Center for the Humanities, University of Washington. Accessed December 15, 2021. https://youtu.be/mINMifB8bm4.
Hodges, Sarah. *Contraception, Colonialism and Commerce: Birth Control in South India, 1920–1940*. London: Ashgate, 2008.
Mitra, Durba. *Indian Sex Life: Sexuality and the Colonial Origins of Modern Social Thought*. Princeton, NJ: Princeton University Press, 2020.
Mitra, Durba. "The Report, or, Whatever Happened to Third World Feminist Theory?" *Signs: Journal of Women in Culture and Society* 48, no. 1 (Spring 2023): 557–84.
Morgan, Jennifer. *Reckoning with Slavery: Gender, Kinship, and Capitalism in the Early Black Atlantic*. Durham, NC: Duke University Press, 2021.
Murphy, M. "Against Population, towards Alterlife." In *Making Kin, Not Population*, edited by Adele Clarke and Donna Haraway, 101–24. Chicago: Prickly Paradigm Press, 2018.
Murphy, M. *The Economization of Life*. Durham, NC: Duke University Press, 2017.
Sreenivas, Mytheli. *Reproductive Politics and the Making of Modern India*. Seattle: University of Washington Press, 2021.
Tadiar, Neferti. "The New Global Political Economy: Life-Times Lived and Expended (a Talk)." *Global Condition* 1, no. 1 (2018). Accessed December 6, 2021. http://livingcommons.org/neferti-tadiar-political-economy.
Tadiar, Neferti. *Remaindered Life*. Durham, NC: Duke University Press, 2022.
Tambe, Ashwini. *Defining Girlhood in India: A Transnational History of Sexual Maturity Laws*. Urbana: University of Illinois Press, 2019.
Zengin, Asli. "The Afterlife of Gender: Sovereignty, Intimacy and Muslim Funerals of Transgender People in Turkey." *Cultural Anthropology* 34, no. 1 (2019): 78–102.

CONTRIBUTORS

CAMERON AWKWARD-RICH is the author of two collections of poetry: *Sympathetic Little Monster* (2016) and *Dispatch* (2019). His creative work has been supported by fellowships from Cave Canem, the Watering Hole, and the Lannan Foundation. Also a scholar of trans theory and expressive culture in the United States, Cameron earned his PhD from Stanford University's program in Modern Thought and Literature. His more critical writing can be found in *Signs, Trans Studies Quarterly, American Quarterly*, and elsewhere. His book *The Terrible We: Thinking with Trans Maladjustment* was published by Duke University Press in 2022. Currently, he is Assistant Professor of Women, Gender, and Sexuality Studies at the University of Massachusetts Amherst.

MARQUIS BEY's (they/them, or any pronoun)* work focuses on Blackness and fugitivity, transness, and Black feminist theory. Bey is particularly concerned with modes of subjectivity that index otherwise ways of being, utilizing Blackness and transness—as fugitive, extra-ontological postures—as names for such otherwise subjectivities. These two analytics (rather than endowments of the epidermis or specific bodily morphologies) are the axes around which Bey thinks about subjectivity formation and deformation, abolition, and political work. Bey's monograph *Black Trans Feminism* (Duke University Press, 2022) attempts to theorize the convergence of Blackness, transness, and Black feminism via the Black Radical Tradition, critical theory, and contemporary literature. Bey's short text *The Problem of the Negro as a Problem for Gender* (2020) deeply meditates on Nahum Chandler's work, putting into conversation his thinking on paraontology and desedimentation with the transness and gender nonnormativity of transgender studies. Bey has also published a collection of autotheory essays meditating on the relationship between Blackness and the category of cisgender, entitled *Cistem Failure* (Duke University Press, 2022). (*Note on pronouns: The "preference" for they/them pronouns is an attempt to mark both the author's irreverence toward the gender binary and a tentative and always-in-process relationship to gender nonbinariness. Put differently, this is not to say the author "is" nonbinary; instead, the author, more pointedly, seeks a nonbinaristic relationship to a self-understanding of gender—an attempted unrelation to gender, as it were. Thus, it matters less what pronoun one uses; the author is, ultimately, pronoun indifferent. That capaciousness is simply another attempt to express an irreverence and disdain for the gender binary and the ways it might inhere in pronouns.)

KAY GABRIEL is a poet and essayist. Her research focuses on contemporary anglophone poetry and poetics, trans studies, tragedy, adaptation, classical reception, and translation studies. She has taught at Princeton, the Prison Teaching Initiative, the Bard Microcollege at Brooklyn Public Library, Naropa University, and the Poetry Project at St. Mark's Church. With Andrea Abi-Karam, she co-edited *We Want It All: An Anthology of Radical Trans Poetics* (2020), nominated for Lambda Literary and Publishing Triangle awards, and she's the author of two forthcoming poetry collections: *Kissing Other People or The House of Fame* (2021) and *A Queen in Bucks County* (2022).

JULES GILL-PETERSON is Associate Professor of History at Johns Hopkins University. She earned her PhD from Rutgers University and has held fellowships from the American Council of Learned Societies and the Kinsey Institute. She was honored with the Chancellor's Distinguished Research Award from the University of Pittsburgh in 2020. Jules is the author of *Histories of the Transgender Child* (2018), the first book to shatter the widespread myth that transgender children are a brand-new generation in the twenty-first century. Uncovering a surprising archive dating from the 1920s through 1970s, *Histories of the Transgender Child* shows how the concept of gender relies on the medicalization of children's presumed racial plasticity, challenging the very terms of how we talk about today's medical model. The book was awarded a Lambda Literary Award for Transgender Nonfiction and the Children's Literature Association Book Award. Jules has also written for the *New York Times*, CNN, the *Lily* (by the *Washington Post*), *Jewish Currents, New Inquiry, The Funambulist*, and more. She has been interviewed extensively by the *Guardian*, CBS, National Public Radio, and *Xtra Magazine*. She also serves as a general co-editor for *TSQ: Transgender Studies Quarterly*.

EMMA HEANEY is Associate Director and Clinical Assistant Professor in the program XE: Experimental Humanities and Social Engagement at New York University. She is a scholar of comparative literature, feminist studies, and trans studies. Her first book, *The New Woman: Literary Modernism, Queer Theory, and the Trans Feminine Allegory* (2017), traces the medicalization of trans femininity and the uptake of the resulting diagnostic in works of literature and theory. Her current research derives a theory of the transformation of queer and trans identities from works of literature spanning the long twentieth century. Emma was previously Assistant Professor of English at William Patterson University and has held fellowships at MacDowell and the Marble House Project.

MARGAUX L. KRISTJANSSON is a theorist, writer, and political organizer whose work centers on a critical anthropology of the intimate and affective economies of conquest and racial capitalism in the Americas. Her book project *Waging Care: Indigenous Economies of Care against the Carceral Child Protection System* argues that Canada securitizes its settler colonial economy of extraction from Indigenous lands through the ongoing apprehension of Indigenous children into the child welfare system. It is based on collaborative research with colleagues in the Algonquins of Barriere Lake First Nation and the National Indigenous Survivors of Children Welfare Network. Kristjansson teaches in the American and Indigenous Studies program at Bard College. Previously, she was at Williams College, where she served as Mellon Postdoctoral Fellow in Native American and Indigenous Studies. Her areas of specialization also include political and legal anthropology, transgender feminisms, racial capitalism, and political economy. At Williams, she designed and taught seminars on subjects ranging from an introduction to Indigenous feminist theory to settler colonialism, care, and kinship.

GRETA LAFLEUR is Associate Professor of American Studies at Yale University. LaFleur's research and teaching focus on early North American literary and cultural studies, the history of science, the history of race, the history and historiography of sexuality, and queer and trans studies. LaFleur's first book, *The Natural History of Sexuality in Early America* (2018), reveals how eighteenth-century race science contributed to emerging sciences of sex in the colonial Atlantic world. They are working on two new projects. The first, a scholarly monograph tentatively titled *How Sex Became Good: The Feminist Movements and Racial Politics That Made Modern Sexuality* (under contract), tracks how cultural and legal responses to the problem of sexual violence shaped the politicization of sexuality in the modern period. The second is a co-authored book of essays, with anthropologist Cal Biruk, on birding, under contract with the Practices series at Duke University Press. LaFleur is co-editor of two collections: *Trans Historical: Gender Plurality before the Modern* (with Masha Raskolnikov and Anna Kłosowska), published in 2021; and *American Literature in Transition, 1770–1828* (with William Huntting Howell), published in 2022. They are the series editor, with Blake Gutt and Emily Skidmore, of the six-volume *A Cultural History of Trans Lives* (under contract). LaFleur is also the co-editor of three journal special issues: a special issue of *American Quarterly*, "Origins of Biopolitics in the Americas" (2019, with Kyla Schuller); a special issue of *Transgender Studies Quarterly* on "Trans Exclusionary Feminisms and the Global New Right" (2022, with Serena Bassi); and a special issue of *GLQ* on "The Science of Sex Itself" (2023, with Benjamin Kahan). Their writing has appeared in *Early American Literature, Early American Studies, American Quarterly, American Literature, Criticism,* the *New Republic, BLARB: The Blog of the Los Angeles Review of Books,* and *Public Books.* Their research has been supported by fellowships at the Institute for Advanced Study (School of Social Sciences); the American Council of Learned Societies; the Massachusetts Historical Society; the William Andrews Clark Library at UCLA; the John Carter Brown Library at Brown University; the Clement Library at the University of Michigan; the American

Antiquarian Society in Worcester, Massachusetts; the Newberry Library in Chicago; and the Baldy Center for Law and Social Policy at the State University of New York at Buffalo. LaFleur holds a PhD from the University of Pennsylvania and a JD from the University of Connecticut.

GRACE LAVERY is a writer, editor, and academic living in Brooklyn, New York. As Associate Professor of English, Critical Theory, and Gender and Women's Studies at the University of California, Berkeley, she explores the history and theory of aesthetics and interpretation, with particular interests in psychoanalysis, literary realism, and queer and trans cultures. Her speculative memoir, *Please Miss*, was published in 2022. Her first book, *Quaint, Exquisite: Victorian Aesthetics and the Idea of Japan*, was published in 2019. Her second scholarly monograph, *Pleasure and Efficacy: Of Pen Names, Cover Versions, and Other Trans Techniques*, was published in 2023, and her scholarly essays have been published in *Critical Inquiry, differences, Social Texts, Transgender Studies Quarterly*, and elsewhere.

DURBA MITRA is the Richard B. Wolf Associate Professor of Women, Gender, and Sexuality at Harvard University. Mitra works at the intersection of feminist and queer studies. Her book *Indian Sex Life: Sexuality and the Colonial Origins of Modern Social Thought* (2020) demonstrates how ideas of deviant female sexuality became foundational to modern social thought. It received a recognition for scholarly achievement with the Bernard S. Cohn Book Prize from the Association of Asian Studies; an honorable mention for the Law and Society Association's J. Willard Hurst Book Prize for the best work in sociolegal history; and an honorable mention for the Feminist Theory and Gender Studies Book Award from the International Studies Association. Mitra's current book project explores the history of Third World feminist thought and South-South solidarity movements. Other projects include a book of essays on sexuality and social science and a collection of interviews with global feminist thinkers. Mitra's work has been recognized with the 2021 Walter Channing Cabot Fellow Award for "distinguished accomplishments in the fields of literature, history, or art" from Harvard University. She is the recipient of the 2019 Roslyn Abramson Award for Excellence in Undergraduate Teaching at Harvard, which recognizes teachers for "excellence and sensitivity in teaching undergraduates" and the 2020 Star Family Prize for Excellence in Faculty Advising. Mitra was named as a "Favorite Professor" for three years in a row by the Harvard College classes of 2021, 2022, and 2023.

BEANS VELOCCI is Assistant Professor in History and Sociology of Science and Core Faculty in Gender, Women's, and Sexuality Studies at the University of Pennsylvania. They are a historian of knowledge production about sex, gender, and sexuality. Their work uses queer, trans, and feminist methods to interrogate classification systems and how they become regarded as biological truths, primarily in the nineteenth- and twentieth-century United States and its colonial and white supremacist context. In their first book project, *Binary Logic*, they look at how sex emerged as a privileged way of sorting bodies not despite but because of its incoherence. Rather than focus on those whom scientists and medical doctors cast out of male and female categories as pathological aberrations, the book traces how knowledge producers brought ill-fitting bodies back into a normative binary with no harm done to sex itself. It follows a sprawling cast of researchers through zoology, eugenics, gynecology, statistical studies of sex, and transgender medicine as they self-fashioned their expertise, created enmeshed fields of sex science and race science, and made science the way to know sex.

JOANNA WUEST is Assistant Professor of Politics at Mount Holyoke College, where she teaches and researches constitutional law, American politics, and gender and sexuality politics. Her book *Born This Way: Science, Citizenship, and Inequality in the American LGBTQ+ Movement* (2023) examines how the natural sciences and the mental health professions have been foundational to LGBTQ+ civil rights victories. Wuest's writing has appeared in academic and popular outlets, including *Perspectives on Politics, Polity, Politics and Gender, Law and Social Inquiry, GLQ: A Journal of Lesbian and Gay Studies, Nonsite*, the *Nation, Boston Review, Dissent*, and *Jacobin*.

INDEX

Note: Page numbers followed by f refer to figures.

abjection, 136–37, 144–47, 152n4; Black, 38, 46; gendered, 138, 140, 142, 151; trans, 38

abolition, 149–50, 166; of borders, 146; of capital, 136, 138; gender, 136, 149, 151, 158–59, 164–65, 167–68; of gendered abjection, 138; of prisons, 146; violence and, 40; of whiteness, 16

abuse: daddy tank and, 74n29; domestic, 57; physical, 70; sexual, 13–15, 30n3, 221–22; shelters, 74n27; sterilization, 64

accumulation, 1, 142; body as strategy of, 140; capital, 28, 29n10; capitalist, 139; by dispossession, 137, 153n7; gender as strategy of, 140–41, 144, 150, 152; primitive, 141; strategy, 136

Affordable Care Act, 177–78

age, 15, 117, 119

Alito, Samuel, 108–10, 112, 124

Alliance Defending Freedom (ADF), 24, 176–78, 182–87

American Civil Liberties Union (ACLU), 73n1, 181

Amin, Kadji, 95, 118–19

animal husbandry, 90–91, 94

anti-Blackness, 12, 23, 62–63, 67, 71, 203

antiracism, 24, 176, 185

anti-trans movements, 24, 212n25

Ask Me First campaign, 24, 180–81

athletes: female, 42, 181; intersex, 41–42

autonomy, 63, 138, 142, 145–48; bodily, 64, 109, 136, 143, 151–52, 153n9; women's, 176, 189

autotheory, 226, 230–33, 242

Awkward-Rich, Cameron, 19–20, 30n24, 242

Baldwin, James, 159, 170n4

bathroom policies, 20, 23, 56, 58, 111, 176, 180–81, 183–84, 186–87

Belcourt, Billy-Ray, 27, 61

Bell, Cei, 69–70

Benjamin, Harry, 121–22, 124n6

Ben-Shalom, Miriam, 179, 190n21

Bey, Marquis, 22–23, 30n29, 60, 127n34, 242

Bhattacharya, Tithi, 139, 148
Biden, Joe, 56, 58
Big Lebowski, The (Coen Brothers), 25,
228–30, 233–34, 236n29
binary: cisness and, 2; cis/trans, 21, 112,
117n122; gender as, 20, 23, 38, 117,
120, 161–62, 168, 170, 171n8, 176, 188,
204–5; heterosexual/homosexual, 114,
127n25; sex as, 1, 7, 9–10, 20, 22, 38, 112,
118–19, 128n38, 179, 204; subversion
of, 169
Black feminism, 38
Black flesh, 60, 64
Black life, 60–61
Blackness, 23, 159, 162, 165–66, 168,
171n16; anagrammatical, 171n13;
forced degendering of, 118; gendered
treatment and, 30n24; nonbinariness
and, 167, 170 (*see also* facelessness);
non-cis operation of, 30n29; sex and,
13; time and, 47; ungendered, 60.
See also anti-Blackness
Black women, 26, 30n26, 41, 43, 46, 64;
exclusion of, 30n25, 40; labor and, 140;
slavery and, 12, 60; transness and, 117
Bostock v. Clayton County, 108–9, 124n2
Brand, Dionne, 166–67
bullying, 24, 201
Burkett, Elinor, 38–39, 51n4
Butler, Judith, 6, 150, 166, 171n8

capital, 23, 60, 136–41, 149–50, 152;
accumulation, 28, 29n10; extraction, 2;
reification and, 22, 136; sex work and,
145–46
capitalism, 2, 16, 152, 171n18; masculinism
and, 71; plantation, 44; racial, 140,
146, 218
carcerality, 60; anticarcerality, 64; of
everyday life, 20, 58
care, 1, 21, 209; access to, 122; for children,
10; collective, 62, 71; gender-affirming,
102, 178, 183, 199, 210–11n1; industry,
189; medical, 57, 149, 200; mutual,
63–64, 70; networks of, 63–64;

practices of, 16, 69, 72; provision of, 15;
reproductive, 146, 154n44; trans, 65,
110, 213n40; trans children and, 197;
transition, 110, 121
care work, 63, 65
caste, 2; gender as, 69
castrati, 98, 104n30, 232
castration, 18, 85, 90–96, 99, 105n33; fear
of, 223; as punishment, 29n18, 84, 86;
self-castration, 21, 84, 97–98, 102; of
a text, 101; unwanted, 100; of young
people, 104n30
childhood, 15, 119, 199, 209, 213n36;
sexual abuse, 222
children, 8, 11, 13, 29n15, 56, 59, 63, 84,
98–99, 119, 146, 161, 182, 189, 201–4,
207–10, 221; Black Panther Party and,
74n25; care for, 10; dead, 198; enslaved,
60; gender and, 111; girl, 248n4; Indigenous, 61; sexual assault and abuse
of, 30n23; white, 206. *See also* trans
children
Chinatown (Polanski), 25, 222–23, 227,
236n19
Christianity, 105n33, 160, 170n5, 190n21
chromosomes, 2, 9, 11, 177
cis people, 19, 27, 67, 110, 112, 115, 117, 123
cis women, 19, 24, 57, 71, 176, 178, 182,
243; privacy of, 185, 188
civil rights, 49, 56, 179, 189, 202; Civil
Rights Act of 1964, 109; discourse,
31n45; law, 183–84, 187; office (Department of Education), 178; struggle, 20
class, 2–3, 8, 171n8; composition, 146;
experience, 87; politics, 189, 236n24;
positions, 22, 136; power and, 10, 15;
relations, 139; sex work and, 29n21;
struggle, 22, 135–37, 146; woman
and, 27
classification, 112, 115–16, 119–21, 126n24
Cohen, Cathy, 26, 28, 31n45
colonialism, 21, 141; settler, 2, 62–63, 67
coloniality, 2, 72
Concerned Women for America, 177,
180, 188

confession, 160–61, 168, 170n4, 242; forced, 167
conquest, 57, 59; of trans-sexuality, 152
consciousness-raising, 5, 69
conservatives, 177, 179; American, 243; Christian, 175–76, 181, 183; social, 23, 176, 178, 180, 183, 189; young, 184
counterrevolution, 1–2
Cox, Laverne, 50–51, 88
cross-dressing, 4, 8, 116, 126n23; laws against, 47, 66, 114

decolonization, 72, 245
deductiveness, 25, 219–20, 222, 228, 230, 233–35
democracy, 189; liberal, 198, 205
demography, 244–48
Department of Housing and Urban Development (HUD), 179–80
devirilization, 90, 93
disability, 15, 97
disappearance, 20, 58
discipline, 105n33, 164–65; gendered, 21, 98; revolutionary, 71; state, 86
Disclosure: Trans Lives on Screen (Feder), 31n47, 88
discrimination, 108–9, 198; employment, 109, 112, 187 (*see also* trans people: job discrimination and); gender identity and, 184; racial, 186; sex, 179, 185; Title IX and, 188. *See also* law: antidiscrimination
dispossession, 20, 58, 136, 140, 146; accumulation by, 137, 153n7; bodily, 15; of gender, 141; settler colonial, 71
diversity, 24, 189; gender, 21, 103n8
domination, 1, 165; bourgeois, 3; of capital and colonial relations, 150; masculine, 241; political, 206
Douglas, Angela, 66–68
Douglass, Frederick, 40, 51n16

embodiment, 29n20, 147, 224; Black trans, 50; Indigenous, 67; sexed, 27; theorizations of, 16; trans, 60–61, 145;

transsexual, 29n10, 153n31; transsexuality and, 22, 136; trans women's, 18
empiricism, 2, 88
Endnotes, 137, 149–51
Enke, Finn, 116, 129n17, 211n18
enslavement, 12–13, 20–21, 37, 58, 63
eugenics, 15, 85

facelessness, 23, 30n29, 158–60, 164–70
false consciousness, 137–38, 142, 150–51, 206
Family Policy Alliance (FPA), 24, 175, 177, 179–81
Family Research Council, 182–83
Federici, Silvia, 139–40
femaleness, 48, 119
feminine, the, 10–13, 16, 71, 241
femininity, 14–15, 28, 60, 71, 94, 119; compulsory heterosexuality and, 69–70; conspicuous, 224; normative, 118, 121; trans, 7, 10, 61, 67–68, 72, 86, 117
feminization, 7–8, 27, 90, 147; foreclosure from, 12; of labor, 5; labor-power and, 145; as tactic of racialization, 13
Floyd, Kevin, 22, 136
Foucault, Michel, 23, 112, 125n13, 158–61, 163, 166, 226
4thWaveNow, 205, 212n29
freedom, 60; language of, 243; sex and gender, 3; trans, 72
Freud, Sigmund, 26, 29n20, 220–23, 235
Fritz the Cat (Bakshi), 226, 227f
futurity, 47, 168, 209; economic, 246–47; trans, 198; of white womanhood, 208

Gabriel, Kay, 22–23, 29n10, 242
Gage, Frances Dana, 44, 46–47, 49
Gay Liberation, 62–63, 70, 72, 151
gender, 2–3, 7–9, 12, 19–28, 42–44, 46–49, 51n3, 59–62, 69–70, 86, 101–2, 111–12, 114–24, 124n1, 136–44, 148–52, 160–69, 177, 179, 200, 202–5, 208, 241–42; abolition, 136, 149, 158–59, 164, 167; alignment, 23, 159; assignment, 121; binary, 112, 120, 161–62,

gender (*continued*)
168, 170, 171n8, 176, 188, 205; Black,
48–49, 60, 62, 87; capital and, 29n10,
140, 144, 150–51; categories, 47, 112,
116, 119–21, 127n25, 127n29, 247; cis,
20, 43; crossing, 124n6; diversity,
21, 103n8; dysphoria, 109, 120, 183,
186–87, 204 (*see also* Rapid Onset
Gender Dysphoria [ROGD]); equality,
185, 190n33; equity, 184; experience,
27, 97, 171n8, 186; expression, 11, 28,
97; genitals and, 99; historians of, 83;
ideology and, 38, 136, 138, 188; liberation, 3, 28, 137; logic of, 146; markers,
237n34; modern understandings of,
95; movement and, 127n24; nonconformity, 49, 101, 116; normative, 58, 87,
89, 121, 168; normativity, 162; norms,
22, 110, 115, 126n15, 141, 144, 177, 189;
politics, 138, 148; reform, 180; religious
tradition and, 190n21; rights, 244;
self-determination, 60, 73n9; self ID
policies, 56; studies, 125n12; third, 246;
variance, 62, 117; whiteness and, 206.
See also abolition: gender; accumulation: gender as strategy of
gender-affirming medical care, 102, 178,
183, 210–11n1
gender-critical moms, 24–25, 201, 203–6,
208, 212n28
Gender Recognition Act, 24, 202
genocide, 8, 20, 57–60, 73n9
Gill-Peterson, Jules, 16, 23–25, 29n15,
52n27, 95, 103n22, 119–20, 218, 242,
248n1; "Estro Junkie," 17–19; *Histories
of the Transgender Child*, 111, 124n6,
125n12, 126n19, 126n23; on trans DIY,
102, 105n35
Gossett, Che, 60, 166, 218
Gould, Elliot, 223, 226–27
Griffin, Pat, 41–42, 50

Hands across the Aisle Coalition
(HATAC), 179–80
harassment, 17, 24, 49, 201, 205; police, 68

Haritaworn, Jin, 146, 199
Hartman, Saidiya, 60, 68, 85, 87,
103n10
Harvey, David, 137, 153n7
Hawley, Josh, 181, 190n23
Hay, Harry, 67, 75n48
Hayward, Eva, 167, 218
healthcare, 144, 146, 178, 183, 207; in
prison, 64; trans, 56, 199, 202, 205;
trans-affirmative, 24; trans children
and, 197–98, 211n5
Heaney, Emma, 31n42, 39, 51n4, 117,
125n12, 223, 241–44
hedonism, 147, 149, 152
Hemmings, Clare, 41
Hennesy, Rosemary, 137, 144–45,
152n4
Heritage Foundation, 177, 180,
182–83
heteropatriarchy, 3, 63
heterosexuality, 26; compulsory, 70
history, 2–3, 6, 19, 47, 87–88, 100, 117,
126n17, 150, 163, 194, 230–32; Alito
and, 110; American, 188, 236n24; of
birth control movements, 248n4; of
the body, 37–38; chronopolitics and,
46; of cisness, 31n46, 245; of cis sexist
feminism, 51n4; of the clinic, 143; conditions of, 16, 26; departments, 125n12;
as dialectical particular, 219; of enumeration, 248n3; facelessness and, 167;
of gender crossing, 124n6; gendered,
169; of hysteria, 211n20; inadequacy of,
241; legal, 190n33; natural, 94; queer,
21; of Schreber, 153n31; of sexuality, 21,
111–15, 145; of slavery, 103n10; of trans
femininity, 86; trans feminist, 62;
of transsexuality, 145; Truth and, 37,
43–45, 49; of Western philosophical
thought, 29n20; of white women's
feminism, 206; of women's rights, 176.
See also trans history
Hitchcock, Alfred, 222–23, 236n19
Hocquenghem, Guy, 151, 226
homelessness, 11, 63, 180

hormones, 2, 4, 9, 11, 18, 64, 66, 126n23, 218; access to, 68, 120, 122; adjustment to, 21; androgenic, 42; role of, 83; sharing, 58; trans children and, 198, 203; trans teens and, 110, 206, 208

housing, 57, 144, 198–99; public, 5, 74n27; universal, 146

identity, 7, 113, 117, 145, 164, 167, 169; denial of, 49; gay, 114; gender, 21–22, 31n45, 109, 116, 126n15, 177–78, 180–84, 186–87; mother/mom as, 15, 24, 203, 212n25; politics, 22, 135, 203, 205, 208, 211n20; racial, 171n16; sex, 5, 11; sexual behavior and, 126n13; social, 7, 22, 136, 144; trans, 24, 110, 140, 143, 159, 187

ideology, 139, 142–44; of anti-Blackness, 12; anti-macho, 71; binary gender, 205; cisness as, 2–3, 10–11, 14, 19, 28, 59; gender, 25, 188; gender and, 138; gender identity, 180, 182; QAnon/Trans, 236n24; of sexual difference, 12–13, 243; TERF, 182; trans children and, 212n36

incarceration, 49, 57, 66, 74n29, 152, 242; mass, 199

Indigenous genders, 67, 75n48

Indigenous internationalism, 69, 72

Indigenous land, 57, 60–61, 65

Indigenous nations, 61, 66

Inherent Vice (Anderson), 25, 228, 236–37n29

intersex, 43; athletes, 41–42; bodies, 59; women, 41

Invisibles, The (Morrison), 225, 233

Irigaray, Luce, 16, 27, 29n20

Jacobs, Harriet, 12–13

Jameson, Fredric, 137, 147–48, 153n5

Jenner, Caitlyn, 38–39

Johnson, Marsha P., 3–8, 62–65. *See also* Street Transvestite Action Revolutionaries (STAR)

Kristjannson, Margaux L., 19–20, 31n45, 242

labor, 37, 137–41, 189, 246; cognitive, 219; convict, 30n26; domestic, 5–6; of enslaved people, 58; gendered training and, 61; informal, 244; intellectual, 41; of *māhū*, 72; manual, 13, 138, 230; markets, 114, 188; plantation, 30n25; reproductive, 5, 10, 19, 28, 29n9, 137, 139–40, 145, 200; subordinate position of, 11; value, 248; wage, 140, 144; women's, 5–6, 10 (*see also* feminization)

labor-power, 139, 145–46

Ladin, Joy, 20, 37–40, 43, 45–47, 50

LaFleur, Greta, 21, 29n5, 29n18, 102n8, 242

Larson, Scott, 117, 120

Lavery, Grace, 25, 203–4, 212n33, 224, 226, 242, 246

law, 47–48, 85, 184–85, 188, 241; administrative, 40; antidiscrimination, 176–77, 181–83, 188; civil rights statutory, 183–84; colonial, 59; deception under, 65; discipline and, 165; of male sex-right, 29n20; natural, 179; sex-based civil rights, 187; trans people and, 171n7

lawlessness, 23, 46, 159, 168

Laymon, Kiese, 13–15

LeFlouria, Talitha L., 13, 30n26

lesbians, 69, 74n29, 123, 179, 202, 207

Lewis, Sophie, 15, 154n44

liberalism, 198, 224

Lightcap, Alexis, 178, 185–88

Linehan, Graham, 225–26, 232

Long Goodbye, The (Altman), 25, 222–23, 226–27, 228f, 234, 236n19

Loop-the-loop, 16–17, 19

Lugones, María, 52n54, 59, 141

Lukács, Georg, 22, 136

māhū, 65, 72

Malantino, Hil, 57, 213n40

maleness, 28, 95, 119

Manion, Jen, 89, 114, 124n6, 125n12, 126n23, 127n25

Maracle, Aiyyanna, 71–72

marijuana, 226, 228

masculinity, 10, 28, 71, 95, 99, 119, 163; animal, 94; counter-revolutionary, 70; hypermasculinity, 162 (*see also* Blackness); ideologies of, 243; normative, 118; trans, 48

Masson, Jeffrey Moussaieff, 222, 233, 236n16

materialism, 6, 8, 19, 154n45

maternity, 15, 30n25, 64

Mattachine Society, 67, 75n48

Mecca, Tommi Avicolli, 69–70

medicine, 68, 96, 198, 208; American, 121; biomedicine, 202, 204; gender-affirming, 102; glandular, 119; trans, 124n1, 128n48, 205; transsexual, 164

memes, 126n18, 218–19; enthymemes, 233–34

men, 2, 12, 27–28, 39, 99, 117, 140, 180, 184, 187; biological differentiation and, 43; Black, 100; Dawes Act and, 61; femininity in, 94; feminization and, 145; gay, 11, 75n48; Her (dating app) and, 232; heterosexual, 4; masculine, 69, 231; movement, 70–71; normative, 119, 121; penetration and, 7; selling of, 6; sexual mastery and, 29n20, 37; slavery and, 59; social subordination of women to, 177; working-class, 224. *See also* masculinity; trans men/trans masculine people

#MeToo, 24, 180

Meyerowitz, Joanne, 109, 120, 124n6

Mieli, Mario, 151–52, 155n58

Miller, D. A., 222, 236n19

Mirage/Moonshadow, 66–68

misgendering, 8, 169

misogyny, 2, 72, 199; new, 182; trans, 20; Trump's, 180

Mock, Janet, 14–15, 19

moralism, 142–43

mother, the, 2, 60; function, 65

motherhood, 16, 44, 60, 63, 65

mothering, 2, 15–16, 65

murder, 20, 58, 200

Murphy, M., 244–45

nationalism: anticolonial, 58; ethnonationalism, 201, 207; homonationalism, 146, 152; Indigenous, 69

New York University (NYU) sit-in, 62, 66

noir, 25; neo-, 25–26, 222–23, 225–28, 233, 236n19, 236n27; slacker, 236n29

nonbinariness, 161–63, 166–70

nonbinary identity, 169, 206

nonbinary people, 27, 49, 89, 154n41

nonprofits, 23, 56, 189

normativity, 121, 170n4; cis, 22, 25, 66, 68, 116, 120, 162, 167; nonnormativity, 168; sexual, 118; trans, 39

Obama administration, 175, 178, 180, 184–85; Title IX and, 184, 188. *See also* Biden, Joe

Painter, Nell Irvin, 40, 43, 45, 51n16

patriarchy, 2–3, 5, 69, 162; femininity and, 224; heteropatriarchy, 3, 63; racial, 43

penetrability, 7, 9, 11, 14, 16, 18–19, 27

penetration, 7, 9, 11, 18

Pineapple Express (Green), 228, 236n29

plasticity, 118, 128n40, 205; childhood, 119; racial, 218

pleasure, 15, 18, 137–38, 147–48, 151; of critique, 204; feminized sexual, 142; gender as source of, 152. *See also* hedonism

pluralism, 24, 186; gendered, 189

police, 17, 47, 62, 64–68, 70, 137; power, 85, 97; violence, 57, 65

politics, 57, 152, 162–63, 213n39, 224, 236n24; anti-trans, 176, 178; biopolitics, 201, 208, 247–48; chronopolitics, 46; class, 189; contemporary, 242, 248n1; electoral, 198; feminist, 45, 188, 244; feminist/LGBT, 39; future, 150; gender, 138, 148, 151; Haudenosaunee, 72; identity, 22, 135, 203, 205, 208, 211n20; of *Moonshadow*, 67; restroom, 181; revolutionary, 137, 149, 151, 159; trans-affirmative, 207; trans cultural,

100; of trans history, 123–24; of trans identities, 19; trans necropolitics, 199; of the United States, 58; of white trans people, 62; white women's moralizing, 212n22. *See also* trans politics

pornography, 23, 143, 146, 181

power, 12, 168, 225; cisness and, 2; of cis normativity, 116; class, 10; disciplinary, 85, 97; dynamic, 69; feminist critiques of, 241, 245, 247; gender and, 149; gendered, 123; heterosexuality and, 26; labor-, 139, 145–46; male, 152; of the past, 88; population and, 246; racial, 10; rape and, 29n20; selfsameness and, 163; sexual difference as ideology of, 243; social, 15, 39; state, 198, 201, 205–6; symbolic, 41; trans history and, 111; woman and, 8

precarity, 142, 144; sexual, 13; social, 144–45

Preciado, Paul B., 142, 164, 231–32

prison, 51n16, 57, 64, 85, 138; abolition of, 146; women's, 74n29

privacy, 176, 180, 182–88; right to, 183–85, 190n33

privilege, 121, 159; male, 162–63

progress, 50–51; colonial, 72; feminist, 41, 51; liberal, 189

psychoanalysis, 26, 143, 220–22

puberty blockers, 110, 198. *See also* children; trans children

public space, 20, 58

Puritanism: American, 224; Left, 137, 147

QAnon, 181, 219, 225, 236n24

queer people, 26, 126n15

queer theory, 27–28, 139, 141–42, 153n24, 225, 233

race, 7–8, 15, 20, 42–43, 59, 87; facelessness and, 168; feminism and, 41; sexed body and, 118; sex work and, 29n21, 146; trans analysis and, 117; womanhood and, 37

racialization, 9, 12–13, 21, 41, 43, 118, 167–68, 242; of European gender norms, 141

racism, 72, 203

Radical Faeries, 67, 75n48

Radical Queens, 58, 69–72

rape, 7–8, 11, 15, 29n20

Rapid Onset Gender Dysphoria (ROGD), 201, 204

Raymond, Janice, 38, 142; *The Transsexual Empire*, 120

reification, 22, 136

rent strikes, 57, 74n27

reproduction, 1, 200, 242; of death, 218; of family, 42; in fungi, 119; of gender, 150; of kinship, 209; of settler nation, 20, 58; social, 16, 139–40, 145, 153n9

resistance, 27, 70, 198, 218, 246; to carcerality, 60; Indigenous, 61; political, 26; trans, 20, 58, 62; to US empire, 65

Ricoeur, Paul, 220–22

rights, 50, 145–46, 185–86; abortion, 64, 210n1; gay, 67; human, 208, 246; individual, 3; lesbian, 179; of physicians and therapists, 23; privacy, 184, 187; sexual, 245–46; state, 57; students', 73n1; tenants', 57, 74n27; transgender legal, 175; trans people and, 39, 110; of trans women, 188; women's, 24, 37, 44, 64, 176, 181, 189, 244–45. *See also* civil rights; trans rights

Rivera, Sylvia, 3–8, 29n12, 62–65. *See also* Street Transvestite Action Revolutionaries (STAR)

Rosenberg, Jordy, 139, 141

Ruble, Mamie, 47–50

Rush, Florence, 221–22, 233, 236n16

Salah, Trish, 144, 153n31

Schuller, Kyla, 117–18, 128n40, 206

seduction theory, 26, 221–22, 235

self-determination, 123, 152; bodily, 64; gender, 60, 73n9

separatism, 66–67

settler colonization, 68, 72

sex, 1–7, 9–17, 19–22, 24, 46–49, 95, 111–13, 115–16, 118–24, 124n1, 177, 205, 208, 241; assigned, 2–3, 10, 15, 61, 115, 121, 124n6, 144, 185; binary, 38, 112, 118–19, 127n25, 128n38, 179, 204; biological, 12, 176, 179, 185, 245; birth, 161; cis, 20, 43, 51n3; difference, 206, 245; discrimination, 108–9, 178, 185; fair, 92–93, 100; as fiction, 59; identification, 144; identity, 5, 11; low-stakes, 234; of material body, 150; material reality of, 7, 27, 244; ratios, 248; religious tradition and, 190n21; segregation, 181, 184; testing, 42; trafficking, 181, 190n23; trouble, 167–68; truth of, 203

sex change, 5, 63, 66, 125n6

sexological sciences, 83, 85, 87

sexual assault, 11–14, 30n23, 70, 86, 180, 204, 222

sexual difference, 7, 9–16, 22, 27, 29n20, 39, 42, 241, 243; Black people and, 46; without cisness, 3, 6, 9, 12–13, 15–16; gender abolition and, 136; as hierarchy, 19, 28; politics of, 247; signification of, 138, 142–43, 147–49, 151. See also ideology

sexual dimorphism, 42–43, 59–60, 117–18

sexuality, 19, 26, 122; embodiment and, 143, 147; feminized, 248n3; historians of, 83, 113, 123; history of, 21, 85, 111–15; reification and, 22, 136; trans-, 151–52, 155n58; value of, 104n33

sexualization, 7; unwanted, 182

sex verification, 42, 48, 108, 165

sex work, 6, 10, 29n21, 63, 143, 145–46; clients, 7; criminalization of, 198; decriminalization of, 146, 153n9

sex workers, 10–11, 17, 58; elimination of, 138; trans, 145, 154n41

shelters: domestic abuse, 57, 74n27, 180; women's, 179, 183, 188

signification, 22; gendered, 23, 138, 159; of sexual difference, 138, 142–43, 147–49, 151; social, 136, 138

Skidmore, Emily, 111, 114, 124n6, 125n12, 126n24

slavery, 12, 37, 59–61, 68, 73n9, 85–86, 118, 141; afterlives of, 60, 72; archives of, 248n3; history of, 103n10. See also enslavement

slave trade, 60, 141, 244

Snorton, C. Riley, 13, 60, 87, 117–18, 125n12, 146, 199

social relations, 2, 7, 15, 138, 144, 148

solidarity, 13–14, 26, 69, 144, 147, 152, 209; Mattachine Society and, 75n48; practice-based, 74n29; solidarity-in-difference, 48; trans movement and, 58; trans sex work and, 146

South Dakota, 182, 197–99

Spade, Dean, 57, 161, 171n7, 213n37

Spencer, Lord John Charles, 94–95

Spillers, Hortense, 30n28, 58–60, 64, 127n37, 141

sports, 24, 201, 210n1; leagues, 39; sex and, 181; trans people and, 56, 183; women in, 41, 43

stability, 22, 124, 127n29, 169; of cis, 38, 51n3; financial, 145; gender, 21, 49; of gender categories, 120

Stonewall, 64–66

Strangio, Chase, 198–99

Street Transvestite Action Revolutionaries (STAR), 58, 62–66, 70, 72, 74n27, 74n29

Stryker, Susan, 103n12, 114–15, 121–23, 124n6, 125n12, 126n22, 127n25, 127n27; Bugs Bunny and, 88; on transness as movement, 128n52; Truth and, 44–45

subjectivity, 113, 142–43, 158–60, 167, 187, 222; gendered, 23, 158–59, 163

subordination, 19, 243; social, 177; of women, 152

Supreme Court (US), 39, 108–10, 178, 184–85, 187, 210n1. See also Alito, Samuel; Bostock v. Clayton County

surgery, 120, 122, 126n23, 162; genital, 5; top, 206; trans, 68. See also sex change

surplus value, 6, 139, 147, 152n4

survival, 64, 72; pattern of, 199; programs of the Black Panther Party, 74n25; sex work for, 6, 63

Title VII (Civil Rights Act of 1964), 109, 179, 187

Title IX, 184, 188; funding, 178; reforms, 175

trans children, 24–25, 111, 185, 197–201, 205, 207–8, 213n36

trans discourse, 38, 203, 206

trans exclusionary radical feminists (TERFS), 23, 175–77, 180

trans experience, 8, 24, 87, 121, 127n29; modern, 85; vocabularies for, 89, 103n12

trans feminine people, 20, 58, 62–63, 66, 70, 72, 73n6, 89, 206

trans feminism, 20, 46, 58, 68, 218, 247; separatist, 66

trans feminist struggle, 41, 59, 72

Transgender Trend, 205, 212n25

trans history, 27, 85–89, 97, 100, 103n8, 108–24, 125n12, 126n19

trans inclusion, 20, 243

transition, 109–11, 121–22, 142–43, 146, 202, 204, 209, 212n29; children and, 201; public, 38; trauma and, 209

Trans Liberation, 22, 68–69, 135–36, 147, 149, 152; bodily autonomy and, 151; milieus, 63; political projects, 20, 58

trans life, 3, 15, 22, 27, 144, 201, 242; assault on, 189; cisness and, 112; defense of, 207–8; Indigenous, 69, 71–72; medical care and, 200; newness of, 31n42; politics and, 57; of Truth, 20, 38–39; writing, 241

trans men/trans masculine people, 11, 39, 48, 69, 114, 126–27n4, 154n41, 206–7

transness, 8, 21–22, 86, 108–18, 123–24, 124n1, 127n26, 161, 217, 242–43; in antiquity, 124n6; of Black genders, 87; Blackness and, 47; cisness and, 127n27; fatal, 207; genealogy of, 60; history of, 120, 125n12; homosexuality and, 126n15; as movement, 121, 128n52; of sex, 43; transitivity of, 38; Truth and, 48

trans pasts, 85, 89

trans people, 19, 22, 28, 39, 49, 56–58, 87, 108–13, 115, 119–24, 126n15, 171n7, 178, 187, 198–203, 212n28, 217, 233, 242–43, 248; alienation of, 145, 148; autonomy and, 138; Black and brown, 62–63; citizenship and, 207; elimination of, 138; gender-affirming care and, 210–11n1; gendered abjection and, 151; job discrimination and, 56, 73n1; nonacademic, 21; non-passing, 144; poverty among, 154n38; representation of, 88; rights and recognitions for, 146; settler nation and, 20; sexual assault and, 30n23; Stonewall and, 64; trans DIY and, 102; white, 62

trans politics, 56–57, 69, 138, 144, 146; anti-trans politics, 176, 178; nationalism and, 207; TAO's, 67

trans rights, 24, 56, 176–77, 179–83, 185, 187–89

Transsexual Action Organization (TAO), 58, 66–69, 72

transsexuality, 22, 136, 167; history of, 145

trans struggle, 20, 27, 57–58

trans women, 11, 18–19, 24–27, 40, 64–68, 187, 199–201; athletics and, 178; Black, 72, 218; cis women and, 176, 182, 186; of color, 49, 58, 65, 67, 72, 199–200, 208–9, 248n1; femininity and, 121; liberal feminism and, 38; pornification of, 212n33; prison and, 51n16, 57; public restrooms and, 176, 224; recognition of, 39; rights for, 188 (see also trans rights); shelters and, 57, 180, 183–84; visibility and, 49; womanhood and, 21; writing by, 16, 19. See also trans feminine people

Trump, Donald, 178, 206; administration of, 23, 175, 178–79, 184, 188; misogyny of, 180

Truth, Sojourner, 20, 30n24, 37–41, 43–51, 52n54, 242–43, 247

Under the Silver Lake (Mitchell), 25, 228, 233–34, 234f, 237n29, 237n37

vagina, 9, 11, 16–17

value, 3, 11, 141, 144, 224; accumulation of, 136; hierarchy of, 19; labor, 248; production of, 140, 142, 150; of sexuality, 104n33; surplus, 6, 139, 147, 152n4; system, 218; Third World human, 246; of women, 244

Velocci, Beans, 21, 31n46, 95, 242

violence, 23–24, 49, 59–60, 68, 70, 85–86, 96, 139, 167, 169, 203–4, 243; in abolition work, 40; administrative, 24, 201, 210n1; anti-trans, 20, 58, 108, 198; of beholding, 163; cis-normative, 68; domestic, 180; extractive, 28; feminizing, 2, 48; gender, 12; gender and, 142; male-perpetrated, 181–82; normative, 161; patriarchal, 100; police, 57; political, 199–200; racial, 67; racializing, 13; sexual, 13, 20, 58, 61, 64, 137; social, 15; state, 64–65, 67, 217; trans women and, 176; white-supremacist, 86, 101

visibility, 49, 146; hypervisibility, 50, 199; nonvisibility, 218; trans, 39, 205, 217

vulnerability, 8, 11–13, 30n23, 137, 144–45, 176, 198; feminized, 203; language of, 243; to premature death, 205, 208

Wachowski, Lilly, 88

whiteness, 13, 16, 27–28, 67–68, 118, 170n4, 205–6; bourgeois, 19, 46; of cisness, 117; womanhood as, 12

white supremacy, 2, 15, 25, 71, 199, 201, 242. See also anti-Blackness

white women, 25, 30n25, 44, 206–7, 212n22, 243; Black abjection and, 46; trans children and, 201, 205; trans-exclusionary, 244

Wittig, Monique, 2, 151

woman, 2, 4–5, 8–10, 12, 16, 19–20, 27–28, 28n1, 29n20, 38–40, 43–48, 50, 61, 66, 89, 117, 170, 177, 179, 182, 224, 247; impersonation of, 118; naturalness of, 123; passing, 113; as property, 71; sexism and, 185

womanhood, 5, 9, 13, 24, 61, 179, 189, 209, 245, 247; biological, 246; Black, 41; cis, 11; expanding, 49; modern, 117; normative, 121; trans, 21, 37, 48, 67; Truth's, 38, 43–44, 50; white, 41, 206–8; as whiteness, 12

women, 2, 4–6, 10, 12–13, 15, 24, 27–28, 28n1, 37–39, 59, 63–65, 69–70, 77, 78, 84, 119, 121, 123, 140, 145, 152, 177, 179–89, 208, 243–46, 248; archives of, 68; Black Panther Party, 74n25; butch, 74n29; distinction between men and, 117; enslaved, 44, 60, 118; feminism and, 1; incarcerated, 30n23; intersex, 41; married, 127n24; masquerading as men, 114; oppression of, 139; poor, 74n27; protection of, 176, 178; racial mobilization of, 29n15; sexual desires of, 142; sports and, 41–43, 178; violence against, 60; young, 206. See also Black women; cis women; rights: women's; trans women; white women

Women's Liberation Front (WoLF), 24, 176–77, 179, 181–82, 185

Wuest, Joanna, 23, 25, 29n19, 242

Young, Tatiana Kalaniopua, 65, 72

www.ingramcontent.com/pod-product-compliance
Lightning Source LLC
Chambersburg PA
CBHW020844270326
41928CB00006B/541